ENTRUSTED TO THE FAITHFUL

AN INTRODUCTION TO PASTORAL LEADERSHIP

Kenneth S. Coley, Editor

Entrusted to the Faithful:
An Introduction to Pastoral Leadership

Published by Rainer Publishing
Spring Hill, TN
www.RainerPublishing.com

ISBN 978-0-9978861-7-7

Printed in the United States of America

Reverend Julian M. Motley

A pastor to many pastors and a Godly role model who exemplifies the instructions for pastors found in Scripture and this text.

MEET THE AUTHORS

Kenneth S. Coley, Ed.D. University of Maryland, College Park

Dr. Kenneth S. Coley is Professor of Christian Education and the Director of the Doctor of Education Program at Southeastern Baptist Theological Seminary, where he has taught since 1996. Ken has been married to Kathy for 41 years, and they have two adult children, Scott and Caitlin. He enjoys playing with his two German Shepherds and kayaking.

David R. Beck, Ph.D. Duke University

Dr. Beck is Professor of New Testament and Greek and Associate Dean for Biblical Studies at Southeastern Baptist Theological Seminary where he has taught since 1995. David has been married to Jeannie for 40 years, and they have one daughter Melissa and three granddaughters who he enjoys spending time with.

Allan Moseley, Ph.D. New Orleans Baptist Theological Seminary

Dr. Moseley is Professor of Old Testament and Hebrew at Southeastern Baptist Theological Seminary, where he has taught since 1996. Allan and his wife Sharon were wed in 1979, and they have three children and six grandchildren. He enjoys hanging out with his family, preaching, reading, and fishing.

Steven P. Wade, Ph.D. Southeastern Baptist Theological Seminary

Dr. Wade is Associate Professor of Pastoral Theology at Southeastern Baptist Theological Seminary, where he has taught since 2004. Steven has been married to Jenny for 18 years, and they have four children, Caleb, Sarah, Lydia and Anna. He enjoys outdoor activities and spending time on his hobby farm.

James P. Porowski, Psy.D. George Fox University

Dr. Porowski received his doctorate in Clinical Psychology from George Fox University, and also holds a Th.M. from Dallas Theological Seminary. Jim is on the full time faculty at Southeastern Baptist Theological Seminary, and directs a counseling practice in Raleigh, North Carolina. He and his wife Ginny have been married for 32 years, and have four adult daughters, Stephanie, Jody, Corinne and Bridget.

Larry J Purcell, Ph.D. The Southern Baptist Theological Seminary

Dr. Purcell serves as Professor of Leadership and Discipleship and Associate Dean of Academic Administration at Southeastern Baptist Theological Seminary, Wake Forest, NC. Larry has been married to Terri over 40 years. They have one daughter, Dawn, and two grandchildren, Abby and Chase. Larry served in the military for a decade and was pastor of churches in Kentucky for over 30 years. He currently serves as a coach and consultant to pastors and churches experiencing conflict.

J. Gregory Lawson, Ph.D. Southwestern Baptist Theological Seminary; Ed.D. UNT; J.D. Campbell University

Dr. Lawson is Professor of Christian Education at Southeastern Baptist Theological Seminary where he has taught since 1996. Also, he is the

Senior Pastor of Union Chapel, Zebulun, NC since 2007. Greg has been married to Betty for 32 years and is the father of James, John and Rebecca Lawson. His hobbies include real estate and going to the beach.

John Boozer, DMA Louisiana State University

John is retired Professor of Church Music and Worship Studies at Southeastern Baptist Theological Seminary, where he taught for 15 years. Before academia, he served as worship pastor in churches in Alabama, Florida, and North Carolina. He is married to Patricia and they have two children, Britt and JoBeth, and seven grandchildren. Although he has retired from participating in triathlons, John enjoys road biking, and cheering for the University of Louisville basketball team.

CONTENTS

INTRODUCTION

Jonathan sat with slumping shoulders on the edge of his bed starring into the quiet nothingness of his bedroom, his wife and kids long since asleep. The fatigue of ministry was almost overwhelming, and he saw no end in sight. Because of his hard work in seminary classes, he had come to his first pastorate with a sense of confidence that was depleting, one problem at a time. He recalled from his days as a pitcher on the varsity baseball team—how he depended on his catcher to communicate the signals from his head coach as he negotiated the subtleties of surviving each batter he faced. In time he mastered several pitches and had earned the credibility with his coaches and teammates necessary to make the strategic decisions on the mound on his own. Now he stood alone on a very different mound of leadership, getting shellacked by every confrontation that he faced. If he could just have some veteran advice from a coach who had been where he was, Jonathan thought he could turn things around in his ministry and regain the trust of his congregation. But where would he go to begin building his competence in the areas in which he was lacking?

With each passing year of the 21st century, pastoral ministry is becoming more complex, and many ministers share Jonathan's frustration—needing sage advice to deal with the intricacies of local church ministry. Most are simply not prepared for the dilemmas that stalk them every day.

One author describes the challenge this way: "No leader can be effective without character, but character does not ensure that a leader is effective. A good leader stands out when character is matched by *competence and the central virtue of knowing* (emphasis added)."[1] Many ministers, who have an authentic call to ministry, lack the virtue of knowing how to fulfill some of the rudimentary responsibilities of the job. The author continues, "The leader is not a superman, but he had better know who he is, what he is doing, what the organization faces as a challenge, and how to move forward."[2]

Entrusted to the Faithful

The contributors to this book have accepted the challenge to assist contemporary church leaders with this very real struggle and deficiency. In Paul's day he recognized full well that Timothy faced demanding difficulties and must prepare the next generation of Christ followers to train successive generations. In his second letter to his young pastor in-training, Paul wrote, "And what you have heard from me in the presence of many witnesses, commit to faithful men who will be able to teach others also" (II Timothy 2:2 HCSB). The NASB version renders the Greek word, *paratithemi*, in verse 2 as *entrust*. Guthrie describes the richness of this text in this way:

> The idea is clearly to entrust something for safe keeping, and in the present context this notion is of great significance. The transmission of Christian truth must never be left to chance, and is clearly not committed fortuitously to every Christian, but only to faithful

> men, who shall be able to teach others also. Two qualifications are demanded: A loyalty to the truth, i.e. a loyalty which has been proved, and an aptitude to teach.[3]

I believe you will agree with me that the authors of these chapters are superb examples of these two qualifications: fidelity to the truth and able to teach. In addition, they celebrate the significance of what the Lord has entrusted to them and eagerly commit it to you in the pages that follow.

This text reflects several of the on-going tensions in contemporary theological education. The authors are at once scholars in their disciplines and practitioners with decades of experience in pastoral ministry. We have spent time both in dusty library shelves looking for clues to the answers to ancient questions and in dusty streets of a developing nation exploring contemporary expressions of these questions. The topics we have chosen for each chapter represent a dimension of significant importance in the local church as well as the subject of centuries of academic research and debate. The packaging and delivery of the content makes use of case studies and problem solving activities, educational techniques that have accompanied instructional episodes throughout history. These approaches are widely accepted as examples of the latest research findings regarding the needs of contemporary adult learners who often meet with instructors and fellow classmates in virtual classrooms. The foundation of each chapter is biblical truth, unapologetic and passionate. But just as the Apostle Paul's instruction contained a balance of theological information and practical application, each chapter of our text contains wisdom and insights that reveal God's design for pastoral leadership along with each author's coaching on what that looks like in contemporary settings.

An Overview of the Layout of the Book

We believe that this book will provide our readers with a valuable tool for an individual currently in ministry or for one who is preparing for future service in the local church. Likewise, a pastoral staff can use these chapters for team building and problem solving. Instructors in traditional classrooms, hybrid courses, or online classes will find the format of the book ideal for university or seminary classes.

With this in mind the substance and format of each chapter are designed to respond to what research states are the needs of adult learners. The contributors to this volume believe that teaching and learning involve change–in perception, in attitude, in awareness, but most importantly, *change* in behavior. And the most effective learning experiences that bring about change are those in which the learner is actively *engaged.* Barkley describes this process well,

> Active learning means that the mind is actively engaged. Its defining characteristics are that students are dynamic participants in their learning and that they are reflecting on and monitoring both the processes and the results of their learning... This definition of active learning, where students make information or a concept their own by connecting it to their existing knowledge and experience, is critical to student engagement. An engaged student examines, questions, and relates new ideas to old, thereby achieving the kind of deep learning that lasts. Active learning is fundamental to and underlies all aspects of student engagement.[4]

Knowles and his colleagues contribute helpful insights regarding what adults are looking for in a learning environment, whether in a traditional university setting or a virtual classroom:

> *Need to know.* Adults need to know why they should learn something and how it benefits them.
>
> *Self-concept.* Adult learners may have difficulty with someone telling them what to do and how to think, which may make them resistant to learning in some situations.
>
> *Experience.* Adult learners have a lifetime experience and want to use and share what they know to enhance their learning.
>
> *Readiness to learn.* Adults become ready to learn something when they have a need to solve a problem.
>
> *Orientation to learning.* Adults want to see how what they are learning will apply to their life, a task they need to perform, or a problem they to solve.
>
> *Motivation to learn.* Incentives such as increased job satisfaction, self-esteem, and quality of life are important in giving them a reason to learn.[5]

As the editor of this compilation, I have challenged my colleagues as experts in various fields of local church ministry to tackle these expectations as each composes his chapter focused on critical issues. To assist us in accomplishing this ambitious goal we have developed four sidebars in each chapter. *Each active learning sidebar is intended to highlight the most significant points of the chapter and invite the reader's engagement.* Garrison and Vaughan in *Blended Learning in Higher Education: Framework, Principles, and Guidelines* articulate the importance of designing instruction in such a way that it creates a "community of inquiry". One of their principles that assists in establishing such an environment is: "Plan for critical reflection, discourse, and tasks that will support systematic inquiry."[6] We have designed the following four active learning techniques for each chapter. Each section contains a sample illustration based on the content of this introduction.

Active Learning #1: Recite and Rehearse

This will be a recommendation for the student to focus on new information presented in the chapter, such as a list of things or an important definition that should be memorized. We view this as the author coaching or reminding a player—you have to practice this and make sure you know this. It will be personal practice. Donaldson and Conrad explain this type of activity as follows:

> Engaged learning stimulates learners to actively participate in the learning situation, and thus gain the most knowledge from being a member of an online learning community. Activities can also serve as memory cues. On several occasions, students have reported remembering the lessons learned from an activity in

order to trigger long-term memory relative to the recall of basic concepts.[7]

Review the needs of adult learners presented in this chapter. Rank order the list, placing the needs in order of importance from 'most important' to 'least important' according to your own personal preferences.

Active Learning #2: Reflect and React

Writing personal reflection essays is a popular way to stimulate higher order thinking and challenge students to do more than memorize, as we did in Sidebar #1. Also, in online instruction, students can be asked to post their reflection essay and then respond to their classmates' papers. So the author will select some aspect of the material and ask the reader to reflect and react to the new material. Based on both educational studies and brain research, Tokuhama-Espinsosa discusses the value of writing reflection essays:

The act of articulation moves reflection beyond superficial learning to deep learning and improves the quality of true understanding. Reflective practice gives the brain time to return to things that are known, ruminate, and sometimes reinforce those pathways, as well as reassess choices by comparing what was thought to occur and what did occur. The neuroscience of decision-making is closely related to reflective practice.[8]

> Write a compare/contrast essay in which you describe two learning environments, including the roles the instructors play. In one of the environments describe a situation that is very effective for your learning styles and preferences. In the other, describe an environment in which you would struggle to learn. Conclude by articulating how you as a teacher are prepared to modify your preferences to meet the needs of students who learn differently.

Active Learning #3: Research and Create

A popular instructional activity for both virtual classrooms and on campus meetings during a hybrid course (in which students meet face to face) is to challenge students to collaborate on a problem/solution assignment. The authors have recommended problems or challenges that a team of students could research, create a solution for, and present to their classmates in a reasonable length of time. For some classes this could actually be the culminating project for the semester. "Problem-based learning works because learning takes place in an authentic context that students can relate to, which easily leads to transfer. Transfer is in part, the ability to view and use information in a variety of settings."[9] Watson and Groh applaud problem-based learning as an approach that allows learners to "develop intellectual curiosity, confidence and engagement that will lead to lifelong learning."[10] Palloff and Pratt also endorse the significance of collaboration stating that

> Collaboration enhances learning outcomes and reduces the potential for learner isolation...By learning together in a learning community, students have the opportunity to extend and deepen their learning experiences, test out new ideas by sharing them with a supportive group, and receive critical and constructive feedback.[11]

Join a team of three other classmates and research one of the following four topics:

Describe current 'best practices' in online instruction, emphasizing the role of the instructor.

Do adult learners from different age groups such as Boomers versus Digital Natives have the same attitudes toward online instruction? Develop a brief survey in which you solicit the differing viewpoints of 50 students in your university. Aggregate the data and draw conclusions. (Check with your university policies about Human Subjects participation in surveys and Informed Consent requirements.)

Collaboration or Problem Based Learning (traditionally called 'group work') is a popular but still controversial approach to learning, particularly with adults. Research the pros and cons of this methodology, including strategies that research says leads to effective structuring of this educational technique.

Will hybrid or blended learning classes lead to increased enrollment in your institution? Take on the role of a dean at a nearby university and decide if you are going to invest in the human resource training and capital expenditures necessary to make this change in the institution's approach to delivering classes. How many auxiliary departments must participate in making this change successful? Outline what each department would be asked to contribute.

Active Learning #4: Respond to a Case Study

The final section of each chapter is a case study. It will be a true to life narrative about some, not necessarily all, of the ideas discussed in the chapter. These case studies have been crafted in such a way that the students' responses can be debated. Palloff and Pratt believe that "the process of arriving at an answer is more important than the answer itself."[12] Here are the guidelines they recommend for students to begin an analysis of a case study:

1. Read the case quickly to get an overview of what is involved.
2. Read the case a second time and list assumptions, hunches, and facts.
3. Identify the major problems and auxiliary issues. Also, list the major players and the part each plays.
4. Reorder the problems, listing each in order of priority. Indicate which problems should be dealt with first.
5. Develop a list of alternative courses of action that reduce the impact of each problem.
6. Outline the constraints that limit the success of the alternatives in step 5. (These constraints could include material resources, human skills, or member attitudes.)
7. Determine the best course of action. Explain how the course of action would work and why it would be the most successful alternative.[13]

Here's an abbreviated Case Study for the Introduction of this text:

Nick is a young seminary student who has recently returned to graduate school after five years in youth ministry. He is highly motivated to prepare for full time commitment in ministry in response to a call he believes the Lord has placed on his life. His brief ministry experience has been generally positive but has left him with more questions than answers. He has a growing list of questions and issues for which he desperately needs practical solutions. Hybrid classes are a new approach to coursework delivery at his seminary and some of his required core include hybrid classes. Coming to campus for three weekends throughout the semester combined with distance learning activities seemed like a great approach at the time, particularly sense his ministry position and family needs are growing with each passing month. And not having the two hour round trip to and from class each week is a huge plus. But now he is not so sure...

Early on in the semester the delivery platform used by the seminary wasn't working consistently. Coupled with his unfamiliarity with online learning,

> these issues created lots of distractions. At the first on-campus session his professor spent the entire two days presenting non-stop lectures, leaving little time to meet classmates with whom he would be corresponding. Nick did well enough on the weekly quizzes not to be worried about his grades, but he questioned the value of the true/false statements he was required to respond to. By mid-semester Nick was struggling, not having really connected with the professor, the content, or his classmates. But it was too late to drop the course...

---

1. What are the key issues in the case study? Rank order your list, with the most impactful issue listed first, and so on.
2. What concepts discussed in this chapter do you believe speak to the issues that you have identified?
3. How should Nick address his issues and struggles? How should the seminary respond?

Case study analysis involves a unique set of problem solving techniques that may be new to some students. Perhaps you will find this list of warning about common mistakes useful:

- Failure to understand or accept the facts of the case.
- Failure to explain exactly what the problems are & why they have occurred.

- Making unwarranted assumptions to try to simplify the case.
- Sticking to generalities, such as "they must try to improve communication."
- Failure to integrate the various points into a preferred solution.
- Seeking ways out of the situation (such as "fire them all") rather than trying to solve the problems.
- Ignoring practicalities.[14]

Concluding Comments about the Book

Over the years my favorite response to a class presentation was to have a student say, "Dr. Coley, if I had heard this presentation five years ago, I wouldn't have been fired from my first ministry position." Simple, direct, and to the point–a student evaluation that says it all. It is the collective heartbeat of all of the contributors to this text on pastoral ministry that the biblical truth and practical wisdom presented here have the ring of truth and an immediate applicability to your ministry setting. You will find that each chapter is carefully crafted in a way that presents God's enduring truths, current scholarship, and the author's personal experience on topics of vital importance to your success in ministry.

1

SHEPHERDING GOD'S FLOCK

David Beck

It was early on a cold Thanksgiving Day in Western Pennsylvania where I served as pastor of a small congregation. I was only a couple of years out of seminary and several years away from God's call to academic ministry. We were looking forward to a quiet day of family celebration when the phone rang. I could barely make out what was being said for the heavy sobbing at the other end of the line, but I knew it was John, an older man in my congregation who served as a deacon and Sunday school superintendent. I knew something was terribly wrong, and I told him I would be right over.

He met me at the door and through tears said simply, "I think she's gone." We went together to his bedroom, and there was his wife he loved dearly, with whom he had shared more than half a century. She had gone to sleep next to her husband she had devoted her life to and woke up in the presence of her Savior.

The time that followed was hectic. I made phone calls for John that he couldn't make for himself. First the funeral director, then his children, and after that his extended family. In between the calls and waiting for people to arrive, we talked, reminisced, cried, and sought God's comforting presence. We remembered His love for us and the sure and certain promises of eternal life.

Thanksgiving dinner with my wife and daughter was late that year. We did not mind; it was a privilege to be serving God by fulfilling His calling to shepherd His flock.

What does the phrase "shepherding God's flock" mean? The imagery was more common in a previous generation, and the traditional terminology of "pastor" for the leader of a congregation reflects that. But today there is much discussion surrounding the correct designation for church leaders. Should they be called *ministers ... pastors ... elders*? Sometimes this discussion is a question of different understandings of leadership functions, and other times it is attempting to be more biblical in the terminology we use. But whatever they are called and however their roles are understood, God's Word mandates that the leaders of His church are called to shepherd the flock of God, regardless of the title they bear or the written job description they were given. As Andreas Köstenberger has correctly observed,

> The mandate to shepherd God's flock is not an optional activity for leaders in which to engage only if they feel they have the right personality or inclination. Pastors will no doubt shepherd in different ways based on individual gifting or temperament, but the obligation to shepherd cannot and must not be delegated to others, and no matter how construed contains a personal dimension. Remote or absentee shepherding is not an option.[15]

After Peter's infamous failure to carry out his promise of loyalty even unto death, he encountered the risen Jesus in the well-known restoration scene in John 21. This is not a detailed explanation of the responsibilities entailed in his apostolic office. It was far more basic and went to the core of his relationship with Jesus and the call upon his life to lead and serve the community of believers. After Peter's renewed affirmation of his love for Jesus, he was informed that the love he declared for Jesus was to be manifested in the feeding of God's flock and tending of His sheep. Without details or specifics of the exact content of his commission, Peter was assigned to be their shepherd (John 21:15–17). In this chapter we will examine the biblical imagery of *shepherd* as it relates to our leadership of God's people and explore how it is fleshed out in ministry.

Interest in leadership as a practical academic discipline has grown tremendously in our culture and within the church. This is appropriate, since clearly leadership is at the core of our ministry responsibility. One of the most basic and common leadership images in Scripture is that of shepherd. Our use of the title "pastor," from the Latin for *shepherd*, and the descriptive adjective "pastoral" is directly linked to this image. The problem for most twenty-first century Americans is that the practical reality behind this image is foreign to us.[16] Our knowledge is mostly secondhand background information acquired from lessons and sermons we have heard on the Twenty-third Psalm, Christmas messages from Luke 2, or other biblical passages referencing this image. What is rarely noted is the richness of this image throughout Scripture for the leadership God intends for His people.

Shepherding in the Old Testament

The most notable biblical use of this metaphor for leadership is applied to God Himself. Many are familiar with Psalm 23, where David identifies *Yahweh*, (translated *kurios* in the LXX, and the LORD in modern English translations) as the shepherd of his life. But this metaphor for God's relationship with His covenant people is not limited to the familiar shepherd Psalm; it is found throughout the Hebrew Scriptures. In Genesis 48:15 in his blessing of Joseph, Jacob identifies God as the One who "has been my shepherd all my life to this day." Moses prayed for God to appoint a man to lead His people so they would not be sheep without a shepherd (Numbers 27:16–17). The same graphic description of leaderless people prompts Jesus' compassion for the people of Israel in Mark 6:34 and Matthew 9:36.

A close examination of Psalm 23 reveals the character of God's shepherding of His flock from the perspective of one who has been a recipient of that care. It is "a Psalm of *trust and confidence*" in God's provision and protection of His sheep.[17] Because of the identity of his shepherd, the Psalmist has been provided for so that there is nothing he lacks, nor any danger he fears. Although paths may be hazardous and valleys may be perilous, the care of the Shepherd is constant and trustworthy.

In today's ministry of shepherding, the task is the same. We must provide the nourishment that will sustain the spirits of God's flock and enable growth in the faith and knowledge of God. An examination of Paul's prayers in his letters reveal that it is not their physical well-being that is the primary content of his intercession on behalf of God's people. It is for them to know God, experience His love fully, grow in their confidence in their positions in Christ, and experience His power to walk in a manner worthy of their callings in Christ.[18] As the sheep of God's flock encounter difficulties as they traverse the pathways of their lives, it is the shepherd who needs to guard and protect, being a visible reminder of God's constant presence and a facilitator who helps them negotiate the rough spots, helping them grasp how God's Word speaks relevantly to everything they encounter. When sheep find themselves in the darkest of valleys, it is the shepherd who shines the light of Christ into their situations and illumines their paths with God's Word.

God prophetically promised to give His people "shepherds after My own heart" in Jeremiah 3:15, a description later used in Acts 13:22 to describe David's leadership of Israel (not his personal character). God pronounced His judgment on those false shepherds who led His people astray (Jeremiah 23:1–2, Ezekiel 34:1–10) and promises, "I will care for my sheep and will deliver them from all the places to which they were scattered" (Ezekiel 34:12). His declaration of His own shepherding activity includes the following verbs, descriptive of the process of shepherding: "I will search" (v.11), "I will care" (v. 12), "I will bring ... and gather" (v.13), "I will feed" (vv.13, 14, 15), "I will seek ... bring back ... bind up ... strengthen" (v.16). Notice these verbs are active, not passive. The shepherd does not wait for the sheep to seek him out; he searches for them when they wander, gathers them and brings them back, ministers healing to their wounds, and cares for their needs.

Recite and rehearse

Selecting from the biblical passages examined in this essay, develop one shepherding principle or practice and list the characteristics in order of importance.

Shepherding in the Gospels

In the messianic prophesy of Micah 5:4, God promises to raise up from Bethlehem One who would "arise and shepherd His flock in the strength of the LORD." Jesus identifies with this shepherd imagery and the Old Testament promise to God's covenant people. He first tells His disciples, then the Canaanite woman, that He and they are sent to "the lost sheep of the house of Israel" (Matthew 10:6, 15:24). In one of His most familiar parables, Jesus tells of the shepherd who leaves the ninety-nine and seeks out the one straying sheep and thereby models His Father's will (Luke 15:1–7). But it is in John where Jesus gives the fullest explanation of this shepherd imagery in His ministry.

In John 10 Jesus identifies Himself as both the Good Shepherd and the doorway by which His sheep enter His fold. As the door of the sheepfold, He is the only means of entrance into the fold, into the salvation God offers (v. 9). As the Good Shepherd, He will lay His life down for the sheep

(v. 11). He knows the sheep, and they know Him (v. 14). The sheep know His voice and will follow His leading (v. 3). Furthermore, He has other sheep, not from this flock, and He will make of them one flock, with one shepherd (v. 16). The qualifications for being the Good Shepherd that sets Him apart from the false shepherds that have preceded are twofold. The first is His absolute devotion to the welfare of His flock, to such an extent that He will die for them. The second is His knowledge of the flock and the depth of the intimate familiarity He shares with them. They know His voice, and He knows their names.

We do not and cannot serve the Good Shepherd's function as the door into the sheepfold. But we must emulate His devotion to the sheep, willing to sacrifice ourselves for their benefit. Our ministry must not be motivated by a desire for accolades or other personal gains, but only what benefits God's sheep. We also follow Christ's example of His intimate knowledge of the sheep, which enables their confidence and trust in Him. Only when God's people learn the authenticity of our walk with God, and the genuine nature of our love for them, will they trust us and allow us to feed, guide, and lead them.

Jesus continues this imagery in John 21 in the restoration scene with Peter. He confronts Peter with a question concerning the depth of Peter's love: is it "more than these?" (21:15). Regardless of the antecedent of the demonstrative pronoun[19] and whether "these" refers to his fellow disciples or the accoutrements of fishing that surround him, it is still a question of the priority of his love for Jesus above all else. Peter answers affirmatively, but Jesus repeats the question three more times. In each instance following Peter's affirmative response, he is given a ministry assignment. It is the same task, repeated three times in different language: "feed/shepherd/tend my lambs/sheep." Jesus' response to Peter's affirmation of love is not an indication that somehow Peter's love for Jesus has qualified him to serve in a role of authoritative leadership. Rather, it is Peter's love for Jesus that motivates him to obey Jesus' command to be a shepherd of Christ's flock.[20]

To understand the full implications of the shepherding assignment Jesus gives to Peter, it is necessary to view it within the context of the entire gospel of John. After Jesus identifies Himself as the Good Shepherd in chapter 10, including His willingness to lay down His life on behalf of the sheep, the following chapters flesh out the precise meaning and significance of the metaphor. In 12:24 Jesus' response to the request of the Greeks to see Him is to announce that now His hour has come, and He clarifies the content of this hour with the statement of the necessity for a grain of wheat to die before it can bear fruit. At the foot washing in chapter 13, Jesus models the heart of the shepherd toward His sheep and their needs. In that context Peter asserts His willingness to die for Jesus (v. 37), a claim that Jesus responds to with skepticism, predicting the unfaithfulness of his denial instead. In the farewell discourse Jesus explicitly ties love to obedience (14:15) and declares that the greatest expression of love is the willingness to die for another (15:13). These portions of the narrative confirm the understanding of the affirmation of Peter's love as the motive for his obedience to Jesus' shepherding command and the prediction of his martyrdom that immediately follows it.[21] He too will lay down his life for the sheep and their Shepherd.

Jesus' final words to Peter in John 21, predicting his martyrdom, reveals an important truth about the task of shepherding God's flock. Faithful shepherding would cost Peter his independence and eventually his life. Obedience to God's command for the leaders of His church to live out their professed love for Him in the service of shepherding requires a surrender of our own wants and goals and priorities to Him. We go wherever He calls, and we expend our energies wherever His sheep have need. We surrender our own control over our lives, yielding to Him and His call. And, if required, we willingly give our lives for His glory.

Shepherding in 1 Peter

This imagery is one that Peter never forgot. In later years when he wrote his first letter and addressed the God-called leaders of the church, his directive to them was that they "shepherd the flock of God among you" (1 Peter 5:2). In this exhortation he gives a descriptive phrase characterizing the function of shepherding, as well as three contrasting pairs that provide the parameters for how shepherding God's flock is to be practiced.[22] What a shepherd does is to exercise oversight. The word here for *oversight* shares its root with the noun "overseer" found in 1 Timothy 3. *Oversight* implies leadership authority and is quickly qualified so as to contrast the godly shepherding oversight Peter is urging, from the world's exercise of authority.

The first qualification is that our shepherding is not to be entered into with reluctance or resistance. Instead, it is to be "according to God." Jesus Himself, God incarnate, provides us the model for our shepherding. Even with what it would cost Him, He did not resist His Father's will, but freely gave Himself on our behalf (Galatians 1:4). We in turn seek only God's will for our lives and willingly follow it. We shepherd and serve because having surrendered to God's control over our lives, after seeking His face to discover how His will is to be carried out in our lives, we can do nothing else and discover the joy in obedience.

The second qualification turns to the motive behind our shepherding. It cannot be for monetary benefits or personal gains. This is not to say it is wrong for church leaders to be paid. There are many Scriptures that confirm the appropriateness of this.[23] However, that compensation can never be the motive for our shepherding. Instead, we are eager to do the ministry to which we have been called, desiring to serve the people of God. We follow the earnest example of Jesus when He lamented, "Jerusalem, Jerusalem, who kills the prophets and stones those who are sent to her! How often I wanted to gather your children together, the way a hen gathers her chicks under her wings, and you were unwilling" (Matthew 23:37). To serve and minister to God's people was the desire of Jesus' heart, not a task He viewed with distaste, nor a means to material gain.

The final adverbial qualifier in this passage addresses the character and temperament with which we exercise the shepherding oversight of God's flock. It must not be an authoritarian dominance with which we rule over God's flock, as if they are our subservient subjects. Jesus warns against this in Mark 10:42–44, when in response to the disciples' indignation at learning that James and John were seeking a favored position for themselves, He said, "You know that those who are recognized as rulers of the Gentiles lord it over them; and their great men exercise authority over them. But it is not this way among you, but whoever wishes to become great among you shall be your servant; and whoever wishes to be first among you shall be slave of all." This precludes us leading with an authoritarian, dictatorial style.

Jesus recognized that it is natural in our fallen human nature to take advantage of those we have authority over. Peter echoes this truth and contrasts it with the need to be models to the flock. Jesus contrasted His warning in Mark with His own example, "the Son of Man did not come to be served, but to serve, and to give His life a ransom for many" (10:45). With Jesus as our example, we must model for God's flock the content of faithfully walking with God, never forgetting that while called to shepherd, we too are still sheep. Our tendency is toward an unwillingness to offer our own lives as an example to God's flock. This may come from an appropriate humility that seeks to grow believers who are disciples of Jesus, not of ourselves. But it may also be motivated by the desire to avoid the pressure of living lives that are "pure and blameless" (Philippians 1:10). Paul did not hesitate to offer himself as an example of the believer's walk that he was exhorting God's people to follow. He wrote to the Philippian believers, "Brothers, join in following my example, and observe those who walk according to the pattern you have in us" (Philippians 3:17). He told the Corinthians, "Be imitators of me, just as I also am of Christ" (1 Corinthians 11:1). Whether we embrace the scrutiny of those whom God has entrusted to us for shepherding or not, they are watching us to see how we practice what we are teaching them. The question is not if we are an example, but is our example faithful and are we consistently living out God's Word in the circumstances of daily life?

Shepherding in Ephesians

In Ephesians 4 Paul also references the ministry of shepherding when he lists the leaders with which God graces His church. Here we find the only New Testament occurrence of the noun *shepherd* in reference to a leader of the church. It is generally translated from the Latin into English as *pastor*. The grammatical construction of this list of grace-gifted leaders in God's church changes for the last two items in the list, pastors and teachers. This leads some to see this as different functions of the same leader, while others view pastors as a subset of the larger group (all pastors are teachers, but all teachers are not also pastors). At the very least the grammar indicates a close relationship between these two ministry functions. Shepherding and teaching overlap and are closely linked.[24]

In Ephesians 4 the focus is not on the particular shepherding activity but God's goal and purpose in the exercise of all the leadership gifts He has provided. His goal is to equip the people of God for service, for the building the body of Christ (Ephesians 4:12). The result will be unity and maturity, a maturity measured not by comparison with other believers but Christ Himself as the only acceptable standard of measurement (v. 13). The result will be stability rooted in God's revealed truth, not susceptible to false teaching and deceit. This is achieved by "speaking the truth in love." It is significant that this oft-repeated biblical phrase, in its biblical context, is addressing the manner in which shepherds guard the flock by faithfully teaching God's truth and correcting any deviation from it.

Reflect and react

Choose the shepherding principle or practice that has the most direct relevance to your ministry context. Briefly explain to what extent it is implemented in your ministry and how you plan to strengthen it.

The Shepherd as Guardian

God's people today have easier access and more exposure to false teachings than previous generations. It is not only the prosperity gospel being proclaimed on the airways and promoted in bookstores, but also the infiltration into popular culture of the radical skeptical scholarship that used to be reserved for the ivory towers of higher education. Today the same denial of biblical truth can be readily accessed on PBS, A&E, and other media outlets through programing promoted with catchy tag lines like "the Jesus you never knew." This exposure increases the shepherding obligation to faithfully instruct God's people in His truth and directly confront false teaching with biblical refutation. Doing so fulfills the admonition Paul gave to the Ephesian elders in Acts 20. To give effective oversight to God's flock, the shepherd must protect his congregation from those who would lead them astray from God's truth.

However, it is not only the flock that must be guarded; the shepherds must also guard themselves. This self-guarding can only be accomplished by allowing God's Word to have its way in our lives before we minister and apply its truth in shepherding God's people. This is explicitly addressed in 2 Timothy 3:14–17, though often missed by modern readers. It is in this context that we find the familiar declaration of the character and function of God's Word. It is "God-breathed," flowing forth from the inner essence of God Himself, and shares His inerrant, trustworthy nature. It is purposeful, God's revelation accomplishing God's purpose of teaching, reproving, correcting, and training in righteousness (v. 16). But what is frequently overlooked is that this is not the shepherd ministering God's word among God's people (that admonition occurs in 4:2). In chapter 3 the pronoun is second person singular, rare in New Testament epistles. Paul is not addressing the church (*you* plural), but the shepherd of the flock, Timothy (*you* singular).

Only after allowing God's Word to fulfill its instructional, convicting, correcting, equipping purpose in the life of the shepherd can the shepherd effectively proclaim it so that it can work God's purposes in the lives of the sheep. Once the shepherd has been equipped by God for the good work of shepherding the flock, he is commanded to minister God's Word to God's flock. The ministry of the Word must be when convenient or not, both when the shepherd feels up to it and when he doesn't, but also when the sheep are receptive and when they are resistant to God's truth.[25] Furthermore, great patience is the manner in which the truth of God is to be spoken into the lives of His sheep. Whenever we are tempted to become exasperated at what we perceive as the sheep's non-responsiveness to God's Word, we must never forget we too are sheep, sometime rebellious, and God is patient with us.

A careful examination of the metaphor of shepherd in general and these texts in particular give insight into the task of shepherding God's flock as church leaders in the twenty-first century. Thomas Golding has summarized the role of shepherds as follows: "guiding, providing food and water, protecting and delivering, gathering scattered or lost sheep, and giving health and security."[26] He further notes that the two emotions evoked by the image are opposites, fear or contentment and security.[27] The mandate to faithful shepherding can be summarized under three categories. The first is providing/feeding, second is guiding/leading, and the third is protecting/guarding. How do leaders in churches today practice the shepherding mandate in the daily ministry to those whom God has given us oversight responsibility?

The Shepherd as Provider

Provision and feeding primarily refers to the ministry of God's Word into the lives of God's people. It is easily identified with the tasks of preaching God's Word in regularly scheduled worship and designated instructional opportunities. It is a joy and delight to stand before God's people and proclaim His truth. It is also an awesome responsibility. If we are to allow God to use His Word for its instructing, convicting, correcting, and equipping purpose, then our proclamation must be biblically sound, spiritually rich, and practically applicable. We must avoid the temptation to be entertaining and amusing at the expense of biblical depth and theological accuracy. If our churches suffer from a biblical illiteracy, who is to blame except those entrusted to feed God's flock? If there is a disconnect in the lives of those who sit under our teaching between what they profess to believe and the practical living of their lives, do we who shepherd not bear at least some of the responsibility? If God's flock walk through their lives without an adequate biblical world view through which they filter everything they encounter, don't we at least have to ask whether we have provided the opportunity for them to develop their understanding of God's point of view?

We must proclaim the "whole counsel of God," teaching His flock the story line of the Bible, connecting the dots in God's grand narrative of redemption in its cohesive whole from Genesis to Revelation. But it is not sufficient to only inform the flock of what His Word says and what He has done. We must also guide them in applying God's truth to every facet and in every corner of their lives. We must provide clear teaching on how to have gospel-centered marriages and families. We must instruct them in how to live out the implications of the gospel in their schools and on their jobs. We must teach them to think biblically about what they hear and observe in the culture that surrounds them. We must help them interpret popular media, entertainment options, political pundits, and every other portion of the world's influence in their lives through the lens of God's truth.

The opportunities to preach, teach classes, and lead groups are not the exclusive opportunities for shepherding the people of God. Guiding and leading God's church has both a corporate dimension and an individual one. It is undeniable that the New Testament understands the Christian life as being lived out in community. To be God's church is to be the people of God, the family of God, the army of God, the body of Christ. All of these speak to the church as a unified, cooperate whole. But it is a whole comprised of individual members, a body that is one, yet comprised of many individual parts (1 Corinthians 12:12–14).

Research and create

List the five primary ministry activities in your church and assess them for how they fulfill the shepherding mandate.

The Shepherd as Guide

Shepherding is not limited to the oversight of a congregation collectively. It has an undeniable individual element as well and necessitates our direct involvement in the lives of individual sheep. Ezekiel 34:15–16 gives us a precise summary of this aspect of our shepherding responsibilities: "'I will feed My flock and I will lead them to rest,' declares the Lord God. "I will seek the lost, bring back the scattered, bind up the broken and strengthen the sick; but the fat and the strong I will destroy. I will feed them with judgment.'" Considering this to be "the perfect outline of the shepherd's responsibilities," Derek Tidball notes:

> Not only is he to feed, guide, and protect the flock but also to understand that there are individual sheep to which he must give special attention. The lost must be found, the wandering restored, the injured tended, the weak strengthened and the strong disciplined. Here so many aspects of ministry come together. We are called to be evangelists who bring the lost home, pastors who go after those tempted to drift and slide backwards in discipleship, nurses and doctors who bring healing to the wounded, educators who build up the young and encourage the vulnerable, and disciplinarians who admonish the arrogant.[28]

In an age when churches are growing larger numerically, it is imperative that we do not lose sight of the responsibility to shepherd the individual members of God's flock. Shepherding God's sheep requires knowing the sheep. In John 10 Jesus identified what set Him apart from the false shepherds who sought to harm the sheep as His intimate knowledge of them. He knew them, and they knew Him. It is impossible to shepherd people we do not know. While numerical growth can be good, we must avoid valuing size as an end in itself and deeming numerically smaller churches insignificant. But even in smaller churches shepherding can be neglected. There is a danger that instead of having leaders who are shepherds, the flock of God has effective administrators leading an organization, skilled communicators addressing crowds, and gifted visionaries charting successful strategy. But who is shepherding the sheep? When numbers increase, shepherding can still occur, but it must be a conscious effort, intentionally planned, and purposefully implemented.

Those who are assigned the shepherding task must involve themselves in the lives of the people they are to lead. They must be willing to make an investment in them, meeting them on their own territory, not just in the vestibules and hallways surrounding worship centers. During crisis times there must be a visible presence, not just an impersonal e-mail. This does not occur by accident. It takes a willful choice on the part of those who would shepherd, and it requires an investment of time. As we involve ourselves intimately in the lives of God's sheep, their real needs are revealed. We remember that when Jesus washed the feet of His disciples, it was not to establish a third ordinance for the church or to illustrate symbolically a spiritual truth. He washed their feet because their feet were dirty and needed washing. He did not consider the task demeaning, nor beneath Him. And when He finished He asked them this question, "Do you understand what I have done for you? ...You call me 'Teacher' and 'Lord,' and rightly so, for that is what I am. Now that I, your Lord and Teacher, have washed your feet, you also should wash one another's feet" (John 13:12–14). The reciprocal effects of knowing the sheep are being known by them and receiving ministry from them.

This means shepherds live out their lives transparently before those who comprise the family of God. We shepherd faithfully by modeling in ourselves how a life is lived faithfully following the Good Shepherd–with humility. We must never exercise our leadership responsibility in an authoritarian manner. We must get to know our sheep and involve ourselves in their individual lives. We respond willingly and joyously to every need we observe in the life of one of God's sheep as an opportunity to serve him and love Christ. No service is too demeaning or beneath us as we faithfully obey the shepherding mandate of the One who washed feet. Only then can the goals of shepherding as outlined in Ephesians 4:12–16 be accomplished: being united as God's flock, knowing His truth, growing mature in faith, recognizing and rejecting what is false, equipping to joyously and fully serve one another.

Respond to a case study

Pastor Joe was sitting in his study, putting the final touches on Sunday's sermon. In retrospect, it had been a good week. The staff meeting that started the week had gone well. Progress and accomplishments had been reported, needs discussed, and ministry tasks assigned. The prayer time that followed had been especially meaningful.

Tuesday's finance committee meeting had been surprisingly non-controversial. He had finished going over the work of the constitution revision committee, and the draft was ready for the

Leadership Team's scrutiny. Planning was finished, and the reorganization transition from Sunday school to small groups was ready for implementation. He had finished the final edits on his manuscript and sent it to the publisher. Joe was looking forward to wrapping things up and spending a couple of hours at home with his family before tonight's meeting.

The knock at his door surprised him. He opened it to find a small group gathered there. They included prominent members of his church family who identified themselves as a "delegation" from the congregation. They were obviously uncomfortable, most unable to meet his eye, each one shifting his weight form one foot to the other. These were people he knew and counted as friends. Much to his dismay, he quickly found out what this was all about. Their self-appointed spokesman, a man Joe had never been able to warm up to, declared that, having carefully followed the guidelines provided in the church by-laws, they had called a special vote tonight on the continuation of Joe's tenure as their pastor.

Joe was caught completely off guard. "What have I done?" he asked. He was quickly assured it was nothing personal. He was a good man and a good preacher. He was an excellent organizer and administrator. "But what we really need," they said, "is a pastor." Joe was floored. What was that even supposed to mean? What was he going to tell his wife? What would he say before the vote tonight? What could he have done differently?

Questions:

1. What do you think the group meant by their assessment of Joe's ministry and their conclusion, "But what we really need is a pastor"?
2. How could Joe defend his ministry activities as fulfilling the shepherding mandate?
3. What do you think Joe should offer to change or do differently if he is to continue to lead this church?

2
PREACHING EXPOSITORY SERMONS

Allan Moseley

Mike was attending his first preaching conference. He sat in an enormous crowd and felt like a lone stalk in a vast field of wheat. As he listened to one preacher after another, he became overwhelmed. All the preachers were articulate, passionate, and seemed so knowledgeable. They all served as pastors in churches with thousands of members, and they all told of impressive successes in their ministries. As they preached, they were displayed on giant screens in the auditorium, which seemed to magnify their importance and expertise. Mike knew that after the conference was over he would return to serve the small church he pastored. No great crowd, no big success stories, and no screen. He found himself envying mega-church pastors and wanting to leave his people to serve in a place where his preaching would look and sound just as impressive. But then in prayer he asked God what *is* great preaching anyway? What kind of preaching pleases God? How can he know he is preaching the right kind of sermon in the right way, even in a place that is not impressive to the world?

"The work of preaching is the highest and the greatest and the most glorious calling to which anyone can ever be called ... The most urgent need in the Christian Church today is true preaching."[29] Thus Martin

Lloyd-Jones began his book *Preaching and Preachers*, based on lectures he delivered at Westminster Seminary in 1969. His words are still true today, and they always have been. God has spoken. What calling could be greater than proclaiming His Word?

Why could Lloyd-Jones write that preaching is the "highest ... greatest ... most glorious calling" and "the *most* urgent need" of the church? First, believing, obeying, and preaching God's Word is primary in the Bible. The first sin resulted from the mishandling of God's Word. Noah was "a preacher of righteousness" (2 Peter 2:5). Abraham was a good steward of God's Word because God said he, "kept My mandate, My commands, My statutes, and My instructions" (Genesis 26:5). Moses received God's Word, recorded it, and proclaimed it. Throughout Israel's history prophets, poets, and sages received and spoke God's Word. John the Baptist preached to prepare people for the Messiah (Matthew 3:1–12). Jesus began His ministry by preaching repentance and "the good news of the kingdom" (Matthew 4:17, 23). Later in His Galilean ministry, Jesus "went to all the towns and villages, teaching in their synagogues, preaching the good news of the kingdom" (Matthew 9:35). After Jesus' resurrection, Peter and John "were teaching the people and proclaiming the resurrection from the dead" (Acts 4:2). All the followers of Jesus who scattered from Jerusalem after the martyrdom of Stephen "went on their way preaching the message of good news" (Acts 8:4).[30] Proclamation of God's Word is clearly central in the Bible.

Second, preaching is important for pastors because God explicitly commands preaching. Paul exhorted Pastor Timothy, "Proclaim the message; persist in it whether convenient or not" (2 Timothy 4:2). Pastors are shepherds (Acts 20:26–31; 1 Peter 5:1–2), and shepherds feed the sheep. God's Word is the spiritual food the people need, and preaching is the way pastors feed God's Word to God's people. Jesus told His followers to make disciples.

After people become His disciples we baptize them and teach them to obey what Jesus commanded (Matthew 28:19–20). Preaching is teaching people God's Word and exhorting them to obey it. Through preaching in corporate worship, pastors feed God's Word to more people in the church than through any other ministry. If pastors do not give significant effort to the task of feeding the sheep, they are not faithful shepherds.

Third, preaching is an evangelistic ministry. As pastors preach the gospel, they can affect the eternal destiny of the hearers by leading them to faith in Jesus. People will not believe in Jesus and be saved without hearing the gospel (Romans 10:13–14). In the preaching of God's Word, much is at stake—the spiritual maturity of believers and the eternal destiny of unbelievers. Faithful pastors respond to those high stakes by preaching all of God's Word to God's people and by preaching the gospel and inviting every person to put their faith in Jesus.

Fourth, expository preaching is essential because God has spoken in the Bible and expository preaching exposes the contents of the Bible. The great priority for pastors is not to be clever, funny, or eloquent, but to present the contents of the Bible clearly and compellingly. The church and the world need what God says in His Word, not what a man wants to say. Yet, the contemporary church faces a crisis of biblical illiteracy. Because the Bible is God's revelation of Himself and the truth to humanity, biblical illiteracy is a tragedy of epic proportions. The church cannot know what God is like, what God expects of humanity, or even the structure of reality if the church does not know the Bible. Therefore, now more than ever, faithful pastors teach the Bible from the pulpit.[31]

Recite and rehearse

What is the source of your motivation to preach the Bible? Is it the size of the crowd? Your own need? Accolades from people? Biblical mandate? Which biblical truth motivates you most to preach the Bible? Which is most important?

A Definition of Expository Preaching: What Are Expository Preachers Trying to Do?

Definitions of preaching are inevitably theological. What pastors believe about God, His purposes, and the nature of His Word will shape their conceptions of preaching. When pastors believe the Bible contains the words of mere humans, they also likely believe their own words are virtually equivalent to the words of the human writers of the Bible. Therefore, their preaching consists of finding a kernel of religious truth in the Bible and expounding on that idea in the way they deem appropriate. Where the truth and power of the Bible are undervalued, the importance of expository preaching is likewise undervalued.

On the other hand, belief in the divine inspiration and inerrancy of Scripture demands the expository method of preaching. What does it mean for a sermon to be expository or expositional? When pastors master a concise definition, they know what they are trying to do in the pulpit every week. A pastor preaches an expository sermon when he explains the meaning of a text of Scripture in the power of the Holy Spirit, follows the form of the text, applies the message of the text to the lives of hearers, affirms that Jesus is the fulfillment of the passage and the only Savior, and preaches for the purpose of changed lives to the glory of God.

Each phrase of that definition calls for explanation. **"Explains the meaning of a text of Scripture"** means that an expository sermon is text-centered. The subject of the sermon is the subject of the text of Scripture. After the sermon, hearers should know the meaning of that text because the preacher explained it to them.

"In the power of the Holy Spirit" refers to the fact that a preacher preaches in God's power, not his own. Throughout the process of sermon preparation and during presentation, the preacher prays for God's power. He asks God to do what only God can do–change lives for His glory through His preached Word.

"Follows the form of the preaching text" means that the main points of the sermon will be the main points of the passage, and the subordinate points of the sermon will be the subordinate points of the passage. "The best homiletical outlines of a passage are those that are derived from the text itself."[32] Furthermore, the sermon should be prepared, written, and delivered with the genre of the passage in mind. For example, if the genre is narrative, the preacher should tell the story. If the genre is exhortation, the preacher should exhort.

The preacher **"applies the message of the text to the lives of hearers"** because a sermon is not the same as a Bible study. A Bible study may include only the communication of information, but a sermon includes application and exhortation. A sermon calls people to be something and to do something in obedience to the text of Scripture. No one should be as prepared to apply the Scripture to the people as their pastor. Faithful pastors spend time with their people, know their people, pray for their people, and love their people. Scripture passages generally have one meaning but many applications.[33] How should a particular passage of Scripture be applied to people in a particular flock? Pastors who know their people know how to answer that question. And they should apply the Scripture to the flock they pastor, not the world in general or hypothetical flocks that exist in their minds.

The expository preacher also **"affirms that Jesus is the fulfillment of the passage and the only Savior."** After Jesus' resurrection He spoke with two of His disciples and "interpreted for them the things concerning Himself in all the Scriptures" (Luke 24:27; cf. v. 44). "All the Scriptures" are about Jesus in some way. Every passage of Scripture points somehow to our fallen condition and our need for reconciliation with God. Jesus meets that need. Since that is true, every expository sermon presents Jesus at some point.

Pastors who preach expository sermons also preach **"for the purpose of changed lives."** God's Word has power. It is "like a hammer that pulverizes rock" (Jeremiah 23:29), like a "double-edged sword" (Hebrews 4:12), and like rain that causes plants to grow (Isaiah 55:10–11). Paul wrote to Christ-followers in Thessalonica that God's Word "works effectively in you" (1 Thessalonians 2:13). Jesus told His disciples that if they continued in His Word they would know the truth and the truth would set them free (John 8:31–32), and "You are already clean because of the word I have spoken to you" (John 15:3). Jesus' words give us the truth and cleanse us (cf. John 17:17).

Why should pastors preach expository sermons? God's Word has power! Sometimes Christians will complement a pastor by saying, "He's a powerful preacher." May God give us fewer powerful preachers and more preachers who recognize their weaknesses and depend completely on the power of God's Word. God's Word has the power to change lives; the preacher does not. The preacher's role is to present what God has said and ask people to believe and obey it. When they do that, their lives are changed.

Finally, expository preaching is **"to the glory of God."** All we do should be for God's glory (1 Corinthians 10:31). In preaching God's Word pastors should be especially jealous for God's glory. Preachers should ask about every line in every sermon, "Does this glorify God?" An expository preacher should be careful about making himself the hero of every story in a sermon, lest he become the center of attention instead of God, thus stealing God's glory. As John Piper wrote, "God aims to exalt himself, not the preacher, in this affair of preaching."[34]

Reflect and react

After committing the preceding definition of expository preaching to memory, write your own definition. Which elements of the given definition would you re-state? How? What elements would you add? Why?

Six Commitments of Expository Preaching: What Is Required of Expository Preachers?

The effectiveness of a pastor's preaching will be determined by the depth of his commitment to excel at preaching. Factors such as the extent of educational preparation and giftedness contribute to the quality of preaching, but nothing is as important as the preacher's weekly commitment to give his best to the task.

First, pastors should commit to diligent preparation. Preaching is work. Preparing to preach is hard work. Of course, shortcuts abound–downloading sermons from the Internet, adopting the lines of popular "communicators," filling the time with storytelling instead of Bible teaching, and cutting and pasting the work of other preachers. Faithful pastors are not satisfied with shortcuts. Each week they meditate on a passage in God's Word, study carefully to interpret it accurately, struggle with its application, pray it into their own souls, put its truth into practice in their own lives, work to present its truth in an interesting way, and preach it passionately and compel people to submit to it for God's glory and their good.

Second, pastors should commit to accurate exposition. In preaching, is anything more important than representing God's words accurately? We dare not misrepresent the holy, perfect words of God. Preaching does not deserve to be called "expository" if the preacher says something other than what the Bible says or if the preacher says more than the Bible says. Still, preachers often say things that are simply not true. To say only what the Bible says, every preacher should make a commitment to accurate exposition. Accurate exposition requires checking and double-checking facts, using multiple sources, and refusing to preach something beyond what the preacher knows to be true. Faithful, weekly Bible expositors can relate to Eugene Peterson's definition of exegesis. He called it, "the discipline of attending to the text and listening to it rightly and well ... rigorous, disciplined, intellectual work." He also wrote that exegesis is "an enormous inconvenience."[35] Every preacher should do the "rigorous, disciplined" work of accurate exposition every week, and it is always inconvenient.

Third, pastors should commit to demonstrative affection within effective expository preaching. Pastors should love every sheep in the flock. When people know the preacher loves them, they will hear and heed his preaching. Such love is not a technique to improve communication effectiveness; it is a biblical imperative. Jesus said that loving God and loving others are God's most important commands (Mark 12:28–31). First Corinthians 13 says that if we have the gift of preaching but do not have love, then we are nothing (1 Corinthians 13:1–3). Every sermon pastors preach should be an expression of love for God and for the people. When a pastor loves the people, he will never preach to vent his frustration or to coerce them to action. Love constrains pastors to preach only for the glory of God and the good of the people. Lack of love undermines the message and the authority of the preacher.

Fourth, pastors should commit to consistent incarnation. Before pastors preach to their people, they have to live what they preach. They incarnate the message. A pastor's holy life amplifies the truth of the sermon. An inconsistent or unethical life mutes the message.

No pastor perfectly incarnates the perfect truth of the Bible. Therefore, every week before preparing a sermon, pastors must allow the Bible to preach to their own fallen hearts. Such an exercise is painful but necessary. If the Bible passage exposes the pastor's sin, he must repent before he preaches. If he encounters a command he is not obeying, he must start obeying before he preaches. Integrity demands such a weekly spiritual discipline, and even "minor" compromises undermine the impact of a pastor's ministry. A pastor cannot preach people into doing something he is not doing. When the preacher incarnates the message, they can "see" the sermon as well as hear it. Only then will the preacher influence his flock for God's glory.

Fifth, pastors should commit to gospel proclamation. Every passage of Scripture points to Christ and His salvation in some way. Pastors have the obligation to find an exegetically responsible way to get to Christ from every text in every sermon.[36] In some corners of evangelicalism, "moralistic preaching" is disparaged. Pastors *should* preach morals! They should tell their congregations what is right and wrong according to God's Word, and they should exhort them to do what is right. However, pastors should never preach *only* morals. Efforts to live morally do not save or sanctify. Only God can do that, and He does it by His saving grace. Therefore, pastors should commit to offer the saving gospel every Lord's Day. People need more than a list of dos and don'ts. They need Jesus, and pastors should proclaim Him every time they preach.

Finally, pastors should commit to compelling presentation. Every biblical text has a spiritual imperative and a moral imperative. The spiritual imperative is to know God in Christ and to love Him. The moral imperative is to live according to God's Word. When pastors preach the Bible, they should call people to obey those imperatives, and it is inappropriate to be indifferent about that call. The first imperative is a matter of life or death. The second imperative is a matter of a joy-filled life or a wasted life of heartache. How can a loving shepherd be dispassionate about issues that affect the health of the sheep and the eternal destiny of people without Christ? Pastors should preach as if such issues matter, because they do.

Research and create

How many of the above commitments have you made in the past? How many are you willing to make now? What important commitments would you add to the preceding list? Write a description of the kind of life schedule necessary to fulfill such commitments. To whom should you make the commitments?

A Preparation Process: How Do Pastors Prepare an Expository Sermon Every Week?

Sermon preparation is like worship liturgy. People who worship more informally sometimes say they don't follow a liturgy. However, they probably do. They stand at certain moments during worship, they sit and pray at certain moments, and they give an offering in virtually the same way at the same time every week. Preachers also follow some sort of process in sermon preparation. Every week they perform certain tasks before they feel ready to preach. We need a weekly process, especially one that insures careful and accurate interpretation of the Bible. "Because it is easy for us to be drawn to a few points that are important to us, we need some objective way of insuring our attention to the entire passage and its major teachings."[37] So preachers should ask whether they follow the *best* process. Preaching will not be improved unless preparation is improved.

The first step in the preparation process is to pray. Actually, it's the last step too. And the middle step. Pastors should pray throughout the preparation process. A pastor who doesn't ask God to help him preach His Word is inconceivable. We pray for the help of the Holy Spirit to illuminate the meaning of His Word. We pray that we will represent His Word accurately. We pray that we will preach with submission to God's Word, love for God, and love for every member of the flock. We pray for the needs of the people, which helps us preach with their needs in mind.

The second step in the preparation process is to select a text. The process of sermon preparation does not begin with a story the preacher wants to tell, an idea he wants to share, or an exhortation he wants to give. Sermon preparation begins with a text from the Bible. In expository preaching, God's Word rules the sermon. Therefore, everything in the sermon—illustrations, anecdotes, exhortations—serves to explain and apply the biblical text. That is the only way preachers can insure they are preaching God's Word, not their own ideas.

Which text should pastors select? First, select a book of the Bible and preach through it in a multi-week series of sermons. If a pastor preaches effectively from Philippians 4:13, his people will gain confidence in their ability to live for Christ in every circumstance through His abiding presence in them. Great! But will they learn the book of Philippians? Furthermore, if a pastor follows that pattern every week—selecting individual texts and preaching selected biblical principles—he is training his people to view the Bible as a collection of spiritual principles for living. After years or perhaps only months of listening to such preaching, when they read the Bible they will look for something like a "principle for today" and ignore the rest. Why? Because that's what their pastor does in the pulpit. The people will not learn the Bible and will not understand the nature of the Bible. Instead, preach through the entire book of Philippians paragraph by paragraph. Listeners will learn Philippians, they will learn what the Bible is really like, they will learn how to read the Bible, and they will even learn more fully the meaning of chapter 4, verse 13.

Second, the selection of a biblical book may be influenced by the maturity of the people in the congregation. If a congregation consists primarily of new believers or people who are not accustomed to expository preaching, perhaps they are not ready for a verse-by-verse exposition of the book of Jeremiah. Start with something shorter and more easily accessible.

Third, preach through books in both testaments. Many Christians struggle with understanding the Old Testament and its relationship to New Testament faith. Pastors can help their people to see the meaning and importance of the entire Bible by preaching from both testaments.[38] Orthodox Christian faith is built on the entire Bible, so pastors should preach the entire Bible.

Fourth, pastors should consider preaching from the various literary genres in the Bible. If a pastor preaches only from the epistles and gospels, how will the people know how to interpret Old Testament narratives, proverbs, or law? Much of the Bible will remain closed to them. The best person to teach them the Bible and how to interpret it is their shepherd.

The third step in the preparation process is to understand what the text says. Reading something into the text that is not there is easy to do. It happens all the time. Our assumption about what the text says gets the best of us, and we preach a mixture of our assumption and the meaning of the text. Such handling of the text inevitably distorts God's Word. Expository preachers carefully determine what the text says and allow the text's meaning to drive every word of the sermon. "There is no greater abuse of the Bible than to proclaim in God's name what God is not saying."[39]

The best way to determine the meaning of a text is to begin by producing an accurate translation from the original language. If a preacher does not know how to translate Hebrew and Greek, he should make every effort to learn how to do so as soon as possible. And regardless of the preacher's ability with the languages, he should check multiple sources to insure his understanding of the text is accurate. Distorted exposition leads to distorted application, and distorted application leads to distorted Christian living.

The fourth step in the preparation process is to consider the context. Context informs the meaning and application of the text. Sometimes considering the context completely alters conclusions about the meaning. A common axiom is, "A text without a context is a pretext."

Many Christians quote Jeremiah 29:11 where God says, "I know the plans I have for you ... plans for your welfare, not for disaster, to give you a future and a hope." Christians often apply that promise by God to any situation they are facing and assume it means that generally God is going to make everything turn out okay. But Jeremiah 29:11 is part of a letter Jeremiah sent to Jewish exiles in Babylon. In that letter, God promised they would remain in exile seventy years as His judgment for their sins. In fact, God said that the prophets who were promising a quick return from exile were prophesying a lie. But then God stated that in those less-than-ideal circumstances they could prosper and He would allow the next generation to return to their homeland. Awareness of the context leads to a different conclusion about meaning. The exiles would continue to experience suffering, and God was allowing it as His judgment for their sins, but God planned to bless His people after judgment. That meaning also leads to a different contemporary application. Jeremiah 29:11 is a call to holiness in order to avoid God's righteous wrath against sin, and it's a revelation that God's ultimate plan for His people is blessing and hope.

The fifth step in the preparation process is to define the meaning of the words. Some words in the text usually deserve special attention because they are theologically important, hard to understand, or determine the meaning of the verse. Faithful expository preachers learn how to study biblical words, and they work hard every week to insure they interpret, explain, and apply the meaning of words correctly.[40] We are handling God's Words; we cannot treat them lightly or incorrectly.

The sixth step in the preparation process is to determine the relevance of the genre. What type of literature is the biblical text? Is it narrative? Proverb? Letter? Apocalyptic? Prophecy? Law? Poetry? The genre usually affects the meaning and application of biblical texts. For example, in poetry some language is to be interpreted, well, poetically. In poetry, we do not take all the language literally because of the frequency of figures of speech and wordplay. When we identify a verse as a proverb, we do not interpret or apply it as an absolute promise because a proverb is a different genre than a promise.[41] Genre identification can make a dramatic difference in the way preachers apply texts to the lives of their hearers.

The seventh step in the preparation process is to identify the main ideas. Every text contains primary ideas that are important to understanding and application. Identify ideas like promises, truths about God, exhortations to godly behavior, keys to relating to God, or affirmations of the gospel. Build the sermon by explaining, illustrating, and applying those ideas. Make sure they arise from the text, and make them the main points of the sermon.

The eighth step in the preparation process is to include the gospel. The greatest need of every person is a love relationship with God. Such a relationship is possible only through Jesus. He is the "one mediator between

God and humanity" (1 Timothy 2:5). Every text somehow reveals human sin and therefore the need for a Savior from sin. Jesus is that Savior. Every text is located somewhere in the history of redemption. Jesus is the culmination of that history. Even when the preacher is relatively certain that every person in the congregation claims Jesus as Savior, he still preaches the gospel. Christians need to be reminded of the gospel truth that we were saved by grace (Ephesians 2:8–9) and we stand by grace (Romans 5:2).

Effective pastoral preachers practice each step of this process every week. They do it because they have made all the necessary commitments to excellence in preaching the Bible, and they affirm the preeminent position of preaching in pastoral ministry.

Respond to a Case Study

When Toby sensed a call from God to preach, he embraced the call and began to prepare by enrolling in seminary. He was called to pastor a small church while still studying at seminary. He enjoyed learning more about the Bible, theology, and ministry. He also agreed that he should follow an exhaustive preparation process for his preaching to ensure that his weekly sermons were Bible-based and effective. However, he struggled with putting all of it into practice, especially with his time pressures. During some weeks he had multiple meetings, pastoral care duties, tests, and family events.

The young pastor hated the idea of the "Saturday night special," but more than once he found himself beginning the Sunday message on Saturday night after his family went to bed. His inner turmoil boiled over one Saturday night at midnight when he suddenly realized that he was half finished preparing to preach on a passage that was preached magnificently by a visiting evangelist just a month before! Was he repeating the same outline of the previous preacher? Could he possibly add any new insights not covered by the more experienced pastor? Close to tears, he stopped his preparation and decided to preach a message he had delivered a year earlier. Toby did not know if the members would remember it, but at that point he was too exhausted to care.

1. What do you consider to be the main issue in this case study? Also, list secondary issues.

2. Discuss with other people in ministry Toby's challenges and decide how you would advise him.

3. Do you believe these issues will change over time? Why or why not?

3
GUIDING THROUGH CHURCH DISCIPLINE

Allan Moseley

Pastor Ronnie was attending a fellowship meal for a Sunday school class in the suburban church where he had served for a year. After dinner people were standing around chatting. When Ronnie went to the kitchen to pour himself some soda, a woman joined him there. She was the wife of a longtime deacon, one of the most respected men in the church. "I want to ask you to pray for me and my husband," she said. "I'm considering divorce. For months I suspected something was going on, and finally I learned beyond any shadow of doubt that my husband has been having an affair." Pastor Ronnie expressed his sadness and disappointment, and he asked about the current status of the affair. "It's still going on," she said. "Sort of, anyway. He's trying to decide whether to continue it or attempt reconciliation with me, and I'm trying to decide whether to take him back if he decides to come back to me." "I'll definitely pray for you guys," Ronnie said. "Is there anything else I can do?" "He'll probably blow up if he finds out I told you. I don't know what you can do." Pastor Ronnie left the party shaken. He had never faced this situation. That night he couldn't sleep as he pondered, "What is a faithful pastor supposed to do in this situation?"

Yvette Cormier walked into the women's restroom of the Planet

Fitness gym where she was a member. Soon after she entered, she stopped in her tracks. Before her stood a man in the ladies' room. She turned around, walked to the front desk, and reported what she had seen. The employee told her that other Planet Fitness members had complained too, but the man was within Planet Fitness policy. When corporate leaders were contacted, the Director of Public Relations, McCall Gosselin, said at Planet Fitness "members and guests may use all gym facilities based on their sincere self-reported gender identity."[42] According to that way of thinking, all people are free to choose their own gender identity, and their "self-reported" gender identity may or may not be the same as their God-given gender identity.

Why include a story about gender identity in a chapter on church discipline? First, it illustrates the extent to which Western culture has rejected morality that is based on transcendent truth, including the transcendent truth revealed in the Bible. Opinion, not revelation, is the moral authority. Western culture has returned to the period of the judges when "everyone did whatever he wanted" (Judges 17:6). Second, the amoral thinking of the culture, according to which preferences rule and eternal moral truths are banished, has been infecting the church for a long time.[43]

Church discipline, however, is based on theological presuppositions that run against ideas commonly promoted in Western culture. The church's presuppositions about morality include the following:

1. The Bible is God's revelation of Himself and His ways.
2. God's revelation stipulates moral absolutes. That is, God has revealed that some things are wrong and some things are right.
3. Since the moral standards in the Bible come from God, they supersede human opinion and even human law, and they do not change.

4. The Bible teaches that followers of Jesus are to live according to the moral standards God has revealed in His Word.
5. Followers of Jesus are to help one another live pure lives as part of the ministry of discipleship (Matthew 28:19).

If a great majority of the members of a local church does not share those presuppositions, instituting and implementing a process of church discipline will be difficult. Before practicing church discipline, church leaders will have to convince the flock to reject the culture's moral relativism and to embrace God's moral truth in the Bible as absolute.

Recite and rehearse

Think about the churches in which you have been a member. How much have they been influenced/shaped by the culture and how much have they been influenced/shaped by the Bible? Rate such influences on a scale of one to ten and explain your rating.

Church Discipline: A Definition

Perhaps the best way to understand the nature and importance of church discipline is to contemplate obedience to Jesus' words in Matthew 18:15–17.

> If your brother sins against you, go and rebuke him in private. If he listens to you, you have won your brother. But if he won't listen, take one or two more with you, so that by the testimony of two or three witnesses every fact may be established. If he pays no attention to them, tell the church. But if he doesn't pay attention even to the church, let him be like an unbeliever and a tax collector to you.

Jesus commanded His followers to confront sin in the church actively and personally. That is church discipline. More broadly, church discipline is part of Christian discipleship. Jesus told His followers to "make disciples of all nations, baptizing them in the name of the Father and of the Son and of the Holy Spirit, teaching them to observe everything I have commanded you" (Matthew 28:19–20).

The mission Jesus gave to His church is to lead people to faith in Him so that they become His disciples, to baptize them, and then to teach them to do what Jesus commanded. Followers of Jesus in a local church help one another to "grow in the grace and knowledge of our Lord and Savior Jesus Christ" (2 Peter 3:18). Hebrews 3:12–13 says, "Watch out, brothers, so that there won't be in any of you an evil, unbelieving heart that departs from the living God. But encourage each other daily, while it is still called today, so that none of you is hardened by sin's deception."

When Christians heed that exhortation, they stay in touch with their brothers and sisters in Christ, they talk with one another about the state of their spiritual health, they urge one another to stay away from sin, and they remind one another of the truth of God's Word so they will not believe "sin's deception" (v. 13). All of that is discipleship, and it is to happen daily. Church discipline is part of that process by which church members help one another reject sin and embrace Jesus' spirit and lifestyle.

What if a church member embraces sin and rejects Jesus' spirit and lifestyle? First, we remember that all followers of Jesus are in the process of growth. The church should be a place where doubting people, wounded people, compromising people, confused people, sinful people, inconsistent people, and uninformed people can have room to grow. So when a follower of Jesus turns from His way, the church *helps* that brother or sister by patiently teaching, loving, encouraging, praying, urging, and modeling the Christ-like life. If a church member walks away from that life altogether, church discipline becomes a process of restoration, returning the wayward church member to Jesus and His way. If the member refuses to return, church discipline will result ultimately in the removal of an unrepentant sinner from church membership.

Every follower of Jesus sins. As James wrote, "We all stumble in many ways" (James 3:2). Why then do some sins compel the church to discipline members and even remove them from membership? What sins make church discipline necessary?

First, the church defines *sin* according to God's Word, not according to personal opinion, cultural standards, or church tradition. Jesus said, "Do not judge, so that you won't be judged" (Matthew 7:1). A church member's dishonest business practices become known. A fellow church member says to a friend, "He's living in sin. We should go to him and urge him to turn from his sin." The friend replies, "Jesus said we're not to judge." That is exactly what Jesus said. *We* are not to judge, but we can and must affirm God's judgment as true. We are not the ones who have determined that lying and stealing are sins; God has done that. Furthermore, some moral judgment is inevitable. In the story about gender identity, Planet Fitness officials sought to portray themselves as nonjudgmental. They would not judge a man for pretending he was a woman. However, in so doing, they made a moral judgment–the man's behavior is acceptable and disagreeing with his behavior is not acceptable. That's a moral judgment, but it was not according to God's Word. The church, however, looks only to God's Word to define right and wrong.

Second, church discipline is reserved for unrepentant, egregious sin. "Unrepentant" sin means that the church member is involved in sin and declares that he or she will continue in that sin. The church member announces a refusal to refrain from practicing sinful behavior. "Egregious" sin is more difficult to identify. In an essay addressing the practice of church discipline in Baptist history, Gregory Wills provided the following list of sins for which church discipline has been practiced: "murder, abortion, arson, assault, theft, fraud, blasphemy, falsehood, drunkenness, abuse, fornication, and adultery ... hostility, anger, slander, or threats ... habitual absence, refusal to submit to the church, indulging in worldly amusements ... and they disciplined those who spread erroneous doctrine or embraced heresy."[44]

Churches do not exercise church discipline for prayerlessness. Churches exercise church discipline for wife abuse. Both are sin, and churches are not condoning prayerlessness by refraining from church discipline. Prayerlessness is, in some sense, egregious. However, such a sin may be seen as part of the typical maturation process for all Christians. We all are negligent in prayer sometimes, but hopefully we are growing in faithfulness. Wife abuse is different. It inflicts great pain on another person and tears apart precious relationships. It is exceptional, egregious. If a church learns about it and remains passive, the church family endangers their public witness because even people without Jesus condemn wife abuse as wrong. If Christians appear indifferent, they seem to be complicit in the behavior and bring shame on the name of Jesus.

Heresy is also egregious sin. None of us are perfect in our beliefs. But the goal of Christ followers is to grow in understanding God's Word and submitting to it. Heresy goes in the opposite direction. Heresy is seeing a clear affirmation of Scripture and denying its truth. When a Christian makes such a denial, his or her church rises to teach, encourage, love, correct, and work for growth. If the denial persists, however, the church begins a process of discipline that may end in the member's removal from the church. Christians who are devoted to God's Word disagree among themselves about the nature and timing of the millennial reign of Christ and other doctrinal matters that could be described as secondary or tertiary doctrinal matters.[45] Church discipline is reserved for unrepentant, egregious sin and denial of primary doctrines.

Reflect and react

Using the information above and any further biblical information that is relevant, write your own definition of church discipline in three sentences or less. Provide an example of a sin that clearly calls for church discipline, one that does not, and one that is unclear.

Foundational Principles for Church Discipline

To practice church discipline according to God's Word, pastors and churches will first commit to biblical principles that govern its practice. The following eight principles approach a biblical foundation for church discipline.

First, the church belongs to Jesus. After the apostle Peter confessed that Jesus is the Messiah, Jesus said, "On this rock I will build My church" (Matthew 16:18). Jesus referred to the church as "*My* church." Since the church belongs to Him, He has proprietary rights. He has the prerogative to determine how His church will be structured and managed. No church should practice church discipline because the pastor decides it's a good idea or because other churches practice it. We practice church discipline because Jesus tells the church to do it and it's His church.

Second, every church member belongs to Jesus. A church is a body of baptized disciples of Jesus who love one another, assemble to worship the one true God, seek to spread the good news of Jesus to the ends of the earth, live filled with the Holy Spirit and formed by God's Word, exercise their spiritual gifts in serving God and others, share the Lord's Supper, and do all this as a family led by shepherds. No church member does all of that perfectly. However, such a definition of a church requires all church members to be Christians, and Christians are people who have ceded ownership of their lives to Jesus. First Corinthians 6:19–20 says to Christians, "You are not your own, for you were bought at a price." Paul wrote in Romans 14:8, "Whether we live or die, we belong to the Lord." Jesus is the Owner and Master of every Christian. Christians who understand that fact will not balk at other Christians helping them to obey Jesus and urging them to walk away from sin.

Third, the new birth in Jesus results in fundamental character change. Why should a church expect members to live differently from the world? Because they *are* different. Jesus said that becoming His follower is like being born again (John 3:1–8). Paul and Peter also used the language of death and new birth to refer to a Christian's new life in Christ (Romans 6:3–12; Colossians 3:3–10; 1 Peter 1:3). Christians are new people, holy people—set apart *from* the old life and *to* new life in Christ. Therefore, Christians relate to sin differently than people who have not been born again. Christians loathe their sin, and people who loathe their sin welcome a process designed to help them stay away from sin.

Fourth, the church is to be holy, and individual sins affect the entire church. Not only are individual Christians to live holy lives, but also every local church is to be holy. That is Christ's purpose for His church. Ephesians 5:25–27 says Christ died for the church "to make her holy ... without spot or wrinkle or anything like that, but holy and blameless." Sin spoils a church's holiness. And the sin of one Christian affects all his brothers and sisters in Christ. Sin is not a bullet to the head; it's a hand grenade. The apostle Paul referred to sin as yeast in dough. "A little yeast permeates the whole batch of dough" (1 Corinthians 5:6). A little sin affects the entire church. As Joseph S. Baker wrote in 1847, "Every offence committed by one individual against another, is an offence committed against the whole body, and against the cause, for the furtherance of which that body was incorporated."[46]

Western culture is highly individualistic. The church of Jesus Christ is not. Western people think, "What I do is my business, not yours." In the church, the holiness of one member is the business of all the members. The church is a body, and what happens to one part of the body affects the entire body (1 Corinthians 12:12–26). So when a church member commits egregious sin and does not repent, the whole church hurts, grieves, and seeks healing. The church is neither indifferent nor passive. The church cares and acts.

Fifth, God forgives and sanctifies. The goal of church discipline is restoration to a right relationship with God and with brothers and sisters in Christ. After any sin, upon confession and repentance, God gives that restoration. First John 1:9 says, "If we confess our sins, He is faithful and righteous to forgive us our sins and to cleanse us from all unrighteousness." When we confess, God forgives us and cleanses us, praise His name. When followers of Jesus pursue a fellow church member who is in sin, they are doing so to lead the member to experience God's forgiveness and cleansing. God forgives and cleanses people made dirty by sin and makes them holy. That is the goal of church discipline—experiencing the forgiveness, cleansing, and sanctification that follow confession and repentance.

Sixth, God has given spiritual leaders to the church. Every organization works more effectively when it has a leader. That is not the reason churches have leaders. Churches have leaders because God's Word directs them to have leaders (Acts 20:17–31; Ephesians 4:11–13; 1 Timothy 3:1–13; Titus 1:5–9; Hebrews 13:7, 17; 1 Peter 5:1–4). The Bible calls servant leaders "deacons." Spiritual, strategic leaders are called "pastors," "elders," and "overseers." Leadership is important to the practice of church discipline because someone must initiate and implement the process of discipline. Usually deacons or pastors should fill the role of leading church discipline since they have been recognized and selected by the church for their spiritual maturity. Pastors especially are to shepherd the souls of the people, and church discipline is part of a shepherding ministry.

Seventh, church membership is a serious commitment. Church discipline makes no sense unless we understand the commitments fellow members of the body of Christ have to one another. The following partial list of Scriptures instructs believers concerning those commitments.

- "Be at peace with one another." (Mark 9:50)
- "Love one another." (John 13:34–35; 15:12, 17; Romans 12:10; 1 Thessalonians 3:12; 1 Peter 1:22; 4:8; 1 John 3:11, 23; 4:7, 11)
- "Accept one another." (Romans 15:7; Ephesians 4:2; Colossians 3:13)
- "Serve one another through love." (Galatians 5:13)
- "Be kind and compassionate to one another, forgiving one another." (Ephesians 4:32)
- "Submitting to one another." (Ephesians 5:21)
- "We are members of one another." (Ephesians 5:25)
- "Teaching and admonishing one another in all wisdom." (Colossians 3:16)
- "Encourage one another and build each other up." (1 Thessalonians 5:11)
- "Always pursue what is good for one another." (1 Thessalonians 5:15)
- "Be concerned about one another in order to promote love and good works." (Hebrews 10:24)
- "Not staying away from our worship meetings, as some habitually do, but encouraging each other." (Hebrews 10:25)
- "Confess your sins to one another and pray for one another." (James 5:16)
- "Be hospitable to one another." (1 Peter 4:9)

Putting all those exhortations into practice is a formidable challenge, but it is what God calls Christ followers to do. Many people do not understand what is involved in church membership: "Uninstructed saints see the local church as a place to hear a good sermon and make a few friends, a place with activities for their children. If that is all it is, then membership is not a serious commitment. Moreover, if it is not, certainly church discipline is ridiculous ... Church discipline must be understood in light of the nature of the local church."[47] The church disciplines members for unrepentant sin out of a desire to relate to fellow Christians in the way God prescribes in His Word.

Eighth, Christians forgive one another. The purpose of church discipline is not punitive; its goal is restorative. If the perfectly holy God forgives sinners, who are we to withhold forgiveness? In fact, as fellow sinners we can forgive with or without confession and repentance. We forgive simply because God commands us to forgive (Colossians 3:13–14).

So we practice church discipline from a position of forgiveness. We do not wait until repentance to forgive; we forgive quickly and unconditionally. Sometimes when church leaders put church discipline into practice and a member is in danger of being taken off the church roll, someone says, "But shouldn't we forgive?" Of course we forgive. But after we forgive, the wayward church member still has not been restored, and the purpose of church discipline is to accomplish that restoration.

Research and create

Write a brief description of your church's process of orienting new members. Does the process include instruction about the nature of the church and the nature of church membership? Is signing a church covenant required? Does the church have a periodic renewal to the covenant? Would any members be surprised that your church believes in and practices church discipline?

The Process of Church Discipline

In Matthew 18, cited earlier in this chapter, Jesus described the process He wants His people to follow. The process may be heartrending and exhausting to implement, but it's simple to understand.

When a church member sins, the church responds first with individual confrontation by rebuking him in private. *Rebuke* is a strong word and may bring to mind a harshness that is not required by the original Greek. One Greek dictionary defines this verb as, "show (someone his) fault or error, convince (someone) of (his) fault or error."[48] The point of this private conversation is to communicate the message, "What you did was wrong. You should confess and repent to receive God's forgiveness, cleansing, and restoration." Such words can be spoken with love and kindness. The hope is that the sinning church member will listen, confess, repent, and be restored to close fellowship with God and with his brothers and sisters in Christ. If that is the outcome, the church is finished with the process of discipline and celebrates the return to holiness and happiness by a fellow follower of Jesus.

If the believer does not confess and repent, the church does not give up. Jesus said to return to the sinning Christian and "take one or two more with you" (Matthew 18:16). Such a visit serves at least two important purposes. First, it is another opportunity for the sinning Christian to confess, repent, and experience forgiveness and cleansing. Second, if the believer does not repent, the second visit provides additional witnesses to his or her spiritual condition. If church discipline must move forward, the truth will not depend on the testimony of only one person. To make this point, Jesus quoted a principle of justice stated three times in Old Testament law: "So that by the testimony of two or three witnesses every fact may be established" (Numbers 35:30; Deut. 17:6; 19:15). The apostle Paul also cited this principle twice (2 Corinthians 13:1; 1 Timothy 5:19). A commitment to truth and justice should permeate our relationships with fellow believers. Church discipline proceeds on the basis of proven wrongdoing, not alleged wrongdoing.

If the erring believer listens to the loving appeal of fellow church members, the church celebrates the confession, repentance, and restoration. If, however, the church member persists in sin, Jesus said, "Tell the church" (Matthew 18:17). How should churches implement Jesus' directions? "The public announcement of an unrepentant life (including the name of the unrepentant believer) will have been preceded by prayer, discussion, and a unanimous vote of the leadership."[49] It is wise to take time. Such time provides the opportunity to pray for the erring member. A waiting period also offers the wayward member time to reconsider and repent. And it gives church members a season to contact the prodigal multiple times in multiple ways to encourage repentance. During this waiting period, church leaders could also send a letter offering the unrepentant member an opportunity to appear before them to say anything he or she wishes to say before the matter is taken to the church body.

Finally, if the church member continues to refuse to turn from sin, church leaders obey Jesus and tell the church. They bring the matter to the entire church in a meeting that includes only church members. When the church votes to remove the unrepentant member from church membership, he or she is taken off the church roll after a specified amount of time to give a final opportunity for repentance and to give the church an opportunity to minister to the member. If the church removes a member from membership because of unrepentant sin, they assure the sinning member that the door to repentance and return to the church is always open, and the church continues to pray for repentance and restoration.[50]

Implementation Imperatives

The Bible provides important guidance in how to practice discipline in a way that pleases God and follows His Word.

First, make expectations of members clear from the beginning. If church members are going to be held accountable for unrepentant, egregious sin, church leaders should tell them that from the beginning. The membership process starts with the potential member's testimony of salvation in Jesus. "The Person must give an account of his Faith; and of the Work of Grace upon his Soul before the Church; and also a strict Enquiry must be made about his Life and Conversation."[51] Thus, a church insures a regenerate church membership.

Beyond being initially assured of conversion, church leaders also provide printed materials that explain the nature of church membership. They also teach a membership course, during which they present the foundational doctrines and documents of the church and teach the nature of the local church. Historic documents concerning church discipline begin with descriptions of the nature of the local church and her officers, and only then address discipline specifically.[52] In the same way, contemporary church leaders can show that church discipline makes sense only when people understand the nature of the church. Churches should also consider requiring the signing of a church covenant and observing an annual service of recommitment to that covenant for all members. Such a covenant expresses the gravity of church membership and binds the member to the church family and the church family to the member.

Second, at every point express love. The imperative for Christians to love one another could not be clearer in the New Testament. Jesus said loving God and others are the greatest two commandments (Mark 12:28–31; cf. 1 Corinthians 13:1–3). In exercising church discipline, church leaders affirm love to everyone involved in every way possible.

Love does not prevent confrontation of sin. "Love finds no joy in unrighteousness" (1 Corinthians 13:6). Sin results in sadness and regret, so failing to call someone away from sin is not loving. Love compels Christians to exhort people to leave sin, and as they do so, they consistently express love. As church leaders perform each step of church discipline, they ask, "Is this the way I would treat a close friend?" Anything less is not doing our best to love.

Third, treat wayward church members with gentleness. When Jewish leaders presented to Jesus a woman caught in adultery, He told her to stop sinning, but He also protected her from public humiliation. He treated her with gentleness and love (John 8:3–11). Galatians 6:1–3 is worthy of meditation and memorization for anyone who must apply church discipline: "Brothers, if someone is caught in any wrongdoing, you who are spiritual should restore such a person with a gentle spirit, watching out for yourselves so you also won't be tempted. Carry one another's burdens; in this way you will fulfill the law of Christ. For if anyone considers himself to be something when he is nothing, he deceives himself."

Every person who speaks to fellow believers about their sin has also sinned. Without God's power and grace, those who perform church discipline today could be in need of church discipline next year. Such facts should result in deep humility on the part of someone confronting a church member with unrepentant sin. An older pastor once told his daughter, "Honey, I have been following Jesus a long time. I am far from perfect. I have fallen many times on that road, but thank God that at least I have never fallen *off* the road." We all fall. So church leaders deal gently with fallen people as those who have also fallen.

To continue the analogy, falling on the road of following Jesus and getting up again is part of the life of discipleship. As the Holy Spirit sanctifies us, we fall less. But when someone falls *off* the road, the church calls for the fallen member to return. If the member refuses to step back on the road, church discipline is necessary. The church must face the truth—the wayward member has chosen to be independent of the life of following Jesus, and removing the member from the church is a formal recognition of his or her choice.

Fourth, involve multiple church leaders. Before the process of church discipline reaches the entire congregation, a plurality of mature and biblically informed believers should be involved. A decision to remove someone from church membership should not be driven by one or two people, with a few others merely nodding in agreement during a meeting with an otherwise packed agenda. The counsel and perspective of others is needed to guard against personal emotions, preferences, or snap judgments.[53]

Fifth, ask the church to make the decision. Jesus said the final step in confronting sin is to "tell the church" (Matthew 18:17). Paul wrote of a case of discipline in the church in Corinth, during which a penalty was applied "by the majority" (2 Corinthians 2:6). "The majority" indicates that most of the people in the church voted for and/or participated in the discipline.

Leaders should tell the church the name of the unrepentant member and the nature of his or her sin. Details are not necessary. The church needs to know only enough information to follow up in meaningful ministry and prayer. For example, a pastor may say, "Church member John Doe has been unfaithful to his marriage with Jane, and he has refused all our appeals to turn from this sin." Leaders should also inform the church of every attempt they have made to restore the unrepentant member to holiness.

Instances of church discipline in the New Testament involve or are addressed to the entire church (Matthew 18:17; 1 Corinthians 5; 2 Corinthians 2:5–8; Galatians 6:1–2; 2 Thessalonians 3:14–15). That fact should be applied in two ways in contemporary churches. First, the final vote to remove from membership should be taken by the entire church. Second, only the church should hear about the matter. Church leaders share the information in a meeting that is for church members only, not in a regular time of worship that is open to guests. Only believers will grieve the sin (see 1 Corinthians 5:2; 2 Corinthians 2:5). Only believers will be able to pray and minister for the purpose of restoration, which is the outcome the church pursues in every case of discipline.

Respond to a case study

A church member named Mark came into contact with an old high school friend through social media. Their correspondence led eventually to unfaithfulness to Mark's marriage and an illicit physical relationship. Mark's wife found out, and he left her. When Mark's wife reported the circumstances to church leaders, one of them contacted Mark and asked him to return to a faithful relationship with his wife. Mark was not responsive. Next, the senior pastor and another church leader visited Mark and asked him to repent. Mark was angry and unrepentant.

Next, the senior pastor reported the situation to the other pastors of the church. They prayed for Mark and waited for his repentance, while additional contacts by phone and e-mail followed. In each case Mark responded negatively or not at all. Mark relocated to a city in another state where the "other woman" lived. For months the pastors continued to pray, while some continued efforts to stay in touch with Mark. They also ministered to Mark's wife who was grieving. Mark made it clear that he was intent on divorce and would not seek reconciliation. Eventually, the pastors wrote a letter to Mark repeating their appeal for repentance, informing him of the possibility of church discipline, and inviting him to meet with them at any time. Again, Mark did not respond. After a few more months of waiting and praying, the matter was brought to the church at a regularly scheduled business meeting. The church voted to remove Mark from membership, and leaders urged members to grieve and pray.

Months later, Mark moved back to the community in which the church was located. His physical relationship with the other woman had ended. Mark confessed to church leaders that he had been wrong all along. However, he and his wife could not agree to reconcile. One of the pastors of the church began to meet regularly with Mark to talk with him about being a godly man. Mark responded positively, though his marriage was not repaired. He began to seek to live as a faithful follower of Jesus in other areas of his life, the pastor affirmed the church's love for Mark, and Mark returned to worship in another church and sometimes in the church from which he was removed.

---

1. In the case study above, what could have been done differently or better? What would you add to the process to make sure a biblical process is followed?

2. In the church in which you worship and serve,

is such a process embraced as part of the "culture" of the church? How would you go about initiating such a process?

3. Interview three church leaders and ask them what they think about affirming a commitment to biblical church discipline and adopting a process to implement it. Discuss the differing perspectives.

4
CONDUCTING BAPTISM AND COMMUNION

Steven Wade

I had rehearsed it in my head a thousand times, practiced out loud at least a dozen, but now I was in front of the congregation who had called me to be their pastor. I was visibly anxious standing behind the table. Sweat was rolling down my forehead into my eyes, and I could not (or would not) wipe it off because I was getting ready to serve the elements with the very hands that would have been used wipe the sweat away (a good reason for pastors always to carry a handkerchief). I was standing in front of the congregation sensing, more than I had anticipated, the weight of holding the bread and the cup before the congregation and declaring, "This is the body of Christ. This is the blood of the new covenant, poured out for the forgiveness of sins." In those moments I prayed that the Lord would guard my mind and my mouth as I led His church, for my first time, to celebrate this memorial meal and experience the spiritual nourishment of Christ together. And after a dozen or more years of leading this same church to celebrate and experience this same Supper together, I am a little less anxious while still being no less overwhelmed by the spiritual weight of the moments we spend at the Table.

Among the most sacred responsibilities a pastor is charged with is the responsibility to lead the church in celebrating the ordinances. When the church is gathered, she is a visible portrait of the bride of Christ, and when she celebrates the ordinances, she visibly displays the good news that made the way for her to become the bride she is. In both baptism and the Lord's Supper, the church is given the opportunity to display and declare the gospel together. The pastor has both the opportunity and responsibility to lead believers to make much of Christ through the ordinances. This chapter examines the pastor's role in leading the church to celebrate baptism and the Lord's Supper in ways that edify the church and glorify Jesus Christ. The pastor's role in the ordinances in general will be considered first, followed by a more specific look at baptism and the Lord's Supper individually.

The celebration of the ordinances of the church gives the pastor a unique opportunity to remind the congregation of Jesus' finished work of redemption and his continuing work in us. In order to do so effectively, the pastor must teach his people clearly about the ordinances of the church. Therefore, let's consider some general principles concerning the ordinances. Throughout church history, two major terms have been used to refer to what Baptists refer to as ordinances. The Roman Catholic, Orthodox, and even some Protestant churches refer to them as *sacraments*, making this the most common term used throughout church history. Coming out of the Protestant Reformation, Baptists, attempting to distance themselves from the meaning imposed upon the term *sacrament* in Roman Catholic tradition, began referring to baptism and the Lord's Supper as *ordinances*. This helped them define what an ordinance is in contradistinction to the Roman Catholic view. While the use of the term *sacrament* certainly did not disappear, the use of the term *ordinance* grew until "by the nineteenth century Baptists had developed an opposition to the term sacrament as a matter of theological principle."[54] While neither word is used in the New Testament to refer to either baptism or the Lord's Supper, both are still commonly used in the contemporary church. Hammett states, "In practice ... most of those who use ordinance accent to the human activity involved in baptism and the Lord's Supper; those who use the term sacrament tend to see an important role for divine activity, though they differ in terms of exactly what that activity is."[55]

This leads to the consideration of a definition of an *ordinance*. Almost every Christian tradition traces its definition of ordinance (or sacrament) back to Augustine's classic definition as a visible sign of an invisible grace.[56] However, Roman Catholics applied this to more than the Lord's Supper and baptism (as did Augustine) and added the clarification that grace was bestowed upon the worshiper in the act of the sacraments and not just signified (*ex opera operato*). However, the reformers were careful to note that grace is signified in the practice of the ordinances, but it is not conveyed by their practice.

With the understanding of the ordinances as signs that symbolize the grace of God bestowed upon the believer, not acts through which God saves, Baptists move to clarify what acts of the church qualify as ordinances. Following the Reformers, Baptists believe that for an act to qualify as an ordinance, it must have been instituted by Jesus as a practice that points clearly to the promise of the gospel. This limits the ordinances to two: baptism and the Lord's Supper. While there are numerous other religious practices that are surely instructed in the New Testament (e.g., prayer), these are the only two that were commanded by Jesus to be practiced as signs of the promise of the gospel.

Baptism

The final instructions from the Lord Jesus to the disciples recorded by Matthew include the command for them to "make disciples of all nations, baptizing them in the name of the Father and of the Son and of the Holy Spirit" (Matthew 28:19 ESV). Baptism is a defining ordinance for believers. It is an act of obedience to the command of Christ, and it symbolizes the believer's identification with Christ, cleansing by Christ and new life in Christ. While Baptists take their name from their views on both the subjects and mode of baptism, there is currently much discussion and even confusion surrounding the major issues of baptism. The pastor must be ready to teach and lead the congregation to carefully consider the biblical teaching concerning the subjects, the mode, and the timing of baptism.[57]

One major distinctive of Baptists is their belief that born-again believers are the only proper candidates for baptism. Every baptism recorded in the New Testament is of a believer. However, other denominations have imported the practice of the sign of the old covenant into the new covenant sign of baptism and baptize babies born into believing families. Hammett states, "The proper subjects for baptism is the topic that has most dominated discussions of baptism for the past five hundred years."[58] The pastor must be clear in his teaching on the proper subjects for baptism, for if baptism is indeed a public profession of faith and a response of obedience to Christ, then it is not for infants but those who repent and believe (which, as all agree, infants are not able to do). The pastor's belief concerning who is the proper subject for baptism has implications for what he believes is the purpose and effect of baptism.

In Romans 6, the apostle Paul shows how baptism is to be understood by the church. In an argument for the believer to live in obedience to

Christ and not go on sinning, he points to baptism as the picture of salvation. He states, "Do you not know that all of us who have been baptized into Christ Jesus were baptized into his death? We were buried therefore with him by baptism into death, in order that, just as Christ was raised from the dead by the glory of the Father, we too might walk in newness of life" (Rom 6:3–4 ESV). Baptism "into Christ Jesus" is a baptism for those who are identifying with Christ. The believer dies to sin and self, is buried in a watery grave, and is raised to live in and for Christ. Baptism is a clear picture of the regeneration of the believer.

Also in Romans 6, Paul provides the primary argument for another major Baptist distinctive: the practice of immersion. Baptists hold that baptism is only properly practiced when the believer is fully immersed in the water. The word *baptizo* means "to dip in or under."[59] The primary symbolism of baptism is seen in both the washing away of sin (cf. Acts 22:16, Ephesians 5:26, and Titus 3:5) and identifying with Christ's death, burial, and resurrection (cf. Romans 6:1–11 and Colossians 2:11–14). Both of these realities are pictured properly only when the convert is immersed in the water. Contemporary churches that compromise their views of the proper mode of baptism take away from the rich meaning given to baptism in the New Testament. Pastors must clearly teach congregants and those interested in joining the churches they lead why baptism is by immersion. While the picture of the gospel portrayed in baptism is not as vital as the issue of the proper subjects, the biblical teaching is clear and the symbolism is too rich for pastors to neglect.

Two issues emerge as the pastor considers the issue of timing and baptism. First, the age at which it is appropriate for a church to baptize a person. While most Baptists doctrinally believe that the only appropriate candidate for baptism is a converted believer, functionally many churches practice a form of paedobaptism. Many churches baptize children who are five, four, and even younger. In order to guard the biblical teaching on believer's baptism, pastors must be clear on what it means to be a believer and be cautious about baptizing young children. When a child makes a step toward acknowledging Jesus, he or she should certainly be encouraged, but making a step toward belief does not mean the child has been converted. In my own ministry I have counseled multiple people who were baptized after being led in a prayer at three to five years of age who as young adults are struggling with whether their baptism was actual believer's baptism or not. In almost every case, the person believes that he or she made some kind of decision but is not convinced there was knowledge of the reality and consequences of sin or the meaning of biblical repentance. Getting a child to confess belief in Jesus is not difficult, so pastors must teach parents and leaders effective ways to speak with children about the gospel and recognize true repentance and faith.

While it is not prudent for a book like this to recommend a minimum age for baptism, it is wise for the pastor to establish some guidelines and strategies to inform and train parents and leaders in teaching the gospel and calling children to repent and believe. I have pastor friends who have set age limits on baptism (i.e., a child must reach the age of nine before the pastor will baptize, etc.). However, I believe that the issue is deeper than chronological age. Therefore, I recommend the pastor consult with parents and make sure a child displays the following fruits of the gospel prior to a discussion of baptism. First, does the child understand the concept of sin? Who is it against? Why is it so bad? What are the consequences of sin? Second, does the child display a genuine sorrow over sin? This is the work of the Holy Spirit in a child, and without evidence of the Spirit's work it is not wise to move forward with baptism. Finally, is there an understanding of what Jesus accomplished on the cross and by rising from the dead? Ask the child to explain his or her understanding of Jesus' work on the cross. It is wise for a pastor to walk through these questions with parents who will see their children in a normal setting at home. Trust parents to recognize fruits of the work of the Spirit both drawing and regenerating children. Once a child can independently share testimony of the gospel in his or her own life, baptism is the next step.

The second issue relative to the timing of baptism is the appropriate amount of time between the candidate's conversion and baptism. Again, there is no clear scriptural instruction as to how soon after conversion a believer is to be baptized. Many churches believe it is best to have the convert go through a testing or teaching period prior to baptism. These churches implement a waiting period during which the convert must complete some type of introductory discipleship training such as a catechism class or basics of discipleship, etc. In this situation, the convert is not immediately baptized but must complete steps in addition to confessing Christ publicly. There is wisdom in this process, as it protects the church from hastily agreeing that one is truly a convert. On the other hand, many churches teach that the *first* step of obedience to Jesus Christ is baptism. These churches tend to baptize converts as soon as it is practically possible to do so. The effective pastor must carefully consider the best course to follow in deciding on the timing of baptism and then be consistent and intentional in his teaching and practice in this area. In all of these areas, pastors must show the church the importance of baptism and lead the church to both understand and practice it in a way that guards the faith, celebrates the gospel, encourages the convert, and brings glory to the Savior.

Recite and rehearse

The chapter mentions "guidelines and strategies to inform and train parents and leaders in teaching the gospel and calling children to repent and believe." Develop an outline of guidelines you believe a pastor and church should have relative to baptizing children. Then discuss with other pastoral students their guidelines and come up with strategies to teach parents about why these are important.

The Lord's Supper

If baptism is the ordinance that serves as the church's gateway to membership, the Lord's Supper is the ordinance that serves as a continuing confession of the gospel by the church. Jesus instituted the Lord's Supper during the observance of Passover with His disciples on the night of His arrest (Matthew 26:17–30; Mark 14:12–26; Luke 22:7–30). The apostle Paul gives instructions on how the church should conduct its celebration of communion in 1 Corinthians 11:17–34. As an ordinance of the church, pastors must lead congregations to understand and practice the Lord's Supper in biblically faithful ways.

In the upper room Jesus instituted the Lord's Supper during the

Passover celebration with His disciples. The Passover was a time to celebrate God's redemption of Israel from slavery in Egypt through the sacrifice of a lamb whose blood was sprinkled and flesh eaten (see Exodus 12). Part of the redemption included the death of all the firstborn of all households and animals in Egypt. Israel was spared only by the blood of a slaughtered lamb. In the same way, Jesus' death on the cross as "our Passover Lamb" (1 Corinthians 5:7) initiated the new covenant, and believers celebrate being in the new covenant by obediently participating in this meal that includes the elements, which represent the broken body and shed blood of Jesus.

Just as Israel was told to celebrate the Passover continually as a memorial and teach future generations of God's deliverance, the Lord's Supper is to be celebrated as a memorial meal in which the church remembers the sacrifice of Jesus and the deliverance that is given through His death. When Jesus gathered His disciples in the upper room during the Passover and instituted the ordinance, He commanded them to "Do this in remembrance of me" (Luke 22:19). Thus, as the pastor leads the congregation in celebration of this meal, it is vital that he do so by calling believers to remember Christ's work on the cross on their behalf. Specifically, it is helpful not only to remind members of the broken body and shed blood of Jesus given as the price for sin, but also to reserve time in the service for reflection and remembrance by members.

Not only is the meal one of remembrance, it is also a celebration of Christ's finished work on the cross. Paul declares in 1 Corinthians 11:26, "For as often as you eat this bread and drink the cup, you proclaim the Lord's death until he comes." At the cross, Jesus Christ accomplished the work of salvation. Therefore, the church is to be led into communion as a celebration of Christ's finished work. Hughes states, "This is by no means a gloomy, funeral pronouncement ... Rather, the Lord's Table proclaims the gospel."[60] In practicing the ordinance, the church is once again proclaiming the good news of Jesus Christ among themselves as a celebration of the Savior.

The ordinance is also celebrated as participation, both with Christ and with each other. The ordinance is referred to in the Bible by different titles (i.e., breaking of bread, Acts 2:42; Lord's Supper, 1 Corinthians 11:20; the Lord's Table, 1 Corinthians 10:21), but none capture the meaning of the Supper any better than Paul's referring to it as a participation in 1 Corinthians 10:16. This is where the title *communion* comes from. Believers commune with each other and with Christ at the Table. As Hughes states, "when we partake of the Lord's Table, we experience a deepened sense of communion with Christ and one another."[61] Pastors must lead the congregation to see the reality of communion with Christ in the Lord's Supper. Dever states, "Paul taught that participating in the Supper testifies to participating in Christ's body and blood. It is the believer's personal identification with Christ's saving work, represented objectively by the elements on the table."[62] Remind members of the reality shown in the symbols of the bread and the cup.[63] By partaking, we are identifying and proclaiming our need of and faith in the work of Christ. This will also require the pastor to call believers to examine themselves and approach the ordinance as a time of renewal of faith and obedience to the Lord so that members do not partake in an "unworthy manner" (see 1 Corinthians 11:28–31).

Believers are not only identifying with Christ through their participation in the Supper, they are also identifying with each other. Pastors must lead congregations to understand that participation is a sign of unity among believers. Wayne Grudem argues, "When Christians participate in the Lord's Supper together they also give a clear sign of their unity with one another."[64] As the church responds in obedience to Christ's command and proclaims the gospel by participating together at the Table, she is unified around the gospel as testimony both to herself and to any who may be watching.

It has been shown that the ordinance of the Lord's Supper is a time to remember, celebrate, and participate. In addition, it is also a time of anticipation. In partaking of the Table, the church is anticipating the impending return of the Lord Jesus Christ as the apostle Paul reminds the believers in Corinth, "For as often as you eat this bread and drink this cup, you proclaim the Lord's death until he comes."[65] "The Baptist Faith and Message" states that the Lord's Supper is a symbolic act of obedience in which church members "anticipate His second coming."[66] As the church celebrates the finished work of Christ, lead members to anticipate His coming and the marriage supper of the Lamb, which believers will share together with Christ at His return (see Revelation 19:16–19).

As the pastor leads the church to understand the Lord's Supper, he will also need to address at least two issues regarding its practice. First, who may properly participate in the Supper? Hammett argues that there is widespread agreement that participants must be born-again believers who have been baptized and are church members in good standing.[67] There are, of course, different ways of applying these standards, so pastors must lead their congregations to understand the biblical teaching and practice participation at the Table in a biblically faithful manner. While Baptists have moved toward the practice of open communion in recent years, they have traditionally practiced a more closed stance toward communion holding baptism (by immersion) and church membership are vital prerequisites to participation.[68] However, a church decides to fence the Table, the pastor must strive to teach and practice communion in a way that honors the sacrifice of Christ and calls people to remember, celebrate, and participate in the gospel and anticipate the consummation of Christ.

The second question that a pastor must address is the frequency of the practice of the Lord's Supper. Some churches gather around the Table weekly, while others celebrate the ordinance less often. There are indications in the text of Scripture that lead the reader to believe its celebration should be often. In Acts 2:46, for example, the believers were breaking bread in their homes "day by day." However, there are no explicit instructions in Scripture as to how often the Supper should be celebrated. While many of the Reformers practiced communion weekly, the Geneva council instituted a quarterly practice (opposing Calvin's desire to celebrate it weekly), and many denominations have adopted that practice.[69] Churches that practice communion weekly point to the benefit of remembering and celebrating the gospel as well as practicing fellowship with Christ and each other often. As Hammett argues, "if the Lord's Supper is given to us as a 'means of grace,' by which believing hearts experience communion with Christ, are nourished spiritually, are encouraged by anticipation of the wedding feast of the Lamb, and are renewed in unity and love by partaking 'of one loaf' (1 Corinthians 10:17) and recognizing the corporate 'body of the Lord' (1 Corinthians 11:29), then such a gift would naturally be something we would desire frequently."[70]

Reflect and react

The chapter mentions the frequency of the celebration of the Lord's Supper. List the pros and cons of both weekly and quarterly (or less frequent) practice. Next, choose which you believe is the best practice for the church and articulate a plan to implement that kind of practice of the Supper.

On the other hand, those who come to the Table less frequently offer two primary reasons for their practice. First, when the Supper is celebrated less frequently, it is less likely to be taken lightly. The argument is that when the Table is added on to the weekly worship service it is not normally given the place of prominence like it is when it is celebrated less frequently (i.e., quarterly). The Table then loses some of its significance, as the worshipers are not reminded of the special nature of partaking as they would (or could) be if the entire service is focused on the Supper. Second, many who lead their churches to the Table less frequently point out that it takes time to practice the ordinance with the meaning that the Bible indicates, and this would be almost impossible to do on a weekly basis without lengthening the worship time. Otherwise, the Lord's Supper can simply become an afterthought to the worship service. In response to this, though, Hammett has a helpful suggestion, "if its value is as great as we have suggested, and its purpose as far reaching, perhaps we need to accustom our people to longer worship services."[71] However, when a church decides to celebrate the Table, the significance of the ordinance should absolutely be guarded.

A man who is called to an existing church as pastor will most likely inherit a particular interpretation of these issues and accompanying practices that have a long tradition. If he believes it necessary to lead the church to change their practices, it would be wise to spend whatever time necessary to teach biblical principles and practices prior to changing a church's current practices relative to the Lord's Table or baptism. On the other hand, if a man is called to plant a church, it would be wise to carefully study the issues surrounding the ordinances and institute practices with intentionality from the beginning. This should be done in the context of the sending church and in consultation with wise pastors. While tradition may not determine the practices of a church plant, it should certainly be consulted and considered as the church planter studies Scripture.

Research and create

The chapter mentions the responsibility of a church planter to articulate doctrine and institute practices relative to ordinances. Imagine that you are preparing to plant a church and have been tasked with thinking through these issues. Interview at least three seasoned pastors and ask them about the current practices of their churches. Discuss why their churches practice the ordinances in the way that they do. Ask them if they could, would they change anything about their current practices and why?

When I was a child, my father served our church as a deacon and assisted the pastors in serving the members the elements of communion.

On the Sundays that he was responsible to set up the table and make preparations, I was especially aware of the service and the special nature of the worship around the Table. The traditions of my home church surrounding both baptism and the Lord's Supper made a lasting impression on my young mind. Now that I am standing behind the table as a pastor leading a congregation, I am even more aware of the significance of leading God's flock in the celebration of both the Lord's Supper and baptism. Both are incredible gifts of God to the church that remind the church of the gospel and allow us to participate with Christ as we live in the power of the Holy Spirit in His grace.

Respond to a case study

Barbara sets up an appointment to meet with you, saying she is interested in joining the church. When she arrives she has two questions, both predicated on the fact that she has been a faithful member of a church of another denomination since childhood. She and her family have just moved to the area and visited the church you pastor. She enjoyed the visit and extolled your preaching and the friendliness of the congregation. After some small talk, she moves to the issue. Barbara has been to "other" Baptist churches in her life and found them unwelcoming and unwilling to accept her beliefs, so she is doubtful and a little frustrated as she explains her situation. She was "baptized" by sprinkling in her church at the age of ten after her confirmation classes. She informs you that she was a believer when this occurred and wants to know: (1) if she has to be baptized in your church (by immersion) prior to partaking of the Lord's Supper and (2) if she would have to be baptized (by immersion) to become a member of your church. In addition, Barbara also speaks of importance of the Lord's Supper for her and her family. She will only come to a church that allows her children (one and three years old) to partake in the Lord's Supper and asks you if it is acceptable for them to partake, even though they have not yet been baptized. How will you respond to Barbara?

To prepare yourself to address these and other issues that will undoubtedly arise around the ordinances, answer the following questions:

1. "The Baptist Faith & Message" teaches that baptism is prerequisite to the privileges of church membership and the Lord's Supper. How does your view of baptism as an ordinance of the church inform the way you respond to Barbara's question about partaking in the Lord's Supper? Get together with other pastors and discuss the issues and implications of allowing or disallowing Barbara to partake prior to

membership and without being baptized by immersion.

2. While Barbara's "sprinkling" was post-conversion, should she be required to be baptized by immersion to join the church? Defend your answer theologically and practically.

3. Should parents allow their children to partake in the Lord's Supper? Why or why not?

4. Carefully think through and write out in a short document how to lead Barbara (or someone like Barbara) through the process of joining the church, including how to specifically teach about the ordinances of the church.

5

OFFICIATING FUNERALS AND ASSISTING WITH GRIEF

Steven Wade

Tuesday morning as pastor Jim steps out of his study to "check-in" with his secretary, he notices that there are three text messages and a voicemail on this mobile phone. As he reads the text messages, he realizes that Margaret, a dear saint of God that has been a longtime member of the church, is close to death. The family had been called in, and they had contacted their pastor to inform him. Pastor Jim makes the necessary adjustments to his schedule and heads to the hospital to be with the family. As he arrives at the room, the family is gathered around the bed, and the nurse steps out of the room after attending to the elderly lady for the last time. The children are holding the hands of their mother as she struggles to breathe. One of the family members notices the pastor as he steps in and motions to him, inviting him into the family gathered in a circle around the bed. He steps in the circle and looks at Margaret and asks the family if he can lead them in prayer. Within a few minutes, as the family stands watching, Margaret takes her last breath and enters into eternity. Pastor Jim stands in the midst of a family that desperately need a shepherd. What is he to say and do in these moments?

I have been privileged on two occasions in 17 years of pastoral ministry to be holding the hand of a saint of God as he or she enters into eternity. Both times have been overwhelming, and the Spirit of God has attended to the departing and the family in incredible ways. It is a weighty task, as well as a great privilege, to walk with loved ones through such an experience. There is a sense of rejoicing because the loved one who was suffering is no longer suffering. She is in the presence of the Lord Jesus and will never experience the suffering of this world again! However, there is also a sense of sorrow and grief with the reality that a loved one will no longer come home and be the vital part of the family that she has always been.

Guiding a family through the paradox of celebrating the home-going and grieving the loss of a believing loved one is a requisite responsibility of pastors. The apostle Paul states that the gospel informs and tempers our grief over those who have died in Christ.

> But we do not want you to be uninformed, brothers, about those who are asleep, that you may not grieve as others do who have no hope. For since we believe that Jesus died and rose again, even so, through Jesus, God will bring with him those who have fallen asleep. For this we declare to you by a word from the Lord, that we who are alive, who are left until the coming of the Lord, will not precede those who have fallen asleep. For the Lord himself will descend from heaven with a cry of command, with the voice of an archangel, and with the sound of the trumpet of God. And the dead in Christ will rise first. Then we who are alive, who are left, will be caught up together with them in the clouds to meet the Lord in the air, and so we will always be with the Lord. Therefore encourage one another with these words. (1 Thessalonians 4:13–18 ESV)

The members of the church at Thessalonica were apparently so focused on the return of Jesus they were worried about the eternal condition of those who died before His coming. Paul assures them that the gospel reality is those who die "in Christ" will rise in a resurrection similar to Jesus' resurrection. This is great news that will assist the pastor in the shepherding task of helping his people deal with death. The intent of this chapter is to assist the pastor to minister to his flock when they are grieving the loss of a loved one. Of course, we cannot be exhaustive in our treatment of such a subject here, but rather will attempt to offer thought-provoking statements concerning major areas of ministry the pastor must consider. As Paul Tautges aptly states, "With compassion, we must learn how to offer Christ-centered comfort to those who grieve."[72]

Be Present

One of the essential elements of shepherding is presence. In times of crisis, the presence of the shepherd gives assurance to the sheep. While the pastor is certainly willing and often asked to do more than be present, a primary concern is to be present as one who cares for those who grieve. I remember one of the first times I walked into the home of a family who had just lost their loved one. I wanted desperately to say something profound and life altering. While I often tried (and failed) to be profound, what I discovered is that it is better to first offer genuine concern for their suffering, a loving embrace, and a willing ear to listen to their struggles. In their helpful book on conducting gospel-centered funerals, Croft and Newton remind us that grieving people "likely will not remember many of our quotes, but they will remember that we stood with them in their loss."[73]

It is important for people to know that their pastor is aware of the situation and is present in the crisis. Your presence will bring assurance, comfort, hope, and peace, not because you bring these things yourself, but because you represent the One who offers them! Often when the pastor enters a home or hospital room where a grieving family has gathered, all of the raw emotion of losing their loved one is renewed. In these moments, the pastor's presence as a representative of the Good Shepherd is impactful in and of itself. Often it is best to simply sit in silence as the person (or persons) weeps. More often than not, though, the pastor will listen with a shepherd's heart as the grieving person lets go of all his desires, fears, regrets, and concerns. It is then, as you hear how the person is experiencing grief, that you can wisely speak truth and comfort into his life. Weep with those who weep and mourn with those who mourn (cf. Romans 12:15).

Often the moments a pastor spends in silence grieving alongside those who mourn will seem awkward to him. Don't let the awkwardness drive you to spewing meaningless jargon that is not helpful in the situation. People, most of the time, will remember your presence more than what you say. They will remember comforting Scripture more than pithy sayings we throw out to be impressive. Your presence speaks volumes about your care for them. I recommend spending those moments of silence in prayer. Pray for God's Spirit to comfort and heal the family and to give you wisdom to know what to say, how to say it, and when to say it.

Recite and rehearse

The chapter emphasizes the character of the pastor; that is, what he needs "to be." List the six qualities. Next, select the one that you are currently best able to exemplify and explain why. Then, select the one quality that you need to concentrate on the most as you prepare for this dimension of ministry. Explain what you plan to do to improve.

Be Word-Centered

There is a time for silent presence when people are mourning, but our silent presence is not sufficient in and of itself. The pastor must be ready to speak gently the gospel truth in love and bring the mourners before the Good Shepherd (cf. Ephesians 4:15). When the time is appropriate, the compassion of Christ will lead us to come alongside and speak words of comfort and encouragement, of truth and promise. Tautges reminds pastors to "make sure your words are saturated with God's words" in those times.[74]

The wise pastor knows he is ultimately not what a mourner needs in the crisis. The pastor's presence points to God's presence. The pastor's comfort points to God's comfort. The pastor's words point to God's words. When ministering to those who grieve, the pastor should have at least three goals: (1) Bring the mourner into the presence of God, (2) Remind the mourner of God's sovereignty, and (3) Offer true hope in the midst of suffering. These goals cannot be attained without bringing the Word of God to bear upon the experience of the mourner.

While there are many places in Scripture that can be used to accomplish these goals, my favorite is perhaps Psalm 46. At a conference I attended when I was preparing for ministry, I will never forget hearing the speaker challenge attendees to be prepared to speak God's words to those who grieve. He rehearsed an experience he had early in his ministry when he had left his Bible in his car. One of the members of his church who had just lost a loved one looked at him and said, "Give us a word from the Word." After fumbling through a smattering of hope from different passages, he resolved to never be caught in that situation again and went home and committed Psalm 46 to memory. He recited it to us in the conference and I, like many other aspiring pastors in the conference, memorized Psalm 46 that week!

Psalm 46 begins, "God is our refuge and strength, a very present help in trouble" (v. 1 ESV). Encourage those who grieve to run to God. He is our refuge. We find strength in His presence. Because we take refuge and find strength in His presence, it doesn't matter what trouble confronts us, there is no reason to fear, even when the earth gives way or the kingdoms of this world fall (cf. vv. 2 and 6). Our God is with us (vv. 5, 7, 11). His presence will keep us and His help is near (v. 5). The psalm invites the one who is experiencing trouble to consider the mighty works of the Lord and know of His power and sovereignty (vv. 8–10). Whether it is Psalm 46 or other passages of Scripture (e.g., Psalm 139, Jeremiah 29, Isaiah 55, John 14, 2 Corinthians 1, etc.) pastors must always know that the Scripture brings assurance of God's presence and sovereignty.

When the words of Scripture are brought to bear upon life and death, they bring great comfort to those whose faith is found in Jesus. However, there are times when the mourner and/or the deceased do not have a relationship with Jesus. Many pastors are tempted to avoid the issue, and the jokes of a wife and children going to the coffin after the pastor's funeral sermon to make sure they had come to the right person's funeral are well circulated as a rebuke upon pastors for being less than forthright. The pastor must be wise in his words, and he should always bring comfort; however, comfort apart from the gospel of Jesus Christ is ultimately no comfort at all. Tautges states, "Any comfort we give to people that lies outside the hope of the gospel is temporary at best and deceptive at worst."[75]

A Word-centered pastor knows that true hope for believers and nonbelievers is found in the gospel and thus must be on his lips when in one-on-one conversations, as well as when he is preaching the funeral sermon. In 1 Corinthians 15, Paul concludes that because Jesus Christ is risen from the dead there is hope for mankind. Jesus was the firstfruits of those who died and all who are "in Christ" will be raised in a resurrection like His. Their bodies will be raised imperishable in glory. This gospel truth must be proclaimed. Even if the deceased was not a believer, there is hope for those who grieve in turning to the Good Shepherd who laid down His life for them and offers them the hope of eternal life. The only true, eternal hope a pastor has to offer is centered on this good news.

Be Personal

As a pastor ministers to a family that is grieving the loss of a loved one, he must know that the hurt is real and his shepherding must be personal. Each individual experiences grief and moves through the grieving process differently. Therefore, the effective shepherd wisely cares for each sheep according to her own need. I encourage you to take three items with you as you go to minister to a family: a Bible, a pen, and a notepad.

When the pastor enters into the grieving process of the family, he should be genuinely interested in the experience of those who are grieving. Remember, the family is grieving the loss of a loved one. Be sensitive to each person and focus especially on those closest to the deceased. Most likely there will be people present and grieving whom the pastor does not know. Graciously introduce yourself and ask about the person's relationship to the deceased. Tell them how you know the deceased and be prepared to listen and care for the person according to his or her own need.

In addition, be personal with the family concerning the deceased. Be inquisitive and prepared to ask questions about memories and experiences that stand out in the family member's memory about the deceased. Ask general questions about the person (e.g., character traits, demeanor, qualities, etc.) as well as specific questions about personal experiences (e.g., events, marriage details, place of occupation, etc.). Take copious notes as you listen (this is especially if you are going to take part in the funeral service). This will help you grieve with the family member and learn more about the loved one she has lost.

When I first started taking notes when I sat with families who were grieving, I felt a bit odd taking out my notepad and pen. However, I simply asked the family if it would be okay if I took notes because my memory was not great. We typically laugh about my memory comment, and they graciously accept. Families have always seemed appreciative that I was so interested in their loved one, and they are especially grateful when their stories show up in the eulogy during the funeral service (if I am charged with it) or when I bring their experiences up later in asking them how they are doing.

As you mourn with those who mourn, be willing to genuinely mourn yourself. Pastors will no doubt be asked to shepherd grieving families that have lost loved ones who are not known personally by the pastor. In these cases, we mourn with those who mourn because we know what it is like to lose a loved one, and we see the genuine grief of our flock. However, the pastor who remains with a particular congregation for some time will undoubtedly be called to minister to a grieving family of a dear member of his own congregation.

The first year of my first pastorate I was a part of ten funerals. It was a thorough introduction to ministering to grieving families. However, I remember specifically receiving the call about an elderly member of our church who was our neighbor in the second year of that pastorate. We had grown close to Ms. Lennie, and it was an entirely different experience as I ministered to that family. My heart was heavy for the family, but we too had lost a precious friend and neighbor. Ms. Lennie had become like a grandmother to us. We had enjoyed many meals with her and learned all about her life and her late husband. She cooked for us, taught us about gardening and exemplified how a woman who fears the Lord trusts in Him to the end.

In those circumstances, avoid the temptation to "be the professional" and suppress your own grief. Rather, genuinely mourn with the family as you minister to them. It is in these times that the pastor has the opportunity to exemplify what it is like to grieve, but not as those who have no hope.

Reflect and react

Reflect on the experience of losing someone close to you and express it in an essay in some detail. What passages of Scripture were helpful in your recovery and why? What other steps do you recall in your process of recovery that may assist you in counseling others?

Be a Counselor

Death often triggers mental, emotional, and behavioral crises in those left behind. The attentive pastor will be sensitive to the special needs of the grieving while ministering to a family during a time of loss. Just as in other crisis situations, the initial moments you spend with a family or individual are pivotal moments in establishing trust and confidence in your ability to guide them through dark moments. A pastor's confidence in God and His Word in the time of grieving will often open the door for people to open up and share deeper (and perhaps even unrelated) hurt and suffering than what comes out in the initial contact. In these times, the pastor must be prepared to be a counselor to the suffering.

I have often had extended family members come to me during my ministry to a grieving family, whether at the funeral home or even after the funeral, and ask me about life issues with which they are wrestling. In moments like these, the pastor must assess the situation and determine how to proceed. First, ask for a brief description of the problem and attempt to discern the nature and depth of the issue. It is often the case that an issue can be addressed in a short (or even, not-so-short), informal conversation. If this is so, eagerly listen to the person's story and speak truth in love (Ephesians 4:15) as much as possible in the time you have. Be careful to point the person to God and His Word as the source of truth, hope, and help. Point him to the body of Christ as the community in which God intends for him to understand and apply the truth, hope, and help of His Word.

If the issue is such that the person needs a more formal counseling relationship, begin the process of moving him along the path toward help. It is wise for the pastor to determine whether or not the person is already an active member of a church. Of course, if the person is already under your pastoral care, then you will know. But if not, it is wise to ask. If a person does not have a church home, then begin the process of connecting him to the counseling ministry of your church. For some this may mean you connect him with a particular counselor (perhaps a staff member tasked with counseling or a lay counselor). For others it will mean you set up an appointment to begin more formal counseling with the person.

If the person is under the watchcare of another church, recommend that he seek out counsel from his own pastor, if at all possible. Even if this is not something the counselee desires to do, it is advisable to have his permission to contact his pastor so that he can be aware of the shepherding issue as the counselee will eventually be turned back over to the normal shepherding process of his own church.

While it is not within the scope of this chapter to offer a full model of counseling, I will suggest a few principles and point to a couple of helpful resources. The Bible clearly instructs us about who we are and why we do what we do. These are key issues when a pastor is counseling people who are struggling with shame, guilt, depression, fear, anxiety, worry, addiction, and a whole host of other issues. The first is the issue of identity. Many believe that what a person does forms his identity. However, the Bible teaches that a person's identity determines what he does. In other words, the essence of who you are determines what you think, say, and do. The Bible uses a couple of illustrations to make this point. For example, Proverbs 4:23 instructs us to guard our hearts (core of who we are) with all diligence, for from it flows the issues of life. In Luke 6:43–45 Jesus uses the image of a tree (type of tree represents identity) and its fruit (fruit determined by type of tree) to make the point that "out of the abundance of the heart" (identity), the mouth speaks (behavior). This is explained well by Tim Lane and Paul Tripp in their book *How People Change.*[76]

In addition to considering why people do what they do, Paul Tripp has written a helpful book that offers a methodology of personal ministry that will be helpful to the pastor who counsels. In *Instruments in the Redeemer's Hand*, Tripp explains that the pastor must love the person, seek to know the person and his situation, speak truth in love, and instruct the counselee on actions to take.[77] These are all key aspects to being an effective pastoral counselor.

Be a Peacemaker

The dynamics of family (and close friends) relationships sometimes elevate the grief process to another level altogether. The mental, emotional, and behavioral crises that are triggered by the loss sometimes create a volatile environment that may explode with emotion and/or confrontation of others. Those associated with the deceased each have their own personal narrative and, while they sometimes share similar views of the deceased, they do not always agree. When these people are family and have deep history with each other, old hurts, jealousy, bitterness, and sometimes even rage can erupt. While conflict will be addressed by another contributor to this volume, it is appropriate to remind the pastor that peacemaking is often a crisis skill he must exercise when dealing with grief situations.

When entering a home or hospital room, the pastor should be aware of the dynamics as much as possible. There are times when there will be a current spouse and a former spouse (or more) with children from multiple marriages. Perhaps there is a feud between siblings or even neighbors. Or perhaps personality differences simply push mourners to be impatient with each other. Whatever the reason, as the pastor becomes aware of these dynamics, he may be invited or forced to act as a mediator. In those times the pastor should remember to be quick to listen and slow to speak. Understand that you most likely do not have all the details of the conflict, so tread lightly. As much as possible, treat all parties equally. Help family members speak openly with respect to each other. As a mediator, make sure all parties' opinions are brought out and considered. Be cautious about taking sides, even if you feel a need to defend one who is a member of your own congregation. Keep the glory of Christ central and know that sometimes a situation like this exposes places where the pastor must help his congregant grow and act in humility toward others as a representative of Christ. Encourage those with whom you have close relations to act as peacemakers, reminding them of the mandate to live out the gospel in their speech, their willingness to forgive, and their work toward restoration.

Research and create

Obtain copies of the following books: *Conduct Gospel-Centered Funerals* by Croft Newton, *Comfort the Grieving* by Tautges, and *Leading Today's Funerals* by Lloyd. Find what they say about funerals for nonbelievers and lead a group of pastors (or pastors-in-training) in a discussion about how to minister to a family whose deceased loved one was not a believer. How would you plan and conduct the funeral? What passages of Scripture might be applicable and helpful?

Be Helpful

When death touches our lives by taking those closest to us, the grief we experience is often intense. When a person must add to his grief the responsibility of handling the details of planning the funeral, the burial, and/or the estate settlement, the situation may become overwhelming. Many grieving loved ones face responsibilities and decisions they have not had in the past. Pastors are in a unique role that allows them to experience and assist in many of the duties loved ones must fulfill when death occurs and can thus be a great help to those traversing this unfamiliar territory.

Planning funerals is not something many people spend much time thinking about. When death occurs, the pastor has an opportunity to assist the family in navigating through some of the darkest waters they may ever face. It is helpful for the pastor to be familiar with the funeral directors in his area. This will allow him to bridge the unfamiliarity of the family with the funeral home during this time. Prepare the family for their conversation with the funeral director, and then, when possible, introduce them to him or her as another member of the family's care team. Be available to the family as they plan the funeral arrangements, but do not overstep your responsibilities by doing the job of the funeral director. Rather, consult with the funeral director and be as helpful as possible.

The pastor's responsibility will be to help plan the funeral service itself along with the family. Therefore, the pastor should both listen to a family, as well as gently suggest parts of a service that are Christ-honoring and helpful in the grief process. Be ready to assist the family by reminding them of the purpose of a funeral in order to help them plan the service. The service is a time of worship of the God who gives and sustains life and the One to whom all will ultimately give account when death comes.

It is a time to both celebrate and remember the life of a loved one as a life that was lived *coram Deo* (before the face of God). Assist them to plan a service that both honors God and helps them celebrate and remember the life He granted to their loved one. Of course, if their loved one was redeemed, the service is a time to celebrate His redeeming power. If the deceased did not know God, help the family to reflect on the gospel and the hope they can have of eternal life. Included below is a brief outline of the elements of a funeral service that could each be used to point the family to the hope of the gospel.

While the funeral director's care of the family is temporary, the pastor's shepherding care does not end with the graveside service. Rather, the pastor should have a plan to provide continual shepherding to the family at least through the one-year anniversary of the death of a loved one. Paul Tautges offers an excellent sixteen-month care plan for following up with grieving families in his book, *Comfort the Grieving*.[78]

Elements Included in a Funeral Service

Prayer	Use times of prayer to intercede for the grieving family. Pray that the Holy Spirit will comfort, sustain, guide, and unify them. Pray that they will have eyes to see the hope that is found in the gospel, even in the loss of a loved one. I always open and close in prayer.
Scripture	The books listed in the resource section below, as well as many pastoral guides, will offer a plethora of Scripture passages appropriate for times of grieving and will be some of the most helpful moments in any funeral service.
Comforting Memories	Sharing memories that you have heard or know personally of the deceased is a great comfort to a grieving family. Take time to learn stories that tell about unique qualities, habits, and hobbies of the deceased. Weave the gospel into the person's story, as these memories will often be what sticks in the minds of those who attend the funeral.
Song	God has given us music as a means of both expressing and leading us in our emotional lives. Songs that focus on the hope of the gospel are always appropriate at funerals.

Sermon Funerals are not times for long sermons, but the pastor should have enough trust in God's Word to point the family and friends to some portion of Scripture and briefly exposit what is there relative to life and death. Reference the books in the resource section of this chapter for many great suggestions.

Testimony It is often helpful for a family to have one or more persons from the family speak and relate memories or a letter or poem written to or about the deceased. If possible, speak with those who share testimony prior to the service and talk about how what they are going to share relates to the gospel.

Respond to a case study

It was Thanksgiving morning when we received the call. A young couple in our church, whom we had grown to know and love, were on their way to the hospital to have their second child. We all should have been thrilled, but instead we began to weep and pray for God's grace in the situation. We made preparations to cut our Thanksgiving trip short and travel back home. Just five months earlier the Smiths had sat at our dining room table and shared devastating news with us about their pregnancy.

The doctors had informed them the baby Mary carried had a condition that would not allow her to survive outside of the womb even if she made it full-term. They recommended an immediate abortion. Mary was in tears as she sought confirmation of her belief that she could not voluntarily take her baby's life, and Chris was wrestling with whether to follow medical advice for the benefit of his wife's emotional health. They were with us to ask for counsel and prayer. We wept that day and prayed just as we had with them for the remainder of the pregnancy. So when we received the call, we left to be with this sweet family as they faced what the doctors had said would be inevitable. On Thanksgiving Day God granted life to Hannah Grace, and she was able to be with her mommy and daddy on this earth for twenty-one minutes before the Lord escorted her into heaven. When we arrived to finally meet with this young couple, there was a deep mourning as we sat down to process all of the events of the past months. I knew there must be hundreds of questions about why all of these things happened and how they happened. Why would God allow this to occur? Did we do the right thing in carrying the baby full-term? What about the eternal destiny of our baby? Can we know she is with Jesus? While the couple desired to trust God through the entire situation, their faith was now being stretched further than they had ever imagined. How does a pastor effectively shepherd in such a time?

---

1. What are some practical ways you could minister to this family the first time you talk with them about the imminent death of their child?
2. When you arrive to comfort the family after the death of the child, what Scripture passages would be helpful to for you to read/quote?
3. Take time to plan out a funeral sermon for Hannah Grace. How would you point the family to Jesus? Specifically write out how you would include the gospel in the funeral sermon in an appropriate way.

6
COUNSELING THOSE DEALING WITH DEPRESSION

Jim Porowski

Caleb walked back into his office at the church. Looking out the window, he thought of his wife. They were close, best friends. He loved her. Ashley was a strong Christian. So when she began showing signs of discouragement two years ago, he brushed it aside as a few bad days. But a few days became weeks, then months. Ashley was not looking like herself: she was too thin, having lost nearly twenty pounds now, and since she wasn't sleeping well, she looked exhausted. She would smile at church but not at home. She cried often, and although she seemed to be happier away from home, she found it hard to get out. Her family physician said it was depression.

Depression? It didn't make sense. Ashley was the most normal person he had ever known. She taught kindergarten. Everyone loved her. Coming home each day was fun.

He looked forward to coming home and sharing his day with her.

What the Bible Says about Avoiding Depression

When Caleb first heard the doctor's words, he was surprised and a little angry. He had studied biblical theology at a reputable seminary. At first he tried to prove the doctor wrong, but the more he studied, prayed, and read, the more he understood. *Webster's Dictionary* provided a helpful starting point by defining *depression* as "A state of sadness, with inactivity, difficulty in thinking and concentration, a significant increase or decrease in appetite and time spent sleeping, feelings of dejection and hopelessness, and sometimes suicidal tendencies." Caleb made several conclusions about depression and how to manage it.

Lesson 1: We all need rest.

Elijah had a tremendous victory in 1 Kings 18. He saw several miraculous things happen: a fierce fire from heaven consumed a burnt offering; Israel turned back to God; justice fell on the prophets of Baal; and a long drought ended. God was God, and He had demonstrated His power to Elijah and all Israel.

But in chapter 19, Elijah's mood quickly changes when he received a death threat from Queen Jezebel and ran for his life. The Bible says that Elijah went into the wilderness, sat down under a juniper tree, and prayed that he might die (v. 4). He went from victory to hopelessness and despair. His experience dramatically illustrates a basic truth of life: anyone can become discouraged.

The last sentence in verse 4 reveals the depth of the prophet's hopelessness: "Take my life, for I am not better than my fathers." Elijah was exhausted and felt like a failure. Have you ever felt like a failure? It hurts deeply to feel you have disappointed yourself, another person, or God. A part of depression is the belief that you have failed and that the future holds no hope for you.[79]

In 1 Kings 19:5–7, God had Elijah sleep, eat, drink, and sleep some more. We often ignore these basic needs in times of stress. Proper attention to the physical needs of the body is essential to spiritual growth and maturity. As humans created by God, we must live within the limitations of the physical body God provided for us. We cannot overestimate the importance of proper diet, exercise, and rest. Care for physical needs is so important that God sent to Elijah an angel, whose only assignment was to help him by taking care of his body.

It's not surprising that current research continues to address the benefits of sleep. "Without restful sleep, mood, concentration, and mental performance suffer. Sleep deprivation is a major cause of car crashes and other accidents, and it has been linked to important medical problems ranging from hypertension, obesity, and diabetes to heart disease."[80]

The body heals itself during sleep. Daniel G. Amen, a prominent clinical neuroscientist, says that "one of the fastest ways to age is by getting less than seven or eight hours of sleep at night. People who typically get six hours of sleep or less have lower overall blood flow to the brain, which hurts its function."[81]

Lesson 2: We all need comfort and encouragement from God, and it usually comes through other people.

Paul writes in 2 Corinthians 1:3–4, "Blessed be the God and Father of our Lord Jesus Christ, the Father of mercies and God of all comfort; who comforts us in all our affliction so that we may be able to comfort those who are in any affliction with the comfort with which we ourselves are comforted by God."

Paul knew that we need comfort in this life because we all face problems. The afflictions and pressures we face can result in deep discouragement and even depression. The word *comfort* is used ten times by Paul in the six verses of 2 Corinthians 1:3–7 (four times as the verb *parakaleo*, and six times as the noun *paraklasis*). The verb is often translated to mean, "comfort, encourage, or cheer up, and the noun, comfort, encouragement, or help."

"Paul wanted his hearers to understand that the merciful Father is the author of all possible comfort and consolation. There is no enduring comfort apart from him ... Paul was certainly one of the most afflicted men ever. He suffered cold, nakedness, beating, imprisonment, criminal assault, shipwreck, betrayal, desolation, desertion, and more. His was a life of perpetual death."[82]

Later Paul writes, "But God, who comforts the depressed (or downcast), comforted us by the coming of Titus" (2 Corinthians 7:6). The emphasis of the Greek word for depressed, *tapeinos*, appears to be on humility, a lowliness of spirit brought on by the hammering of difficult circumstances. It especially carries the idea of discouragement.[83] God is aware of our afflictions and provides comfort—primarily through other people.

Lesson 3: We all need hope and confidence.

Many of the Psalms express our personal thoughts, feelings, and dreams. We can quickly relate when the writers declare: "The Lord is my Shepherd" (Psalm 23:1), or "I will give thanks to the Lord with all my heart" (Psalm 9:1). God cares for us individually and personally.

Kidner describes Psalm 42 as "one of the most sadly beautiful in the Psalter."[84] The writer is a temple singer separated from Jerusalem and the temple worship. He expressed his longing for God. Far from Jerusalem, he felt sadly distant. It is possible to understand that Jesus is close, while at the same time to feel painfully distant from Him.

"As the deer pants for the water brooks, so my soul pants for Thee, O God" (42:1). The Psalmist knew that God refreshes and gives life, but he felt distant from the Lord. His faith was shaken by the taunts of nonbelievers because they matched his doubts. "My tears have been my food day and night, while they say to me all day long, 'Where is your God?'" (42:3).

Finally, the writer asks himself an important question, "Why are you in despair?" He faced his painful feelings squarely and directed himself toward the only One who could satisfy his thirst.

Psalm 42 reflects a personal conflict. Several times the writer indicates he was discouraged and "in despair" (vv. 6, 9, 11) only to reassert his hope in God. The Psalm ends with confidence: "I shall yet praise Him" (42:11).

These were three conclusions Caleb reached that were hard to admit to himself: He hadn't encouraged Ashley to get the rest she needed, even when he saw that she was struggling. Since he had always viewed her as positive and resourceful, he hadn't provided enough of the comfort and encouragement she needed. As she became more depressed, he grew frustrated, not realizing the extent to which he needed to walk with his wife through her difficult times. It was only later that he realized that biblical hope and confidence are not one-time events; they are a continual expression of faith in Christ.

Recite and rehearse

Take a moment to write down the three needs that people have described above. Which have you found to be the most important in your life? Why?

What Is Depression?

Many people who love God face times of intense discouragement. Some of their experiences fit what we would expect to see in an individual who is depressed. Nearly all people face discouragement. It may last for several days, but most individuals gradually begin to feel more positive about themselves and their circumstances. Depression, on the other hand, is a state of prolonged sadness and despair. Feelings of exhaustion and hopelessness are common. The following chart summarizes the symptoms of depression:

Symptoms of Depression[85]

To be considered depressed, you would experience five or more symptoms almost every day for two weeks.

Depressed mood most of the day, nearly every day for two weeks

- Person feels sad or empty, cries often

Loss of pleasure in formerly enjoyable activities

- In a way that is uncharacteristic for the individual, he or she is bored with their job or faces marital difficulty.
- Cooking or gardening were once enjoyable but are now burdensome tasks.

Significant changes in weight or appetite

- Person has gained fifteen pounds or doesn't feel like eating (a 5 percent change in one month)

Can't fall asleep at night, or wakes up repeatedly throughout the night

- Person may sleep too much

Fatigue or loss of energy

- Person just can't do what they once did. To fix the gate of the fence or clean the house is overwhelming

Feelings of hopelessness, worthlessness, guilt, or withdrawal

- Pain in being with others with no light at the end of the tunnel

Inability to concentrate or make decisions

- Individual may spend an hour on paperwork with no progress. Making simple daily decisions becomes a chore.
- This is sometimes described as "painful thinking"

Recurrent thoughts of death or suicide

If a person experiences five out of these eight symptoms, it indicates that his or her depression is serious. This is especially true if the first two of these symptoms have persisted every day for two weeks. This person should seek professional help, beginning with a medical doctor.

Reflect and react

This chart gives eight symptoms of depression. Take a moment to consider one individual that you think might be experiencing depression right now. Highlight the symptoms that they are experiencing.

Five Causes of Depression

There are five main causes of depression. Each by itself may lead to depression, but when an individual encounters more than one of these five, depression is far more likely.

1. Loss

We all have experienced loss or will experience it. No bridge spans the pain of losing people and things we care about. Each of us must eventually wade slowly through these streams. At times others are there to walk beside us, but frequently we find ourselves alone.

The normal grief process is covered in another chapter. However, I place it here because when a person becomes depressed there are often a number of factors that have led to it. Serious depression is usually multifactorial. That is, a person has lost something or someone who is significant to them, and then other issues, or causes of depression, are experienced.

This was true with Caleb's wife, Ashley, in our lead story. A year before her doctor diagnosed her with depression, her grandmother died of cancer. Ashley appeared to handle it well, but when other issues arose in their church, things she would have talked to her grandmother about, Ashley was overwhelmed and became angry.

2. Anger

There are two types of anger people display toward others. People with aggressive anger often get what they want but leave behind an unfortunate trail of hurting people. People with passive anger, on the other hand, tend to be their own worst enemies, causing themselves considerable pain by failing to speak up about the situations or actions that anger them. In the end, they also leave behind a trail of confused, hurting people. Both forms of anger damage relationships and leave the angry person alone and discouraged. When people hold onto it for a long period of time, it leads to discouragement and a sense of hopelessness. And if the individual cannot, or will not, let it go, it manifests itself as depression.

People who are aggressive in their anger must learn to control it. The Bible warns against even associating with a man given to anger: "Do not associate with a man given to anger; or go with a hot-tempered man, lest you learn his ways, and find a snare for yourself" (Proverbs 22:24–25).

Buzzell writes,

> The warning here is against being a friend or even associating with a hot-tempered man (lit., "an owner or possessor of anger;" cf. 19:19) or one easily angered (lit., "a man of wrath") because such an association leads a person to take on wrathful ways, which are foolish (14:17, 29), divisive (15:18), and sinful (29:22), and become ensnared (cf. 29:6), caught up in a situation which is hard to get out of.[86]

Clearly this is not a prescription for happiness! Aggressive anger leads to personal problems. And personal problems, the longer they continue, can leave a person trapped in depression.

People who are passively aggressive in their anger, on the other hand, can experience God's peace by following a simple plan for speaking clearly and honestly. They need to ask themselves three questions as they plan a conversation with someone whose words and actions have left them feeling hurt or angry:

1. What did the person do or say that made you angry?
2. What sort of changes are you hoping to see?
3. What might be the result if the situation does not change?

Taken together, it looks something like this: *When you keep reminding me of what I did five years ago in front of others, it makes me angry. I want you to be more respectful of me in public. If you won't respect my feelings and the fact that God has forgiven me in Christ, our friendship will not be able to remain as close as we would both like it to be.*

3. Poor Personal Choices: Our Own Sin and Our Response to the Sins of Others

God allows us to experience sadness, discouragement, and depression when we sin. He does this in order to motivate us. One of the great consequences of sin is how a person feels as a result of his or her behavior. It is not God's desire for us to perpetually have these feelings, but He does allow them so that we will adopt His attitude toward sin and pursue a life of obedient service to Christ.

Our poor choices affect how we feel. In Psalm 32:3–4, David describes the misery he felt when he refused to respond to God: "When I kept silent about my sin, my body wasted away through my groaning all day long. For day and night Thy hand was heavy upon me; my vitality was drained away as with the fever heat of summer."

Chastened by the Lord, David felt physically, emotionally, and spiritually miserable. Ross writes, "This psalm may be a companion to Psalm 51, referring to David's sin with Bathsheba. At that time David refused for a year to acknowledge his sin. Psalm 51 was his prayer for pardon; Psalm 32 would then follow it, stressing God's forgiveness and the lesson David learned."[87]

David points to the happiness we can experience by being open to the Lord's counsel when he rebukes our sinful choices: "Many are the sorrows of the wicked; but he who trusts in the Lord, lovingkindness shall surround him" (Psalm 32:10).

Paul wrote the Corinthian Christians what he considered to be a severe letter because he wanted them to experience the joy of obedient living. In the letter Paul encouraged them to forsake their complacent attitude toward the sinful behavior of one of their members.

Paul maintained that he did not regret any sorrow he had caused them by what he had written, because it was the type of sorrow God intended—sorrow for sin:

> For though I caused you sorrow by my letter, I do not regret it; though I did regret it—for I see that that letter caused you sorrow, though only for a while—I now rejoice, not that you were made sorrowful, but that you were made sorrowful to the point of repentance; for you were made sorrowful according to the will of God, in order that you might not suffer loss in anything through

us. For the sorrow that is according to the will of God produces a repentance without regret, leading to salvation; but the sorrow of the world produces death. (2 Corinthians 7:8–10)

Clearly, the Lord is always looking out for our long-term benefit and contentment. While He may allow us to experience some discouragement to motivate corrections in the way we live, God's ultimate goal is for us to experience joy.

4. Anxiety and Stress

Stress is a person's response to overload–the accumulated effect of the pressures of life. And as these pressures grow and are not addressed in a healthy way, the likelihood of depression increases. I discuss anxiety and stress in another chapter but include them here since they are also a significant contributing factor in depression.

5. A Painful Childhood

Deuteronomy 6:4–9 was at the heart and center of Israel's relationship with God. There is only one God, and they must love and obey Him alone. This passage contains clear directives for strong, godly families:

Love the Lord with all your heart, and with all your soul, and with all your might (*v.* 5). "In some respects it can be argued that the whole book of Deuteronomy is simply a commentary on this one verse."[88] Moses spoke to the families of Israel and reminded them to love the Lord supremely.

God was to be the object of their love. Today, God intends for our homes to radiate our love for Him and for our relationship with Him to be more important than work, hobbies, money, or anything else. Healthy families need a solid foundation built on the love of God.

Set God's Word on your heart (*v*.6). Merrill describes these commandments (literally *these words*) as "a term that encompasses the full corpus of the covenant text communicated by Moses but which is encapsulated especially in the Shema of vv. 4–5 ... To 'be upon the heart' is to be in one's constant, conscious reflection."[89] The commitment the Israelites had to God and His Word was to be more than mere external ritual. The Word of God was to be set in the hearts of parents. When we were children, God desired that our parents model to us a deep personal closeness with the Savior and adherence to His Word. He intended for us to consistently see, hear, and experience our parents' love for God.

Teach your children to love God and His Word (*vv*. 7–9). Israel would "ensure continuity of this allegiance and this covenant faith by diligently teaching her children."[90] Parenting must be intentional. Parents must make a concerted effort to communicate to children their relationship to God and love for His Word. Healthy parents seek to instill a love for God in their children. Deuteronomy 6:7–9 explains how and when God's Word should be taught: "You shall teach them diligently to your sons and shall talk of them when you sit in your house and when you walk by the way and when you lie down and when you rise up."

These principles were so important to God that he had Moses declare them to Israel just before entering the Promised Land. They are timeless. And as such, chaos enters a child's life to the degree that they are missing. Jesus said that a house built on sand will fall (Matthew 7:26). Many children grow up with scars from a fallen home. They do not all become depressed as adults, but when other difficulties are encountered later on in life, a serious depression may occur.

Final Thoughts

We have considered five common causes of discouragement and depression. Now we need to ask the practical question: How do I make (or help someone to make) the changes necessary to recover?

Research and create

Look at the following description of a Change Process. Critique this process and make changes where you think necessary. Be sure to provide footnotes and citations to support the Change Process that you believe is the most accurate. Include biblical theology, recommendations by pastors, biblical counselors, etc. (Paper minimum: ten pages, double-spaced).

Awareness

Change often begins when God suggests a new and specific direction for us to go. He can speak softly or strongly. Because Caleb heard a strong word from his wife's doctor, he had to face reality. Ashley was not doing well—she was trying with all that was in her but was steadily slipping backward. It was an adjustment for Caleb. How had he missed her struggle?

For Ashley, hearing her doctor say that she was depressed was a relief. She did not know what she would do about it. She still felt the same way, but she began to feel hopeful because she finally knew what it was.

Understanding

In the end, Caleb became a better husband and pastor. When he was in seminary, he was surprised by how much he did not know about the Bible. Those three years marked a huge turning point in his life. This experience with his wife's depression elevated his understanding of people.

Ashley began to sort out the hurtful parts of her life. She saw a female counselor, a strong Christian who valued the Scriptures. They talked about each of her problem areas, making adjustments where necessary. Most importantly, Ashley's faith grew. The Bible, talking to God, and listening to His Word were more important than ever. One of the issues encountered was her need for several good friends. She began to call and spend time with some women near her home whom she knew and liked but had become too busy to see. Now she enjoyed an occasional lunch with them, having someone to text when prayer was needed, or just having a friend to share with when something made her laugh.

Action

You do not need to possess complete awareness and understanding before acting. Caleb began by helping his wife to clear her schedule. Ashley asked Caleb to go with her to her grandmother's grave several times. She talked about the woman who had led her to Christ as a teenager when her brother fell into drugs. They talked about how they would raise their children. Jesus Christ and His Word were central in their life together.

Change

Change comes when awareness, Understanding, and action are a part of life. Change does not mean perfection. It means walking with Christ and living out more of what He is teaching us today than we did yesterday. For example: "Today I didn't get angry when (he or she did or didn't do ________, or this particular event happened) like I might have in the past."

Just as Paul writes, "I can do all things through Him who strengthens me" (Philippians 4:13). I agree with the Apostle Paul when he writes, "I can do all things through Him who strengthens me" (Philippians 4:13).

Respond to a case study

David, a deacon's son, shot himself on Saturday night. Today is Sunday, and the mood at church is subdued. Some heard the news the night before; others heard as they walked through the parking lot and greeted friends. Andy was called to the hospital early Sunday morning. He had been the youth pastor for nearly a year, but as he waited for worship to begin, he could only think of David's face–bright and full of energy when he first met him, but over time it became sad and distant. David's parents spoke to Andy as their son began to question the purpose of life. He lost interest in youth group and later quit the high school basketball team. His grades were slipping, as he complained that his concentration was gone, and he was often too tired to get out of bed. Andy had not known what to say at the time. He assured David's parents that he was a great kid and would probably pull out of it. "Make sure he comes to youth group next week," he told his parents. "I'll be able to talk to him then." That was one week ago. Andy felt awful. David's death was not his fault, but he had an opportunity to get involved, and let it slip away.

1. Look back at the Symptoms of Depression chart. List David's symptoms.

2. What would you have done when you saw David's countenance changing?

3. We opened this chapter with three lessons Pastor Caleb had learned. How might Pastor Andy have applied them in working with David?

7

COUNSELING THOSE DEALING WITH ANXIETY AND STRESS

Jim Porowski

Eight a.m. and Jason already feels tired. The list of tasks he needs to accomplish at the church today seems endless. A screen full of e-mails await him, several asking if he received their previous e-mails. Some quit asking. The rest of the week? The more he thinks about it, the more exhausted he becomes. He feels like a runner at the two-mile marker of a marathon with a long, hard twenty-four miles to go.

At home his list of chores continues to grow. His inability to complete them causes friction with his wife. His lack of time with the kids leaves him guilt-ridden. Jason feels he is failing in most of life's significant areas.

Lately, he's been plagued by physical problems. His body cries out to him through headaches, back and shoulder tightness, stomach problems, and exhaustion.

Jason quickly walks to the front of his office and closes the door. Back at his desk he sits down and waits for the intense feelings of panic to end.

What Is Fear?

There are several terms to be aware of. Fear relates to an identifiable object or event, something that is taking place right in front of you. It is a reaction to a loud noise or seeing a snake on the path ahead. Anxiety is free-floating apprehension. Normal fear addresses a realistic danger.[91] As such, we say that fear is within the normal range of emotions and keeps us safe from danger. The first principle in the book of Proverbs, "the fear of the Lord is the beginning of knowledge" (1:7), is closely related to the idea of fear as safety. Kidner states, "The beginning (i.e. the first and controlling principle, rather than a stage which one leaves behind; cf., Ecclesiastes 12:13) is not merely a right method of thought but a right relation: a worshipping submission (fear) to the God of the covenant, who has revealed himself by name (the Lord, i.e. Yahweh: Exodus 3:13–15)."[92]

The fear of the Lord ultimately keeps our life safe because, out of submission to Him, we are alerted to and kept from things that would hurt us.

What Is Anxiety?

Anxiety, on the other hand, is best addressed by Jesus in the Sermon on the Mount: "Do not be anxious for your life, as to what you shall eat, or what you shall drink; nor for your body, as to what you shall put on" (Matthew 6:25). Five times in Matthew 6:25–34 Jesus uses the word *anxious*. The Greek word *merimnao* has the meaning concern in the sense of anxious worry.[93] It is nebulous than normal fear and constantly gnaws at a person's soul.

Commenting on the words of Christ, John R. W. Stott points out that "Jesus mentions both today and tomorrow. All worry is about tomorrow, whether about food or clothing or anything else; but all worry is experienced today. Whenever we are anxious, we are upset in the present about some event which may happen in the future."[94]

Jesus provides us with one primary goal in Matthew 6:33: "But seek first His kingdom and His righteousness; and all these things shall be added to you." The more we focus ourselves on this goal, the less concerned we are with the details of our future and the less anxious we become. Pentecost adds, "Instead of devoting one's life to the pursuit of material things to provide security for the days ahead, Christ commanded that (we) put God's work and His righteousness before all. It is fruitless to be concerned about the future when no promise is given to us of a future here on this earth."[95]

Jesus is saying that we should not be anxious but should have faith in God. This sounds simple, but remember He said other things in the Sermon on the Mount as well: don't be angry at another person; if anyone asks you for something, give it to him; love your enemies and pray for them; forgive anyone who has wronged you. "These are the standards, the values and the priorities of the kingdom of God."[96] We all face concerns for the future. When brothers and sisters in Christ are anxious, we need to be humble, pray for them, and encourage their faith.

What Is Panic?

Jason, the pastor in our opening case study, was experiencing symptoms of panic: he felt faint-headed and dizzy, his heart was racing, and his hands felt numb. Jason felt like he was losing control. What was he experiencing?

According to the Mayo Clinic, "Panic attacks typically begin suddenly, without warning. They can strike at any time—when you're driving a car, at the mall, sound asleep or in the middle of a business meeting. You may have occasional panic attacks or they may occur frequently."[97]

But how do you as a pastor or Christian worker help a person who is experiencing panic? Here are a few points to keep in mind:

1. Whenever you are speaking with someone who complains of extreme physical symptoms, refer him to his medical doctor. This protects the person in case there is a serious medical issue that has not been identified. If he does not have a doctor he normally sees, have several names of trusted medical doctors whom you can recommend to him.

2. Recognize that panic is a normal adrenaline emergency response that God has created in us to experience for our safety and for the safety of others around us. "Whenever we are threatened physically or psychologically, a complex chain of responses is set in motion to prepare us for what has been described as the 'fight or flight' response. It's as simple as that. When we are under stress, our bodies are prepared either to attack what is threating us or to run away from it."[98]

If a person encounters the proverbial bear on the path, an adrenaline response will occur. The heart will beat harder, sending blood to the large muscles of the body. An extra supply of blood will also leave the hands, feet, and skin, and move to the larger muscles. This creates a side effect of tingling and numbness, but also reduces the threat of bleeding in those areas. The need for a fighting blood supply will also cause digestion to stop.

Jason was experiencing an adrenaline response. His focus on the impossible task of completing all his responsibilities was triggering the fight or flight response. And because there was no bear to fight or run from, the preparation of his body was in vain.

Later in this chapter we will talk about what individuals like Jason can do to live without a constant experience of stress. However, it is important to remind the person who is struggling that God is always near and ready to help.

3. Know that you, as a Christian, hold the key to helping a person who is experiencing panic because you understand God's Word. You know that God does not want us to live in a constant state of fear and anxiety: "Do not fear, for I am with you; Do not anxiously look about you, for I am your God. I will strengthen you, surely I will help you, surely I will uphold you with My righteous right hand" (Isaiah 41:10). Young writes:

> Israel is not to fear at all; there is no enemy, no sudden change upon the scene of history, nothing that should cause her to fear, for her God is with her. She is the seed of Abraham, and to Abraham God had once spoken, "Fear not, Abram: I am thy shield, and thy exceeding great reward" (Genesis15:1).[99]

Hebrews 13:6 says, "So we confidently say, 'The Lord is my Helper, I will not be afraid. What will man do to me?'" So we may not fully understand everything there is to know about the physical mechanisms of panic, but we do know the God of the Bible, and we can offer significant help to another person.

What Is Stress?

Not all of us will have an experience of a panic attack, but each of us will face times in our lives when we become overloaded.

Simply stated, stress is a person's response to overload. The accumulated effect of the pressures of life. Daily tasks, job-related duties, and volunteer projects may not appear staggering when viewed individually. But when they begin to layer one upon another, they reach overwhelming proportions.

We actually need stress in God-managed proportions for normal growth and development. Referred to as *eustress* from the Greek prefix meaning *good*, good stress motivates us to get our tasks accomplished. Often accompanied by an adrenaline flow, eustress provides the added energy level for peak performance. But problems occur when we assume burdens and responsibilities that God did not plan for us. We take on more than God intended. When we accumulate too much stress, we move from eustress to distress.

God created us with a limit to our capacity to carry stress. We can be overloaded with disastrous results. If we choose to consistently pile task upon task, the consequences are predictable: we will crash and burn! On the other hand, if we choose to run the marathon of life within our God-given limits, we will reach the finish line in good time by His grace.

Recite and rehearse

Take a moment to write simple definitions of fear, anxiety, panic, and stress in your own words. Three needs that people have are described above.

Which have you encountered in your own life or in someone close to you?

Understanding Stress and Human Limitations

1. Time Limitations

How often have you planned a day filled with chores, tasks, and activities, only to complete half of what you planned to do? When your time expectations are unrealistic, not even the best time-management system will help. We all have twenty-four hours a day to use; no more, no less.

We are limited by the number of activities we can handle at one time. We wish you could be the best pastor, parent, spouse, friend, coach, business owner or employee, small group leader, or friend. But the truth is you never will be the best in all of these roles. You must choose a few areas in which to concentrate and invest your time wisely.

2. Physical Limitations

We all possess a limited amount of daily physical energy. Once we exhaust our allotted reserve, we must replenish through rest, exercise, and proper nutrition.

Our bodies warn us of physical limitations through pain. If we lift too heavy a weight, our bodies hurt. Likewise, if we ignore our bodies as they cry out for proper rest, diet, and exercise, we will likely experience physical symptoms of stress. Life is a distance race, but all too often people live as if life is a sprint. We can push ourselves for short periods of time (and at times we need to), but not for weeks and months without physical consequences.

Experts report that our culture is plagued by sleep deprivation. What does that mean? It means that most Americans live their lives with too little rest. Rest is even more necessary for those experiencing anxiety, discouragement, or depression. Brandon Peters, MD at the Stanford Center for Sleep Sciences and Medicine speaks to this point: "Not only can someone become cranky or irritable, but difficulty sleeping often contributes to anxiety and depression. Impairment of the frontal lobe of the brain may also interfere with higher level cognitive processes called executive functions. This can undermine judgment, critical thinking, relationships, problem solving, planning, and organization."[100]

There are four things a person can do to reestablish regular sleep patterns:

- Increase your sleep time by at least one hour. You need one hour more sleep than you think you need. For example, if you sleep for six hours, you actually need to sleep for seven hours.
- Practice a consistent bedtime routine. Establish a set bedtime each night, even on the weekends. Refrain from eating high sugar content foods or drinking caffeine beverages after 7 p.m.
- Give your body opportunities to rest during the day. Consider a short nap. To prevent a lethargic feeling, keep the nap less than thirty

minutes. If you can't nap, set aside a few minutes to relax your mind. Thinking on Scripture (not the passage you are preaching this Sunday) or listening to relaxing music is often helpful.

- Plan your monthly calendar to include some relaxed weekends. Say no to intense activities that threaten to invade those times. Scheduling requires work, but the physical and spiritual benefits are immense.

3. Relational Limitations

When we overload our lives with too many activities and responsibilities, key relationships tend to suffer. Family members may complain that we do not spend enough quality time at home. Spouses may feel threatened and unloved. Children may have difficulties at school or church.

Stressful times tend to maximize irritability and minimize patience. As a rule, relationship intimacy decreases as stress increases. Unfortunately, in our hurried lives we minimize the significance of relationships. Instead, we place value on accomplishment. Important relationships require careful attention on our part, for nurturing and care.

4. Spiritual Limitations

Heightened stress affects our spiritual lives. Even though it is God's continual desire that we remain close to Him, we begin to limit the amount of time we spend with Him and in His Word when we are overloaded. We neglect Him during the time we most need Him.

Stress impacts all areas of our lives simultaneously. Consequently, when we feel distant from God and hopeless in our pursuit of Him, it may be time for a good night's sleep. Remember our study of Elijah in the chapter on Depression? When he became discouraged to the point of giving up, God first ministered to him through food and rest. Then God provided the spiritual encouragement Elijah needed to fulfill his service to God.

Paul encouraged the Philippian Christians to draw on God's strength. He understood the human tendency to pull away from God when anxious. "The apostle's teaching on prayer in (Philippians 4:6–7) is one to which Christian people have turned for guidance, and from which they have received encouragement and blessing, in every age.[101]

> Be anxious for nothing, but in everything by prayer and supplication with thanksgiving let your requests be made known to God. And the peace of God, which surpasses all comprehension, will guard your hearts and your minds in Christ Jesus.

God wants us to remain focused on Him. When the cares of life become too great, we need to bring our concerns to God in prayer.

Reflect and react

To manage our stress, we often need to begin with an objective look at our responsibilities. List the hours of the day from the time you usually arise until the time you are usually asleep. Beside each hour, list what you would do on a typical weekday. Then make separate lists for Saturday and Sunday.

Fill in how you use your time, concentrating on activities you regularly accomplish. As you make your lists, consider personal time, family, work/ministry, church, social activities, and free time or recreation. Analyze your list by asking the following questions:

1. Do I typically have built-in free time during the day?

2. Am I getting the amount of sleep I need to feel rested?

3. Is exercise a regular part of my week?

4. Have I made time for eating two to three balanced meals each day?

5. Do I enjoy regular time and activities with family and friends?

6. Do I experience positive times with God, or is my relationship with Him a source of guilt and shame?

7. Rate your life on a scale of one to ten (ten = well balanced, one = very unbalanced)

What Is Burnout?

We have concluded that stress is a person's response to being overloaded. An illustration from the tech world provides more insight: "Stress testing is the process of determining the ability of a computer, network, program or device to maintain a certain level of effectiveness under unfavorable conditions."[102]

When a computer or network can't hold up under pressure, it crashes. When a person sustains continual stress over a long period of time, he or she also crashes. This is what we call *burnout*. It looks like this:

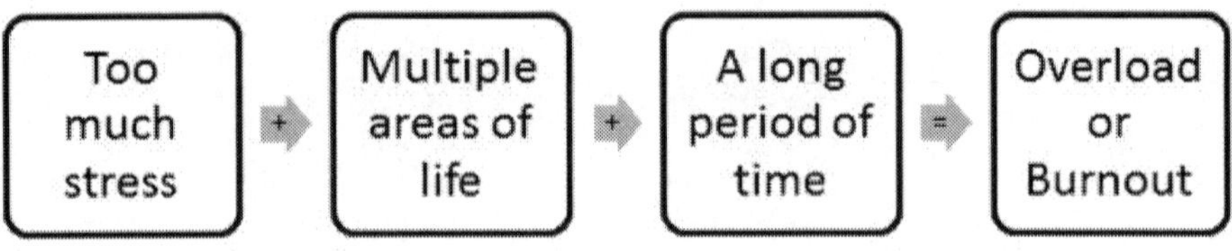

The unknown factor is your capacity for stress. We really don't know if you can handle ten pounds of stress mentally and twenty-five spiritually. Whereas another person may handle twenty-five pounds of stress mentally and ten pounds of stress spiritually. God has created each of us as unique individuals. What may be stressful for you may not bother another person at all. A ride in a hot air balloon may be relaxing for one person but extremely stressful for another. Yet if a person pushes his limit in a number of areas of life for a long enough period of time, he may become burned out.

Learning Your Capacity for Stress

Let's consider a simple approach to understanding your capacity for stress. There are two types of stressors or life pressures:

1. Predictable stressors. These are the things in life that we can plan. The things that we know will take place. These include monthly bills, job pressures, family obligations, and ministry commitments. Even a move to a new location is stressful, but it's still predictable.

2. Unpredictable stressors. These are the things in life that come at unexpected times. A member of your family has a heart attack or is diagnosed with cancer. Your company is purchased, and your job is eliminated. You are on staff at a church, and the senior pastor steps down for infidelity.

The stressors that we do not see coming and cannot plan for are the ones that may push us over our limit. Our lives are often so busy that we make no allowance for the unexpected stressor. The real danger is in living as if we know all that will come our way tomorrow. The truth is only God knows what the future has in store for us. We are reminded of this in James 4:13–17. James tells the merchant not to plan ahead as if next year's profit was a certainty. He provides this wise advice, "Instead, you ought to say, 'If the Lord wills, we shall live and also do this or that'" (v. 15).

James directs us back to God for our own benefit. Since we know that unexpected stressors will come, we need to re-embrace our dependence on the Lord. "What must be recognized is that this world is not a closed system; that an influence quite outside the material sphere ultimately determines the success and failure of plans–indeed, the very continuation of life itself."[103] This is a biblical worldview.

Research and create

Consider the words of James. Your team assignment is to expand on the idea of predictable and unpredictable stressors. Develop a thirty-minute message (in written form) that you would give to a gathering of approximately twenty-five college students from James 4:15 (or 4:13–5:11). Be sure to provide footnotes and citations. Include Scripture, biblical theology, and commentaries, etc., (paper minimum: ten pages, double-spaced).

Affirming our dependence on the Lord and accepting a biblical worldview of history, we must do what all successful Christians attempt to do: manage the predictable stressors but leave enough room for the unpredictable.

Learning to Live Without Constant Stress

Perfect balance is rarely possible. But we can learn to live without experiencing constant stress. Think back to our definition of *stress*, a person's response to overload, the accumulated effect of the pressures of life. Keep in mind the following two points:

1. Although God allows stressors into our lives, He does not choose for us a life of total stress. We can respond to stressors in faith. In the words of David: "From the end of the earth I call to Thee, when my heart is faint; lead me to the rock that is higher than I" (Psalm 61:2). "David, feeling faint and inadequate, found assurance in the strength of his Rock and encouragement in God's enduring promises."[104]

Often a glance upward is all it takes to put the cares of this life in proper perspective. We need to live in the expectation that there is a *rock that is higher than I.*

2. Often burdens are the result of our own actions. Whether our stressors are predictable or unexpected, we still can choose how we create or respond to them. For example, moving to another state or deciding to buy a house may be manageable at one time, while unmanageable at another. Both decisions will involve stress.

You Cannot Control All Variables

Often stress results from our tendency and desire to control everything around us. Even when we take complete responsibility for every aspect of our lives, many factors remain out of our control. Consequently, control is not the mechanism we should use to balance our lives. Our Lord sees the big picture, knows every contributing variable, and wants us to take comfort in His sovereign rule. And with this in mind, let's turn our attention to the things that we do have control over as we seek to maintain balance in our lives.

Four Keys to Balanced Living

1. *Live by faith in Jesus Christ.* Take a look at the words of Paul to the church at Galatia: "I have been crucified with Christ; and it is no longer I who live, but Christ lives in me; and the life which I now live in the flesh I live by faith in the Son of God, who loved me and delivered Himself up for me" (Galatians 2:20).

All attempts at balance ultimately flow from our connection with the hub of the universe–Jesus Christ. Our example is Paul, and he explains his relationship with Jesus. "Christ is the sole meaning of life for him (Philippians 1:21): every moment is passed in conscious dependence on Christ, to whom he looks for everything."[105]

2. *Live by the Word of God.* The Bible provides keys to living a purposeful life. Bible reading and study keeps us from living life in an arbitrary hit-or-miss manner. Following the examples of the godly in Scripture could prevent many mistakes and misjudgments that cause us stress. The Bible also includes negative examples to show us what does and does not lead to healthy, balanced living. The Scriptures teach principles for life management. We need to continually evaluate our lives in the light of God's Word.

3. *Live according to your priorities.* A balanced life requires priorities in keeping with the Word of God. A priority is defined as something that goes ahead of or takes precedence over something else. Consequently, when we refer to something as being first priority, we mean it takes precedence over all that we do.

Priority does not mean a measure of time. We can make personal prayer and Bible study a priority, yet few of us are going to spend eight hours a day in quiet time. We should, however, plan to get approximately eight hours of sleep. Priority means *this will get done, no matter what else has to go.*

Unfortunately, we all have experienced times when we neglect the most important matters in our lives and give attention to the trivial and unimportant issues. While seeking to schedule time and activities, I would suggest the following order of priorities: time with God, time with family, time for work, time for ministry, and time for personal recreation/renewal.

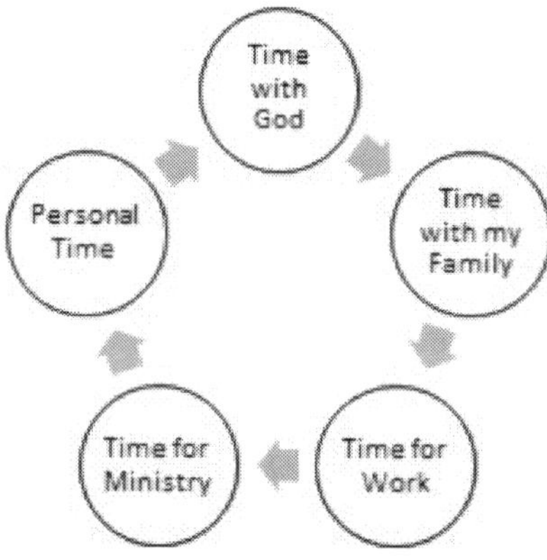

4. *Live your goals.* No person determines or arrives at the important priorities in life quickly or easily. We need to set specific goals that, when followed over a period of time, accomplish our life priorities. Goals represent specific plans we intend to carry out. When setting individual goals or helping others to do so, remember the following three simple tests of a good goal.

- *Brief* enough to be remembered–Is my goal simple enough that I can discuss it with a friend without referring to notes?
- *Specific* enough to be written down–Can I write it down in one sentence?

- *Clear* enough to be achieved—Will I know when I've accomplished my goal?

Respond to a case study

A tired looking couple sat in John's office at the church. The looks on their faces and the slump in their shoulders spoke volumes and indicated a hurried lifestyle. They began their visit by saying, "Sorry we're late, but we need to leave by 4:30." They loved Jesus Christ and were active in the church, and their marriage was strong. Well ... maybe not like before, but they were working on it. Their three school-aged children were happy and growing. So what was the problem? They couldn't see how they could maintain their hectic lifestyle. They asked a simple question: How does anyone do it?

John assured them that they were already doing a great job. As they were leaving, he asked if they had any interest in becoming small group leaders.

1. Look back at the chapter and the Four Keys to Balanced Living. How would you have responded to the question asked by the couple: "How does anyone do it?"

2. How would you recommend John handle this

couple's concerns and the similar concerns of others within his church?

(Note: Begin with a series of messages that target a biblical response to their concerns.)

8
LEADING CHANGE MANAGEMENT
Larry Purcell

Joe just arrived as the new lead pastor of a long established church. It was time for the nominating committee to begin filling leadership positions in the church. The new lead pastor discovered that there were forty-four different committees. When asked, the nominating committee could not identify to the new pastor the purpose of most of the forty-four committees. The nominating committee was challenged to find enough warm bodies to fill each spot. The new pastor desired to move the congregation from committees to a team-driven model of leadership. How could he do this effectively and so soon in his new position?

Change is a word that brings fear to so many leaders. We live in an era of rapid change that is accelerated because of globalism. How we travel and how we communicate has made the world much smaller and forced new pressures on old ways. Churches are not immune to the forces of rapid change in a global society. Joe realized this would be his first test of being the pastor-leader. Joe saw that by capturing this change event as an opportunity, he could lead other critical improvements. He realized the change may seem like a simple one to many, but it could be costly if mishandled. He understood that some welcome the change because they are getting what they want. Likewise, a change could be viewed as bad because it requires someone to give up something. Some pastors may believe that a leader should never make changes the first year of a ministry position. There is a lot of truth in the statement because of the risk, but often the systems at a church do not wait for the leader to know all the issues. As the body of Christ, churches are both organic and organizational units. The church of which Joe was the pastor continued to view the world as it did in the 1970s. Joe understood that because the church was a system; he could influence one change in any area, and it would affect the entire organizational system. Joe desired to capture the energy of this opportunity. The leadership expressed that it was tired of feeling as if they fill meaningless positions to satisfy the demands of the past.

> I teach ministry leaders the principle, *to the degree that a congregation believes there is a crisis, the congregation or group empowers the leader to make change.*

Joe saw a crisis looming by the number of committees requiring attention, which is a 1970s way of ministry. The number of open positions to be filled by the congregation yearly is dominating the attention of the flock. It would be left to committee members to call a special meeting to identify expectation and identify a reason for existing. The new pastor desires to shift the focus of the congregation upon developing a vision that will guide the assembly into the future. Joe had fresh eyes but was challenged by the need to move carefully as he evaluated the situation. The move from committees to ministry-teams is a radical shift. Committees are institutionally driven and seek to protect the organizational systems and programs of a church. A team-driven model of ministry is driven solely by purpose.

The key characteristic of a team is that it exists only to accomplish a clear and common purpose. If the team has no purpose, it does not exist. Joe wanted to resist changing the names of committees to teams, but he also wanted to resist focusing upon a name. The church's leaders had become focused upon continuing the past into the future–institutionally driven. This is a common problem in many established congregations. A leader who makes one simple change can add up to more changes that will promote a profound shift in the DNA of the church. Joe desired to capture this momentum for a greater good. Leaders must offer *hope* to their followers. Kouzes and Posner state that in all of their studies across the globe, characteristics of a leader who scored consistently over sixty percent of all the votes were honest, forward-looking, inspiring, and competent. The characteristic of being forward-looking meant it was critical for the pastor to demonstrate that he has a sense of direction and a concern for his new church.[106] Kouzes and Posner write that it is the energy of the leader and his optimism that signals hope to the followers.[107] Joe understood that the church is the body of Christ and that the church is organized. As the new shepherd-pastor, he had to chart a new course if the congregation was to have hope to be alive in a few short years. Creating a sense of urgency was critical if a new leader is to capture the attention and energy of the followers. John Kotter offers insights into elevating the sense of urgency in an organization. He observes that any organization can become complacent. He defines complacency as "a feeling of contentment or self-satisfaction, especially when coupled with an unawareness of danger or trouble."[108]

The new pastor understood he must elevate the level of awareness of the future. If things remained unchanged, the church would no longer exist in a few years. The new leader needed to look at the history of the church, the growth or decline of its membership, and the health of its ministries. Joe led a survey of available data by looking at the population in the church and the area surrounding the church. In a rural area, it may be accomplished by drawing a circle around the church at five-ten-fifteen-mile radius. Since this was a city and has a shifting population, the surrounding neighborhoods were studied. The pastor would compare the inside population to the surrounding neighbors to evaluate how the congregation reflected its community. The ministries of the church were studied for strengths, weaknesses, opportunities, and threats (SWOT). Leaders of the existing ministries were involved in gathering this information. The pastor wanted the leadership to get first-hand knowledge and a much clearer picture of the condition of the church's health. The data was analyzed, and it demonstrated a rapid decline in the life and health of the church and its ministries.

Recite and rehearse

This chapter includes three strong models for you to consider:

Kotter, Drucker, and Nehemiah. Rehearse each of the lists associated with each model and determine which is most valuable for you at this point in your ministry.

Kotter describes the differences in false urgency and true urgency.

False urgency is exhibited in frenetic-activity, in many meetings, lots of writing, going-going-going, task forces, and projects. False urgency can exhaust people and provide the image of busyness and momentum. It will lead to greater amounts of stress and the possibility of members becoming frustrated, anxious, and angry. True urgency is dedicated to action, alertness, focused, while removing irrelevant activities. Pastor Joe would discuss this valuable topic with his staff and key leaders. Busyness is not a sign of life and vitality.[109] Kotter's eight stages to leading change were carefully reviewed during a leadership retreat.

Kotter's Eight Stages to Leading Change[110]

1. A sense of urgency
2. A guiding team
3. Visions and strategies
4. Communication
5. Empowerment
6. Short-term wins
7. Never let up
8. Making change stick

Joe had enough information to see the present condition of the church and its surrounding neighborhoods. He had to develop a passion for critical changes with the church's leadership. It was not sufficient to share numbers or data. People make changes because of their hearts, not just their heads. He asked critical questions that should be asked by all leaders.

Joe recalled reading "that when Abraham was called by God, he obeyed and went out to a place" (Hebrews 11:8). Abraham moved by faith without knowing all the specific details of where he was going. He had a confidence that was expressed in Hebrews 11:10, "For he was looking forward to the city that has foundations, whose architect and builder is God." Living a life of faith is one displaying trust with confidence that He who "started a good work in you, will carry it on to completion until the day of Christ Jesus" (Philippians 1:6).[111] The life of Abraham was a clear demonstration of one motivated by passion and not just the available facts. Change leaders understand it is the principle of passion that leads church revitalizations and gain greater buy-in from members. So Joe began meeting with church leadership to talk through critical questions, such as how they presently see the church's situation, where they see it moving to in the future, and what changes they each see essential in order to make progress. Peter Drucker, leadership guru, challenges large corporations across the globe with these critical questions:[112]

1. What is our mission?
2. Who is our customer?
3. What does the customer value?
4. What are our results?
5. What is our plan?

In these meetings, Joe wanted to assess the view of the church's condition from key leaders. Leaders should be concerned about understanding the perceptions of key leaders, whether it is a church or in any organization.

Joe thought that if he could communicate with the staff and key leaders some of the analysis of the data, complacency could be challenged. The data would alarm the leadership, but this would not be sufficient to move any significant changes. Joe used these earlier meetings with staff and key leaders to demonstrate how the shift from committees to ministry teams could have a ripple effect upon how the church is organized. He knew their perception would be critical to guiding where he would begin in casting a new dream and direction for the church. Joe used the meetings as an opportunity to build stronger relationships, greater communication, and a sense of hope. Joe knew that only God's Word could build the leadership and congregation's confidence in implementing long-term and lasting changes. However, a number of good books on business leadership, Christian leadership, and church revitalizations were identified by the pastor for the leaders to begin reading together.

Reflect and react

Looking back at the opening scenario, respond to these questions:

1. Should Joe make any changes this early in his tenure?
2. Is this change worth the effort?
3. What should be Joe's initial steps, if he is to make this change?

Lessons from Nehemiah

On Sunday mornings Joe began preaching a series from the book of Nehemiah. He desired to only lead the changes that were directed by the Lord and would honor Him. A pastor has the opportunity to communicate in purposeful ways that can build the flock and provide critical wisdom. It is the Spirit of God who uses the Word of God to direct the hearts of the people of God (2 Timothy 3:16).

Prayer Builds Passion

Nehemiah is a book that offers insights on leadership during a time of great crisis in Jerusalem. The crisis was one of apathy and indifference. It appeared that the people of God who had returned from captivity would rebuild the great city, Jerusalem. However, the report received by Nehemiah from his brother, Hanani, once he returned from a visit to Jerusalem was distressing (Nehemiah 1:1–4). Nehemiah was so troubled by the news about Jerusalem's walls being broken down and its gates burned that he sat and wept (vv. 3–4). The citizens of Jerusalem had returned over ninety years previously. Nehemiah was broken-hearted because a defeated people accepted living a defeated life. The broken walls would be a symbol of a broken relationship with the God of Israel. Nehemiah was being prepared by the Lord to accept a new assignment. He would lead rebuilding the walls of Jerusalem and accomplish in fifty-two days what had been left untouched for over ninety years. The success of Nehemiah to lead this significant change would come from passion and not simply facts.

Pastor Joe knew it would take more than facts to motivate any significant changes in his new church. Joe's time in prayer would provide strength and wisdom from the Lord. This time in prayer would build his passion for the sheep that God had sent him to lead. Joe would look to the inside and outside of the church and its community. This required looking at all the church's documents: constitution/by-laws, budgets, ministry teams, etc. He would carefully review the history of the church for the highs and lows of its lifecycle. It would be insightful to investigate how the congregational demographics reflect the local community. The new pastor was not simply collecting facts, but he was getting to know the heart of the people of God. The role of the shepherd-leader involves knowing the sheep (John 10). A leader who is to influence a congregation must see his role as more than a CEO or manager of a business. It is more than mere facts, but the documents, demographics, and statistics represent persons he learned to care genuinely about. The conversations Joe had with the accepted leadership at the church would deepen his resolve. It was critical for Joe to spend valuable time with leadership and members of the new congregation to better understand its culture.

Nehemiah determined the needs of Jerusalem by personally viewing the city's walls, gates, and surroundings (2:11–20). It was essential for Nehemiah to have this firsthand knowledge because opposition would arise. Passion takes root in caring about the people and desiring to do whatever is essential to improve their condition. Joe understood that hearing leaders describe their views of the needs facing the church was critical. It was equally important for him to personally look at the church's condition, then pray and seek understanding from the Lord. Prayer is not just a step in solving a problem. Prayer deepens the minister's relationship to the Lord and to the people of God. Leading change in a church should deepen our communion with God, or we may crumble under the burden. This would be one of Joe's biggest challenges since his calling to be a pastor. He anticipated opposition and would not be shocked when it occurred. The change-leader in most all circumstances will face opposition. The opposition must be understood as not merely flesh and blood but of spiritual warfare (Ephesians 6:10–20). Joe learned a valuable lesson from his study of Nehemiah—months of prayer and fasting were valuable communion with the Lord. In those times Joe, as Nehemiah, would discover wisdom and strength for the challenges that would lie ahead.

We need to have a face-to-face encounter with God to confront God-sized tasks. Could it be that not many big things occur in our lives or our churches because of too little prayer? Nehemiah would seek the King of Kings, before facing King Artaxerxes. Joe knew he had problems, but his would pale in light of those faced by Nehemiah. We should find confidence as we study the Word of God and seek wisdom from the Lord before all decisions. The time in conversation with the Lord should help a leader overcome fears as he faces tough decisions, just as it did for Nehemiah. It is essential for the pastor to involve more of the church's leaders in a season of prayer before moving to a decision. As more of the leadership and the congregation seek the Lord's direction and wisdom, the closer they can move in collective choices. I have often experienced the greatest connection with church leaders during these prayer events that increased our resolve.

Communication Is Critical

Joe collected the necessary data, talked with trusted leaders, and spent a season in prayer with the leadership. The assessment a leader must make at this stage is to see if the church is ready to move forward. Nehemiah would approach the people at Jerusalem with the challenge about the trouble they are in, and how the mighty hand of God had been on him, and what the king said to him. The people joined Nehemiah at that time stating, "Let's start rebuilding" (2:18). Joe knew he could not force the people to make any changes. Communication is critical to leading change at all stages, but especially in building a sense of urgency.

Change moves at the speed of communication. A leader must insure he is sharing valuable insights and information with the leadership, staff, and the congregation. Joe recognized the congregation was sidetracked from ministry opportunities by filling valuable energy and time by so many committees. Preaching through Nehemiah provided numerous opportunities for the pastor to biblically educate the flock, while sharing implications for the church in the present situation. The opportunities taken by a leader to communicate from a need to share and not just a need to know[113] serves well in building trust and overcoming confusion and suspicion.

Communication is critical to clarifying the vision God has for His people. The Lord sends a pastor to a congregation to lead them to know God's vision. Identifying the difference between mission and vision are essential to build urgency for a change. The Bible commonly identifies the Great Commission as the *mission* of the church (Matthew 28:18–20; Acts 1:8). *Vision* is specific to how each congregation responds to or contextualizes fulfilling the Great Commission as commanded by God. Joe understood this definition and desired to lead the church in a gospel-focused direction. The value of the process of leading a church to identify its vision helps the members see where God is at work. This process can take anywhere from months to years. The issue of having too many committees at Joe's new church is a result of continually adding new layers of structures when an issue or challenge is faced. The structures were never reviewed and aligned with the vision of the church. Churches, or any organization, will face the dilemma of realigning structures to support its vision or allowing the structures to govern the vision. The overwhelming number of committees created an institutionally driven church, not a mission-driven model.

On Mission with God

The shepherd-leader must equip and empower others to lead the vision. Joe and the church's leaders met to identify its primary ministries and teams. All committees were reviewed as to purpose and whether essential to each of the ministries. Committees were transformed to ministry teams as each related to ministry support. This process would slowly convert the church to being mission-driven, aligning structures to vision and recruiting members to an area of ministry service. Pastor Joe would continually share with staff, lay leadership, and the congregation upon every opportunity the value of aligning the structures with the direction the church was moving. The pastor would present this new model as a shared-ministry model (Ephesians 4:12). Members would no longer just be assigned to a committee but would serve as an active member of a ministry team. The congregation was led through a study of spiritual gifts and personality. A number of committees would be retired, and members were encouraged to volunteer to serve on a ministry team. The use of spiritual gifts inventories and personality surveys provided valuable conversations to involve the congregation in making the change from committees to teams. The pastor taught a course on high expectations membership during the Sunday evening services. This led to new members' classes, teacher training, and staff development. Joe's church would be practicing discipleship or servant leaders developing servant leaders.

Family: The Strongest Link

Nehemiah assigned the work of building the wall in Jerusalem according to family units (3:10). The strength of the wall would depend upon the strongest link, individual family units. The builders of the wall would be contributing to the long-term security of their families. Nehemiah did not depend upon professionals to build the wall. Assigning family units to build a portion of the wall behind their houses would tap into the passion of each spouse and parent for his or her family.

Pastor Joe was shepherding an older church with a multigenerational congregation. Joe saw connections to one of the greatest influences in a community and a congregation. Family at many established churches crosses numerous generations and can be seen as a force for good. Joe communicated to the leadership that the changes would strengthen the membership's families, while attracting newer ones. Joe desired to establish with the congregation that the vision God was providing would support families and build a mentality of *us* and not *me*.

Families can be described in many different ways. While serving in the military, I found that my small Bible study group and church would be my family. Serving as a pastor in a rural setting, I have found that *family* would best be described as those sharing generational connections. For the churches I served in a more mobile area of a city, the small group ministries were their family units. The strength of family will cross many boundaries and is not limited to generational connections.

Silos are often developed because ministries, committees, or teams do not have a common purpose or vision. A church can build its ministries around a common vision or sets of goals in the beginning, but too often structures shift to survival mode. This will result in layering more structures with a number of ministries and committees that no longer serve the mission and vision of a church. Realignment is challenging but worth the effort when it is led to fulfill the demands of the gospel.

Spiritual Warfare

Nehemiah experienced resistance to building the wall (chapter 4). The cause of building the wall around Jerusalem was a noble cause, but Nehemiah did not have the support of everyone. The Scriptures do not tell us if Nehemiah was shocked by this response.

Resistance to change can come from both inside and outside the congregation. There are those persons who want to keep structures as they presently are. Pastor Joe felt his cause was equally noble in realigning the church structures to support a biblical mandate of advancing the gospel.

He was not naïve but prepared for resistance. A leader must recognize that resistance to change is a normal response. The human body builds muscle by overcoming a certain amount of resistance. It is critical for a change leader to grasp the concept that building a congregation, like building muscle, must be accomplished over time.

Nehemiah faced a group of persons who mocked and ridiculed the citizens of Jerusalem in building a wall. Nehemiah led the residents of Jerusalem to praying as they faced the anger and opposition. The can-do attitude of the citizens of Jerusalem was built through prayer and directed to building kingdom purpose. It is critical that a change leader not settle for using anger against anger. Pastor Joe was preparing the leadership and congregation to face challenges through communication with God and with each other.

Lessons from Nehemiah 4 taught Pastor Joe to know the attitude of the enemy. General Patton states in the Movie, *Patton*, that he would defeat Rommel, his adversary in North Africa during World War II, because he read his books. He knew his enemy. The desire of Nehemiah's opponents was to create fear and stop any progress on the wall around Jerusalem. Just as Nehemiah and Patton understood their opposition, Pastor Joe must understand who his enemies are.

The spiritual weapon or tactic to overcome fear and anger used by Nehemiah is offered to all: prayer. It is prayer that would assist Nehemiah and the citizens of Jerusalem to keep their focus upon the God-given task of building the wall. Prayer, not anger or fear, would unite the people of Jerusalem. It is natural to want to answer anger with anger. Anger can be turned outward and results in aggression and appears disgusting to all. Anger turned inward can lead to depression and the feelings of being a victim. Anger turned upward will demonstrate the true character of a believer and builds dependence upon the Lord. Extreme anger takes extreme prayer.

Some things can only be taken care of by our trust in a sovereign God. Nehemiah, the leaders, and the citizens of Jerusalem put their trust in the Lord to shut the mouths of the mockers. They had been given a God-sized task, and this challenge must not divert them from the task at hand. Those who conspired against Nehemiah and the citizens of Jerusalem would attempt to use threats and confusion to distract the workers from building the wall (chapter 4). The response of the builders of the wall was one of resolve. "So we prayed to our God and stationed a guard because of them day and night" (4:9).

Pastor Joe embraced these lessons from the example of Nehemiah and taught them to the congregation. Joe would face opposition and reminded the leadership that it should not be a surprise. Christian leaders are to be developing godly disciplines long before facing spiritual battles. It is the soldier's training that he must depend upon when in the midst of conflict. War has been described as "organized confusion." Christian leaders have been called by God to not be entangled in worldly concerns that may distract them from the task (2 Timothy 2:3–4). Joe sought to develop the practice of having seasons of prayer before, during, and after times of resistance. He saw these as teachable moments for both newer and weaker believers.

Value of Community

A pastor must recognize the value of community to the life of a congregation or to any group. The term *band of brothers* is used often to illustrate the bond that exists between soldiers who have shared time together in combat. As a young marine, I shared experiences with a group of men that will last a lifetime. Jerusalem experienced this bond during the rebuilding of the wall. The challenges faced by Nehemiah and the citizens of Jerusalem created an environment of dependence. Citizens of Jerusalem learned to depend upon Nehemiah's leadership, each other, and, most critically, the Lord.

The wall was being built by the families in the city and not by expert craftsmen. There were a number of issues facing the builders of the wall. Nehemiah sought guidance from the Lord in approaching the king for permission to build the wall and for provisions. Nehemiah expressed to the people of Jerusalem his dependence upon the Lord when he responded to the anger of his enemies in prayer. Family units must learn to depend upon each other to build a sturdy structure behind their own houses. God would provide the assurance essential to complete the task in the face of many challenges and threats. The dependence of Nehemiah and the citizens of Jerusalem are the key ingredients to building stronger community.

The crucible is the moment true leadership is tested and the quality of a bond is strengthened. Warren Bennis and Robert Thomas describe the crucible as "a transformative event, severe test or trial. Crucibles are intense, often traumatic—and always unplanned."[114] Nehemiah found meaning in the challenges that he faced, and it verified his godly leadership to the people.

Pastor Joe would likewise face negative comments and threats. The pastor would learn to demonstrate dependence upon the Lord during these times of turmoil. By turning to prayer and dependence upon the Lord in his meetings with staff, key leaders, and the congregation, he would demonstrate dependence upon the God of Israel.

The fear of God would serve Nehemiah as both motivation and restraint (5:14–15). The culture around Nehemiah or any leader can consume them. Nehemiah had the approval of King Artaxerxes, but it was the fear of God that would be his motivation in living his life and leading the rebuilding of the wall at Jerusalem. A spiritual leader must realize what temptations can sidetrack him from doing God's work. Nehemiah had gained a level of prestige and access to wealth. He could use the positions of power and wealth provided by God for good or evil. The fear of the Lord would serve as his guiding star. All leaders have strengths and weaknesses that can build the Lord's kingdom or their own fame. A pastor on mission to revitalize a church must be committed to the health of the community, not just how large it becomes. It can be easy for a pastor to become so focused upon bodies, buildings, and budgets that he begins building his own kingdom instead of the Lord's.

Pastor Joe learned from the example of Nehemiah that experiencing conflict can serve to build dependence upon the Lord and one another. Community can be strengthened as leaders and followers move toward the Lord. The more Nehemiah and the families of Jerusalem depended upon the Lord, the more they would depend upon each other. We read the promise of God: "I will never leave you nor forsake you" (Hebrews 13:5). It is during the times in the crucible that we experience this promise, not while sitting comfortably on the sidelines. Nehemiah and the citizens of Jerusalem would risk failure and ridicule. Joe, the leadership, and congregation would potentially risk failure and ridicule following the desires of the Lord.

Celebrating Wins

The rebuilding of the wall around Jerusalem was accomplished in record time. The citizens had been in Jerusalem for over ninety years, and yet the wall remained broken down. The rebuilding of the wall took only fifty-two days (6:15). The desire of Nehemiah was to build a wall around the city of Jerusalem. Nehemiah had the resources to have professionals rebuild the wall, but he led the citizens to do the work (chapter 7). God used Nehemiah as a means to an end in building the people, not just build a wall. A new team leader, Ezra, came on the scene during the time of celebration of completing the wall (chapter 8). Ezra, the priest, had returned to Jerusalem twelve years prior to Nehemiah. Nehemiah was the role leader of organizing the wall's construction. Ezra was the role leader for the worship and celebration. The celebration would lead the people of God to a renewal of reading the Word of God and the worship of God.

Research and create

1. If I have critical data but do not have a clear enough vision, where do I begin?
2. How do I elevate the level of urgency in a congregation or group that operates in a culture of how it has always been done?
3. What is the most important task of this church?
4. What biblical processes will guide this endeavor?

The forward-thinking man, Nehemiah, provided an example to Joe to remain focused upon the vision the Lord would provide. Joe desired to see his new church refocused from busyness to building a standard of excellence in worship, service, and Bible study. He knew the long-term goal was to see every member actively engaged in an area of ministry, weekly worship, and meaningful Bible study. The short-term objectives for Pastor Joe, the leadership team, staff, and congregation to celebrate would be the emphasis upon time in communion with the Lord. This resulted in greater cohesion among the leadership team and trust by the congregation. Increased communication with the Lord and between leaders and followers would develop a new sense of excitement and expectation. The pastor would acknowledge and celebrate each time ministry teams achieved any success. The emphasis upon excellence in all endeavors would take hold and build momentum as the leadership recognized the achievements. Pastor Joe did not take the credit but publicly acknowledged ministry teams. He would utilize the example of Nehemiah to rely upon leaders, rather than thinking he must do all the work. Joe would hear the comment at times, "I thought this was your job" or "What do you do?" Leaders must capture such moments as an opportunity to gently confront misguided members with biblical teaching. God has not called a pastor to do all the work. Churches that are identified in the small, medium, or even large category can have a misguided view of the role of the pastor.

Sizes of a Church:

Small (100 members or less)
Medium (100–300)
Large (300–1,000)

The numbers should be seen as arbitrary numbers. The perception of the pastor and congregation has significant influence upon what constitutes when one size begins and another size ends. These measures are only designed to assist leaders to see that as a ministry or congregation changes, so should its style of leadership.

Many smaller churches, typically less than one hundred attenders, see the pastor as chaplain. The medium (typically between one hundred and three hundred attenders) to larger church (typically between three hundred and one thousand attenders) may see the pastor as the primary "doer of ministry." The perception of the membership and the leadership may see the role of the pastor as small, even though the membership has grown from sixty active members to five hundred active members. A pastor is only able to effectively minister to one hundred and fifty persons. The pastor has a diminishing return after the active membership grows beyond one hundred and fifty. The organizational system must change to adapt a new view of the role of membership and pastors. The New Testament teaches a different model than was being practiced by Joe's church (Ephesians 4:11–12; 2 Timothy 2:2; Titus 1:5). Joe would seek to equip members called by the Lord, empower them for works of ministry, and thus edify the Lord (Ephesians 4:11–12).

Making It Stick

This last stage will take longer since it is a cultural shift. Culture can be described as habits, norms, and rituals. You know you have experienced culture when you hear the famous words, "We have never done it that way before." Sometimes it can be humorous, but most of the time it is a comment that someone is not pleased. Embedding new changes takes longer because of transitions. Leaders need to realize that change is not a one-time event. Transition is the psychological adaptation to the change, which takes a long time.

It is much like someone I knew who lost his leg to a disease but still has phantom pains. This is the phenomenon of the nerves sensing something is wrong in his leg. He expressed this feeling as his foot itching. Church members will have habits and rituals that are harder to adapt to new ways. When we change the times for a worship service, even if advertised, our bodies alert us to what is normal to us. Transition is also a time of grieving a loss. The longer a member has participated or led in an area of ministry, the more he or she will grieve its loss. This is a phenomenon that is hard for the newer members or new leader to grasp. It is critical to allow the membership time to both grieve the loss and celebrate the new path. This time can resurrect new rituals and build a healthier congregation and leadership.

Respond to a case study

While running errands in a part of the community Jamie did not frequent, he observed a sizable neighborhood of mostly Hispanic residents. As he drove down several streets, he was reminded of the joy that he and a few church members had experienced recently on a short-term mission trip to Latin America. He began to contemplate if the Holy Spirit could be doing something in his heart as he meditated on his new discovery.

Jamie had been at his current pastorate for less than a year and had gotten actively involved in the local association of churches. This familiarity with the wider community provided him with the insight that there was no current Hispanic ministry in any of the evangelical churches with which he was familiar. Maybe the Lord was directing his church, Suburban Community Church, to initiate a new ministry.

Later that afternoon Jamie began to put some plans for his new ministry on paper. He had just finished a six-week series of sermons based on the book of Nehemiah, so he was confident his people were spiritually ready to tackle a new ministry. He began to jot down the changes and adjustments that would need to take place in order to create a welcoming atmosphere for this community of Hispanic neighbors. Parking, signage, staffing, translators, childcare, food pantry, clothing distribution ... the list was growing by the minute and so was Jamie's enthusiasm.

That is until he gathered the church's leadership team together to outline his plan. Though he knew most of the leaders that were present, Jamie was adept at reading the body language of both friends and strangers during the brief rollout meeting. The best way he knew to describe his audience was: "They were looking at me like I had two heads!" He left the session confused and deflated. Enthusiasm and passion gave way to doubts and discouragement. He was at a loss for his next move.

1. State what you believe are the major concerns/issues in this case study. Include a list of secondary ideas that maybe in play.
2. Based on the guidance presented in the preceding chapter, evaluate the change process the young pastor initiated in this scenario.

What would you have done differently?

3. Imagine that Jamie calls you for advice on how to move forward. Outline the steps you would recommend. Where applicable, cite sources from your reading.

9
LEADING CONFLICT RESOLUTION
Larry Purcell

Bob became the pastor of a church that had experienced a significant conflict two years prior. The conflict resulted in the loss of half of its membership. A number of members lived in the community but had either stopped attending church or began attending another church. The congregation continued to be divided. Bob knew of the conflict and had resisted an earlier invitation to be pastor of the church. He was confident now that the Lord desired him to shepherd this flock. As the new pastor he desired to develop a biblical understanding of the congregation's conflict and realized that he faced a challenge early in his new ministry. He wanted to utilize the early stages of this new endeavor to build strong relationships with the people. He wanted to get to know them and learn to love them. He knew this strength of the relationship would be critical to facing the causes of the conflict. But just where he should begin, he couldn't be sure.

Biblical Foundations of Conflict

When you hear the term *conflict*, what are some words that come to your mind? Anger, sin, confrontation, battle, fight, and tension? The words used to describe conflict speak about our perception of *the conflict as a threat to our comfort or as a challenge.* What does the Bible teach about conflict?

Genesis chapters 1–3 are essential for grasping some of the root causes of conflict.[115] It is here we see the beginnings of Adam and Eve, the harmony that existed on the earth before the fall, and their relationship to God. For the sake of this writing, I do not have sufficient time, space, or skill to address all the issues related to humanity being created in the image of God, the fall, and its impact. Genesis 3 provides the reader insights to the effects of the fall, and that this was not limited to only Adam and Eve, but all humanity (Romans 5:12). Sin created a broken fellowship between Adam and God, as well as Adam and Eve; this brokenness was passed to all generations. The stories of the Bible demonstrate in the lives of Abraham, Isaac, Jacob, King David, and all the effects of the fall have been passed along to all.

It is instructive to view the effects of the fall from a New Testament perspective. James 4:1–3 says, “What is the source of wars and fights among you? Don’t they come from the cravings that are at war within you? You desire and do not have. You murder and covet and cannot obtain. You fight and war.” James provides the inner turmoil churning in all humanity. The introductory conflict being experienced at Bob’s new church was continuing to fester. Persons involved in the conflict looked the other side as the reason for the problem, and the solution was simple: the problem would end when the other side gave in or left. The text from

James challenges this thinking and reveals that conflict begins from within each of us.

Bob decided to spend time studying these passages to grasp the depth of their truths. He would seek to teach these truths to the congregation and its leaders. He knew he must be aware of presenting only the tragic side of humanity in these verses. The rest of the story crucial to conflict resolution, whether internal or external, is found in the gospel. The Genesis account provides a promise and hope (3:15). The entire Old Testament is the account of God seeking to redeem humanity. This would find its fulfillment in Jesus Christ (Romans 5:6–11). The life, death, burial, and resurrection provide reconciliation to those who trust in Jesus the Messiah (1 Corinthians 15).

It is never enough to face conflict without hope. A critical aspect of Bob's leadership was to be the shepherd to the flock by loving them. He did not wish to share only from his head, but also his heart. A good leader is a good listener.

Common Sources of Conflict

Roy Pneuman offers nine common sources of conflict in chapter 3 of *Conflict Management in Congregations.*[116]

1. *Disagreement about Values and Beliefs*

This is a major division in the congregation about what the purpose of the church ought to be about. What is the mission or vision of the church? When this occurs the church lacks clear direction, goals, or objectives. This can be experienced because of competing views between older members and newer members. It can occur naturally in an intergenerational congregation. The leadership working closely with the members in developing a new mission/vision statement can manage the issue of competing values.

2. *The Structure Is Unclear*

Structural ambiguity can be the result of confusion surrounding the existing guidelines related to the roles and responsibilities of the pastor. Sometimes members or leaders do not follow the written guidelines, creating confusion among the members. This is more evident when a church experiences a change in size but the structures remain the same. An example of this can be when a church grows and adds new leadership, and the written guidelines as to the expectations of the position are not clear.

3. *The Pastor's Role and Responsibilities*

A new pastor can too often assume he is empowered to lead and administer as he did in a previous church. It is also a common experience among Baptist churches to have the role of the new pastor defined by a search committee and then redefined by elders or deacons. It is wise for the new pastor to understand that pastoral expectations may not all be on paper. I recommend a new ministry leader seek wisdom from some of the key leaders at the new church. Identify early in a new ministry the amount of authority and accountability for the position. This will provide empowerment and opportunity as you build relationships with the membership and discuss critical areas of needs.

Recite and rehearse

Sidebar #1 Recite and rehearse several of the biblical passages included in this chapter. As you do so, select one that is most meaningful to you and begin today to practice saying it from memory. In a short paragraph write down why you selected that passage and why you believe it will be important in future ministry.

---

4. *The Structure No Longer Fits the Congregation's Size*

Pastors want a healthy church and a growing church. Changing the size of the church can be a real source of trouble.[117] When a church is smaller, it is easy for the members to know everyone. The pastor is able to personally manage the work of the ministry. The members can sense they are losing community because as the church grows they do not know everyone. The pastor can feel overwhelmed because he is not able to personally manage the entire ministry.

Sizes of Churches

The numbers are arbitrary and the member's perception is most critical in understanding how each views their church.

Family or Chapel Church—typically a smaller sized church of less than one hundred attenders. The pastor is seen more as a chaplain. He is expected to preach, teach, visit, and perform weddings and funerals.

Pastoral-led Church—typically called a medium sized church of approximately one hundred and fifty to two hundred attenders. A strong pastor is expected to make critical leadership and management decisions, in addition to preaching and teaching.

Ministry-driven Church—typically called a large church that may range in size from two hundred and fifty to three hundred and fifty attenders. The pastor moves the congregation to identify key ministries and add additional leadership. The demands of ministries begin to build greater structural challenges.

Team-driven Church—typically a larger church that may range in size from three hundred and fifty to seven hundred attenders. The pastor begins building a team of ministry leaders. The church's structures must adapt to a new style of leadership by the lead pastor.

Elder or Board-led Church—typically the larger to mega church model that ranges one thousand or more attenders.

---

5. *The Pastor's Leadership Style*

A growing church requires a change in the leader's style. Reviewing the previous material on the sizes of churches, you may recognize that each level of growth requires a different leadership and management style. If a pastor wants to do all the weddings, funerals, sermons and visit all the members, he may not be a good fit if the church grows larger than the pastoral-led model. When calling a new ministry leader, the search team must look at the leaders past experiences and leadership style. A new pastor should talk with members about congregational expectations. Are the size of the church and the expectations of the congregation aligned?

6. *The New Pastor Rushes into Changes*

The pastor's new perspectives provide new ideas. Some leaders say make changes quickly because you can ask for forgiveness easier than you can get permission. Other great leaders say to wait for one year or more to make changes. The pastor who desires to build a long-term ministry will be careful not to make unnecessary changes or to make changes the congregation is not ready to accept.

I have coached many young pastors over the years and suggest three objectives during the first year of a new ministry. First, ask the membership what they expect from the new pastor. You have written expectations, but you need to hear what their expectations are. Second, get to know the heart of your people and let them know your desires and thoughts. This process builds a shepherd's heart for the sheep, and it builds the heart of the sheep for the new shepherd. Third, ask key leadership and team members some critical questions. What are the church's strengths? What are some areas we need improvement?

The new pastor can begin building strong ties to the congregation. He has opportunity to hear and share in their concerns, desires, and hopes. He has heard their concerns and has a better idea of where there is common consent for changes. The pastor may have discovered as well areas that are off-limits for now.

7. Communication Lines Are Blocked

Pneuman states, "often communication problems are more a result of conflict than a cause of conflict."[118] As conflict grows and factions develop, the faction's perceptions become distorted. The lack of communication between factions develops more misinformation and miscommunication. Conflict will increase during such times. A word of caution: during times of increasing conflict, it is not advisable to have an open microphone. An open microphone can increase the divide. Wise leaders must seek avenues to bring resolution to such conflicts, such as small meetings with various groups, increased information flow, and meeting with staff and key leaders regularly to ask for clarity. Set clear guidelines for acceptable communication. It may be advisable to bring in an outside consultant or mediator to assist.

8. Church People Manage Conflict Poorly

Some people view all conflict as evil and attempt to avoid it or ignore it. It would be good for a pastor to lead his staff, key leaders, and congregation through a study on managing conflict.

- Conflict is inevitable.
- Conflict is a part of life.
- Conflict creates the energy that makes change possible.
- Conflict becomes destructive if it is mismanaged.

9. *Disaffected Member Hold Back Participation and Support*

When a conflict has not been managed well, it leads to a struggle over power and control. Churches of all sizes have limited resources and during times of conflict these limited resources become the primary focus. The leadership taking ownership of the vision and dream of the church is key. Working with and through the congregation builds greater ownership of the vision and dream of the church.

Reflect and react

Refer back to the opening scenario to this chapter. After considering the situation, craft a one-paragraph description about a conflict that could produce this imaginary situation and answer these questions in a paragraph or two:

1. What are some of the causes of conflict?
2. What is the biblical view that might speak to this conflict?
3. Where would you begin to resolve the scenario you describe?

Diagnosing a Conflict

Why do people fight at church? Speed Leas offers, "Differences ... center on facts, methods, goals, or values."[119] *Facts* may relate to how a problem is defined differently by opposing parties. *Methods* relate to the differences in tactics or strategies used to reach a goal by opposing revelries. *Goals* relate back to perceived mission and differences in the desired objectives by various groups. *Values* relate to how power is used to obtain a goal or objective. A wise leader gets to know his people. Some involved in conflict may feel powerless or become frustrated, feeling or thinking his or her opinion no longer matters. It is easy for a soldier to get caught up in the battle and begin to see others as a threat. I will deal with the toll of conflict later in this chapter.

Speed Leas offers the following paradigm to assist in diagnosing a conflict:[120]

Five Levels of Conflict

Level One: People who are in a disagreement stay focused upon the problem. The focus continues to be on the problem, and the parties are not panicked.

Level Two: People become much more self-protective. In fact, self-protection becomes their priority and the problem is second. They talk about trust and communication.

Level Three: People become more interested in winning. They begin talking about us and them.

They become expert mind readers and tell others what someone is thinking to divide and conquer.
Level Four: People move from self-protection and winning to getting rid of someone. Someone has to leave.
Level Five: People become religious fanatics about their positions. They begin telling others what God wants to be done or it's time for the pastor to leave.

The Role of Personality in Church Conflicts

In over thirty years of ministry experience, I am yet to pastor a church that experiences any measure of conflict and does not wish to stop it immediately. The congregation and its leadership both feel it is bad and must be stopped. Yet, conflict is a natural part of life. We must learn that conflict is not necessarily destructive or undesirable, but rather the manner in which we seek to handle the conflict can be bad. Congregations are not immune from conflict, whether a new church plant or a traditional congregation.

And yet, conflict can be an avenue to growth. An athlete must experience some level of discomfort or conflict to grow stronger and more resilient. Likewise, a soldier must endure conflict to learn to be resilient and stronger when facing the challenges of fighting a war. Paul uses this metaphor to challenge Timothy, saying a soldier must endure "hardship"

(2 Timothy 2:3). In order for a church to maintain spiritual health in a rapidly changing world, conflict will be a natural phase of growth. The presence of conflict will cause a congregation to become more dependent upon the Lord for guidance, responsive to a changing context, and more resilient.

An article in *SBC LIFE* from October 2012, lists the top five reasons pastors are terminated by congregations: Control issues ("Who's going to run the church?"); poor people skills on the part of the pastor; the pastor's leadership style is too strong; the church is already in conflict before the pastor arrived; and the pastor's leadership style is too weak.[121]

As you can see, the personality of the pastor influences or directly relates to conflict. In the many years I have been a pastor, I have learned that I cannot control the thoughts and actions of others, but I have found my own personality can influence others. I have found that my personality could be both a strength and weakness. I had to make significant adjustments switching from a military environment of leadership to a church environment. I had to better understand how God designed me to respond in various and changing environments. Some define *leadership* as influence. Christian leadership is more than influence, but it is never less than influence. The personality of the pastor necessarily influences those he shepherds.

Paul writes in 1 Thessalonians 5:14 about three different personalities we may encounter in a congregation. The first person knows the law, refuses to obey; he is to be confronted. The second person is discouraged and needs to be comforted. The third person is weak and is to be helped. Still, we are to be patient with all men. This challenges all pastoral leaders not to adopt a "one size fits all" approach to conflict resolution. I think each of us can relate to one of these responses to someone's behavior.

Which one best fits you: confront, comfort, or help? I am comfortable at confronting behaviors, but I am taught in the passage that not all persons are to be confronted. So a key to understanding these verses is seeing the leader's response to various personalities.

Speed Leas identified a variety of responses to conflicts. Each of the responses can be appropriate, depending upon both the persons involved and the issues being faced. Can you identify which best describes you?

1. **Persuasion: attempts to change another's point of view.**

"I am going to win" This is a style comfortable to a pastor or staff minister because we are in the task of persuading persons to know Christ and follow Him.

2. **Compelling: the use of physical or emotional force, authority, or pressure to constrain another to do something.**

This is seen when a crisis exists such as a fire, medical emergency, or even as a parent prevents her child from running into a street.

3. **Avoiding, Ignoring, Accommodating, or Fleeing.**

Avoiding is putting a tricky item at the end of the board meeting. Ignoring is acting as if there is no conflict. Fleeing is actively removing yourself from the arena in which conflict might take place. Accommodating is when one goes along because the relationship is more important to them than the issue.

4. **Collaborative: to work together with the people with whom you disagree.**

Too often seen as the best method, but it is only best when all are willing to play by collaborative rules.

5. **Bargaining and negotiating: assumes that those negotiating will get as much as possible, but will not get everything.**

It is a sorta-win-sorta-lose strategy.

6. **Support: often called communication skills and active listening.**

Major assumption of this strategy is that the other person is the one with the problem.

Leadership Styles and Best Fit: Timothy and Titus

We see a variety of personalities leads to different responses to managing conflict. These differences require pastors to shepherd their people with God-given wisdom and not only out of their own personality.

The apostle Paul was a wise leader and mentor. Paul would leave Timothy at Ephesus to lead the congregation. The apostle would leave Titus at Crete to lead in the midst significant challenges. Reading the pastoral letters, 1 and 2 Timothy and Titus, can assist the reader in discovering some of the personality strengths of both men. Let me preface this section of the chapter by acknowledging that the purpose of the pastoral letters is not to be a complete description of the personalities of Timothy and Titus. I have gleaned insights into how Paul wrote to each of these men in a personal letter. The apostle had knowledge of the strengths and weaknesses of both men, and he knew firsthand the challenges each faced. Of course, these are merely observations I have made and do not serve as an in-depth study of the texts. Timothy was encouraged by Paul to remember his mother and grandmothers influence upon him (2 Timothy 1:5). He was equally reminded of the suffering and sacrifices of the prophets, Jesus, and Paul. Paul knew Timothy and would speak words of encouragement into his life at a critical time. Paul continued his encouragement to Timothy in the remainder of the epistle with examples of "be strong in the grace that is in Christ Jesus" (2 Timothy 2:1); "share in suffering as a good soldier" (2 Timothy 2:3); "keep your attention on Jesus Christ" (2 Timothy 2:8); and "I solemnly charge you ... Proclaim the message; persist in it" (2 Timothy 4:1–2).

Titus appears from a casual reading of the letter to be a more aggressive personality. Paul would approach Titus much differently than he did with Timothy (2 Timothy). Paul moves quickly to his instructions for Titus: "The reason I left you in Crete was to set right what was left undone and, as I directed you, to appoint elders in every town" (Titus 1:5). I call Titus a marine because he has been given the command of making significant changes and dealing with challenges immediately. I served as a marine, and I know when called into action the motto is "Lead, follow, or get out of my way." The text does not give us the benefit of knowing how the people of Crete became believers or how many converted. We do read Paul's comments, "Cretans are always liars, evil beasts, lazy gluttons" (Titus 1:12). Titus was given the charge to immediately establish a godly leadership and set processes in place for the churches to effectively preserve and proclaim the gospel. Titus would have to be comfortable with confronting, as we see words such as *set right, appoint*; *rebuke sharply*; *say these things, and encourage and rebuke with all authority*; *let no one disregard you* (1:5; 1:13; 2:15). Titus was on the island of Crete with specific orders to make his life an "example to all the believers by his good works with integrity and dignity in your teaching" (2:7). The role of the shepherd can be one of demonstrating his love for the sheep by being tender and at other times stern. Leaders can take a lesson from Timothy and Titus: serve where God leads you. Accept that sometimes you may not be called to the specific position or location you thought was what you wanted. A sovereign God will guide your steps to the place He desires you to lead.

Research and create

1. What are some of the personality differences you recognize between Timothy and Titus? Do a thorough exegesis of 2 Timothy 1 and Titus 1.
2. Do you see yourself more as Timothy or Titus?
3. What are the strengths of your personality?
4. Ask three friends to describe your strengths or weaknesses: introvert, extrovert, dominant personality, people person, detail person.
5. What are some of the weaknesses related to your personality type?
6. If you have not already done so, take the DiSC inventory. Discuss your thoughts with a trusted mentor.

The Ministry of Reconciliation

There exists a strong relationship between the terms *discipline*, *discipleship* and *reconciliation* for the Christian. Poirier writes that today we do not like to use the term *church discipline*. Church discipline is interpreted by many as punishment. When our new pastor, Bob, used the term of *reconciliation* during a sermon, it was received well. Church leaders have ignored biblical discipline until it has become as rare as the dinosaurs.

Second Corinthians 5:16–21 declares that believers have been given the ministry of reconciliation. The basis of our reconciliation is the ministry of Jesus the Messiah that by means of the His life, death, crucifixion, and resurrection He reconciled believers back to God the Father. The church is made up of believers who have been forgiven and thus reconciled back to the Lord. We, therefore, are ambassadors because we have a message to tell. The message we have to tell is not about you or me; it is about the Savior. The beginning of conflict resolution and reconciliation is when one or more of the offenders or offended takes seriously the message of reconciliation as presented in these verses.

The Lord, during His earthly ministry, provided the steps to church discipline (Matthew 18:15–20). Poirier writes that church discipline does not begin with verses 15–20, but instructs us to look back verse 1.[122] Jesus provides a lesson on humility in verses 1–5, when asked by the disciples, "who is the greatest in the kingdom of heaven?" Conflict can find its roots firmly embedded in the human interests and pride. The parable of the lost sheep follows in the next section (18:10–14). The pastor is to see himself as a shepherd all the time, but especially when in the midst of conflict resolution. The example of the shepherd represents one who cares, nurtures, and protects the sheep. This will defy what some may seek during a time of conflict resolution.

The over thirty years I have had the honor of serving as a pastor, and I have always looked at the flock of God as my own child. My wife and I were blessed with one child, a girl. I told her once that nothing she can do would ever make me not love her. Certainly, a child can go astray, and it will inflict pain into a family. I knew I would love my girl and seek to bring her back home if she strayed. I was committed never to give up on her.

I have been blessed and can say that she did not stray, but I had a clear determination. I obtained this resolve by the example of my parents. I also knew how many times the Lord has forgiven and restored me into His fold. I want the same fortitude that I had for my daughter for the sheep the Lord allowed me to shepherd.

When a pastor sees his role as shepherd and not just as a CEO or as a celebrity, it transforms the purpose of discipline. Discipline should be seen as one aspect of discipleship. The new pastor, Bob, found that the conflict resulted in some members who left, some had just stayed home to escape the battles, and some continue to fight. Pastor Bob was called to shepherd all the sheep in the fold, and certainly some were easier to lead than others.

The "go to" verses for church discipline are Matthew 18:15–20. The offended person is to go to the offender to talk privately, not publicly. If the person listens to you, you have won your brother. If he refuses, then in the presence of two or three witnesses you are to seek to establish the facts of the offence. If he still refuses to listen and pays no attention to the church, then he is to be treated as an unbeliever. The directive is to treat him as an unbeliever, which is to pursue him with the gospel. The apostle Paul would confront the divided church at Corinth with a matter directing them to exercise church discipline (1 Corinthians 5).

When a pastor and the church's leadership see discipline through the lens of discipleship, it can bring new life into the body of Christ. Exercising public rebuke is not easy, but it can bring fruit. The sinner is restored to God in worship, to others in shared life and peace, and to self in changed character. The purpose of discipline and restitution is peace in Christ[123]

Principles for Discipline and Restitution[124]

Be Gentle–Galatians 6:1; 2 Timothy 2:25

Be Relational–Galatians 6:2; Romans 15:1

Be Beneficial–Romans 6:20–22

Be Purposeful–The purpose of discipline and restitution is restoration.

Toll of Conflict

The term *stress* comes from the world of physics, and relates to the amount of pressure it takes to bend steel. This term has been applied to humans because of the effects of the body to resist change and maintain its balance. I never recalled having chicken pox as a child, but one day I discovered some painful sores on my body. The medical doctor informed me that I had shingles. *Shingles* is the term used to describe the process of how the mind affects the body. The term *psychosomatic* is often used to describe this phenomenon. When the mind senses stress, the body will secrete a hormone creating the fight or flight response. This is a natural aspect of human survival. It can get out of control when we allow our minds and bodies to get out of balance. Western cultures, as in much of the developed world, do not encourage time away from work for meditation and reflection. Ministry leaders feel the demands and burden of ministry, and too often give up time in prayer for the demands of visiting or meetings. The daily work of the shepherd, because of the increased use of technology, requires less and less physical exertion. Pastors can sit, stew, and stuff.

When I left the military life after a decade, I found that being overweight or out of shape was acceptable. The military would penalize service members who did not maintain physical conditioning. I found that my studies, demands of planned and unplanned meetings, or visits would steal my time with God and my family. The day was finished before I had spent adequate time in prayer, devotion, exercise, and relaxing with my wife and daughter. This became too evident when I recalled looking at my daughter and realized she was growing up so quickly. I determined at that moment that I did not wish to lose years with my family. God had provided me with a family before I had become a pastor. I had an obligation to them, but even more I found life and energy as I spent time with them. Family time is critical to the ministry leader in order to model before the church the love between Christ and His church (Ephesians 5:28–32).

A problem that many pastors can develop is the urge to take care of everything. The Bible confronts the work of ministry as a developer, not just a doer of ministry (Ephesians 4:11–12). As the pastor grows in faith, he is to develop/equip the called, empower them for works of ministry, in order to edify the body of Christ. The key to this process whether the church has fifty members or five thousand members is to not go alone. If someone else can do what you are doing in organizational matters, begin praying and seeking to develop someone. The early church had to make significant adjustments to an early crisis (Acts 6). The apostles were to be devoting their time to the talk of prayer and the Word. This is not an expression that waiting upon tables was a lesser work. Acts 6 is an organizational principle employing believers where needs exist, believers are investing in the church and kingdom, and the called are valued for his/her contribution to the work of God.

J. Oswald Sander in his classic, *Spiritual Leadership*, speaks about the cost of leadership. Pastors and staff ministers are normally taught the competencies of the position, too often may not be prepared for its effect upon their spiritual, physical, or emotional being. Church leadership will take a toll on the minister's family, especially during times of increased challenges or conflict.[125] Jesus asked His disciples, "Can you drink the cup I drink or be baptized with the baptism I am baptized with?" (Mark 10:38).

Respond to a case study

Jack had an ever-increasing burden for his community. As he got to know more and more families, he became aware of a significant problem with heroin addiction and the devastating effects it was having on the addicts, their families, and the people with whom they came in contact.

The young pastor wanted his church to be viewed as a safe place people could come to receive counseling, friendship, and material support. Extending an invitation to non-church attenders to attend support groups would run counter to the "members first" mentality that many had grown used to over the years. But Jack did not realize just how deep this sentiment ran.

All ministers are familiar with the countdown to kick-off–the rhythms of activities just prior to worship service. And most are also experienced with satanic attacks that threaten to disrupt the pastor's focus during these quiet moments. Such was the case this particular morning, a day in which Jack was preparing to baptize one of the heroine users his outreach had been ministering to. The woman had been reunited with her family, had gotten treatment, and had given her life to the Lord. But these successes would not go unchallenged.

A knock at his door broke Jack's concentration, and he reluctantly opened it and greeted a leader of one of the adult Bible study classes. The man could not hide his frustration with the "trashing" of their classroom by a counseling group that had used "their space" the night before. Similar things had happened in the past, but things had reached a boiling point this morning. The reasons for their demands included, "furniture out of place, trash, food, and odors" ... the list went on. The group was issuing an ultimatum through their spokesman, the counseling group had to go. Down the hall, to the mobile unit, anywhere but their room, even if it meant eliminating the outreach.

Jack squared his shoulders, remained calm, and did not reply other than to say that he would be in touch later in the week. Tears came to his eyes once the door closed and he was alone again. He knew conflict was brewing and supernatural wisdom would be required.

1. State the central point of conflict in this case study in your own words. What underling issues are at work in this conflict?
2. What points in the reading speak to the issues you listed in your responses to number one?
3. What would you recommend Jack do if he were to call and ask for advice? Will you recommend including others beyond the counseling group and the Bible study leader as he works toward resolution of this conflict?

10
EQUIPPING BIBLE STUDY TEACHERS

Ken Coley

Brandon roamed the wing in which 175 church members were involved in Bible study prior to worship service. This brief exploration of the Sunday morning groups was not an every week activity for him, but he had finished reviewing his sermon notes and had ten minutes to check things out. The engineer side of him was pleased—all the classes were orderly, well maintained, and appeared properly overseen by their teachers. But as he slowed to observe through the windows of several classes, the senior pastor noticed a sameness in each class: no one was engaged but the teacher. It was actually startling how regimented the environment appeared. Reflecting on his memory of the plateau and recent decline in Bible study attendance, Brandon now had a theory of why this was happening. The church's Bible study programed appeared to have "flat lined." The young pastor recognized that this dimension of the church needed his immediate attention.

Excellence in teaching God's Word is a critical component when developing a Bible study program that glorifies Christ, stimulates spiritual growth in believers, and ministers to both the members and the community that God has called them to serve. The apostle Paul said it best when he wrote and expressed his gratitude for the inspiring growth he saw in the saints at Thessalonica: "For this reason we also constantly thank God that when you received the word of God which you heard from us, you accepted it not as the word of men, but for what it really is, the word of God, *which also performs its work in you who believe*" (1 Thessalonians 2:13, emphasis added).

The litmus test for excellence in teaching is the transformation of believers' lives by the power of the Holy Spirit, and one of the major sources of this change is the influence of God's Word on an individual's thinking, believing, and behaving. Where there is effective teaching, there is *change*—in knowledge, in perspective, in attitudes, and ultimately, in behavior. Where there is no change, no teaching and learning has occurred. Yes, there can be passive consent, or short-term memory of a set of facts. But long term, a lasting change in a person's life is necessary to say that teaching and learning has been successful and effective, and that God's word is "performing its work in you who believe." This chapter will examine the *Why*, the *Who*, the *What*, and the *How* of developing the Bible study program in your church.

The Why: Connecting Your Bible Study Program to the Church's Mission

Simon Sinek, author of popular books on leadership, challenges today's executives to "start with why," which is also the title of his first book. Sinek argues emphatically, "Very few people or companies can clearly articulate WHY they do WHAT they do ... By WHY I mean what is your purpose, cause or belief? WHY does your company exist?"[126] When it comes to a discussion on the purpose of the church, one of the most frequently cited passages in the New Testament is Acts 2:41–47. It reads,

> And they devoted themselves to the apostles' teaching, to fellowship to the breaking of bread, and to prayers ... Now all the believers were together and had everything in common. So they sold their possessions and property and distributed the proceeds to all, as anyone had a need. And every day they devoted themselves to meeting in the temple complex, and broke bread from house to house ... And every day the Lord added to them those who were being saved.

In one brief description we see a powerful portrait of the early church involved in Bible study, worship, fellowship, ministry to others, and evangelism. We also see pictures in this passage of the church in Jerusalem meeting in large gatherings and in small, intimate groups. Barclay summarizes the passage with these phrases: learning, fellowshipping, praying, reverent, sharing, worshipping, and winsome.[127]

Taylor describes the seamless connection between the church's mission and the Sunday school program at First Baptist Woodstock in this way. "We have adopted a fourfold mission for our church that we refer to as our church's DNA: Worship God. Love others. Serve God. Invite others ... We have the purpose in our heads and hearts; Sunday School moves it to our hands and feet. Sunday School affords every member a natural way to express the church's mission."[128] As Taylor develops his thesis in favor of small group Bible study on Sunday morning, he continues, "There are three foundational purposes of Sunday School–reaching people, teaching people, and ministering to people."[129] Parr articulates the why in a similar fashion: "The lost will be reached ... Lives will be changed ... Leaders will be sent."[130]

The Who: Characteristics of Teachers of Influence

Paul, Timothy, and Silas arrived in Thessalonica after a brief period of imprisonment in Philippi. Paul preached in the synagogue for three Sabbaths (Acts 17:2) and saw a number of converts accept Christ. "The chief success of the mission clearly lay among those Greeks who had attached themselves to the synagogue."[131] The leaders of the synagogue reacted against Paul and his followers, and the riot and legal proceedings that were generated by their jealousy led Paul and Silas to leave and head to Berea.[132] Against this backdrop of dynamic conversions of new believers and violent backlash by Jewish leaders, twenty-first century pastors and leaders can glean powerful insights about discipleship and influencing others to grow as a result of studying God's Word.

Let's enumerate what we see in the passage. The apostle Paul paints a moving picture of meaningful discipleship in his letter to the church at Thessalonica:

> We cared so much for you that we were pleased to share with you not only the gospel of God but also our own lives, because you had become dear to us. For you remember our labor and hardship, brothers. Working night and day so that we would not burden any of you, we preached God's gospel to you. You are witnesses, and so is God of how devoutly, righteously, and blamelessly we

> conducted ourselves with you believers. As you know, like a father with his own children, we encouraged, comforted, and implored each one of you to walk worthy of God, who calls you into His own kingdom and glory. (1 Thessalonians 2:8–12 HCSB)

1. *Teachers of influence share the gospel.* The rock-solid basis of every outpost that Paul began was the preaching of the gospel. Often pastors and Bible study teachers are tempted to stray from a gospel-centered message to other topics that appear to have current relevance. It is my experience that the best approach to Bible study is to select resources that are based on specific books of the Bible, not contemporary issues. As we teach the entirety of Scripture, intersections with concerns of our day will naturally reveal themselves.

2. *Teachers of influence share themselves.* Is it not startling that Paul would communicate such a deep affection for a new group of converts that he got to know in such a short period of time before having to leave abruptly? Paul and his associates shared "our own lives, because you had become dear to us." Morris points out that some translations use "souls" or "lives" for the Greek word *psyche*, but that in this context it stands "for the whole personality, 'our own selves'" (RSV). "Paul is speaking of that giving of oneself ... that is of the very essence of genuine Christian teaching and evangelism."[133]

3. *Teachers of influence model the way.* In verse 9 Paul reminds his readers that he worked two jobs while he was a part of their community, so as not to burden them financially but also to communicate authenticity. Our post-Christian culture is starving for Bible study leaders who have deep affection for the individuals in the group and who are "the real deal"–devout, righteous, and blameless.

4. *Teachers of influence challenge believers to grow.* "Paul uses three verbs to convey the manner of the preaching, the combination giving the impression of urgency."[134] The challenges of being a new convert in the first century were many, so in keeping with the tone of affection and tenderness, Paul reminds them that he offered both *encouraging* and *comforting* words. But he also *implored* them to make progress as they "walked in a manner that is worthy." Morris notes that these words were delivered to "each of you." The Greek construction makes this more emphatic than a simple "each one" and more individualized. Perhaps this was accomplished in private conversations.[135] Lay teachers have the privilege and opportunity to be the primary influencer/discipler who is closer to fellow believers than the pastoral staff.

5. *Teachers of influence see believers transformed by the Holy Spirit through the power of His Word.* As we mentioned at the beginning of this chapter, Paul rejoiced that they received his preaching, not as words spoken by a mere man, but they understood the message as coming from God. And the result was that the Word was "at work in you." This verb comes from the Greek word *energein* and gives us our English word *energy*. Here the verb tense is passive, meaning God is the One doing the work and it is a supernatural activity and result.[136] Each pastor and each teacher should view this opportunity as a special stewardship assigned to him as a representative of Jesus Himself.

Recite and rehearse

Using the material presented in this chapter and other Scriptures that you select, make a list of qualities you believe Bible teachers at your local church should possess. Organize your list into two categories: qualities that are prerequisite before beginning to teach and those they may be expected as he/she grows as a teacher.

Recruiting Bible Study Leaders

Asking someone to participate in a significant role in the church is a weighty task. The word *recruit* comes from a French word *recroistre* that means, "to grow up again." The primary goal of the recruiter is to strengthen the ranks of the unit, but perhaps in an unintended way, the enlistment of a new recruit can be viewed as providing the individual with a fresh opportunity for growth. If you are going to lead a growing ministry, this must be your mindset. Taylor puts a great deal of focus on proper recruitment: "You cannot build a great organization without great people. Therefore, the importance of proper enlistment of teachers cannot be overstated ... The teacher is, in fact, a "miniature pastor"; and his class is his "miniature congregation."[137] Below is a discussion of proven methods for successfully recruiting new teachers to lead your Bible study groups:

The place ...

Make an appointment with the person you wish to recruit. Plan a suitable place where you can talk for fifteen to twenty minutes without interruption. You might suggest meeting him at his home or a coffee shop near his work. Never recruit in the pews, the parking lot, or the men's room at church.

Your preparation ...

You will want to refer to the church's overall vision for discipleship and the purpose of the Bible study program, so bring along any material that you have that describes this. Also, have a copy of the teacher's job description and a sample of the curriculum resource (preferable a teacher's edition.) Know as much about the person you are meeting with as possible, such as past or current positions held in the church.

Your presentation ...

After a brief time of informal conversation begin by clearly stating why you made the appointment and what you want to discuss. First, connect the teaching position to the overall mission of the church, emphasizing the significance of the responsibility. Do not minimize the importance of the position for which you are recruiting the individual. Second, articulate why you have approached that person. For example, you might refer to past interaction or leadership qualities you have noticed. Connect this person and his unique qualities to the position. (Of course, this must be authentic and genuine and will not be possible if you know little about the prospective teacher.) Third, ask if he is familiar with the Bible study program and has a feel for what the position entails. At this point invite him to look at the job description and pause to see if he has any questions. Fourth, explain details about moving forward if the recruit appears interested in knowing more. At this point two pieces of information can cement the individual's interest—offer a copy of the resource material and briefly outline opportunities for future training events. Never request a response at that moment but ask if he is willing to pray about accepting the position. Set a specific date you plan to check back (suggestion: one week) to see what his thoughts are and if there are further questions. (Yes, valuable time is invested here on one recruit, but this avoids two negative results: strong-arming a decision from someone who may not really be the right person or rushing/losing the best person for the job.)[138]

Once again I refer you to Taylor's exceptional book on the topic of developing your church's Bible study program. He recommends presenting a potential teacher with a *Sunday School Covenant*, which includes the standards and expectations for those who lead Bible study.[139] If your church lacks such a standard, I recommend that you and your teachers review sample covenants from other churches before launching into requiring your current teachers to sign such a document. Another approach is to begin with a blank white board and challenge your current teachers to fashion their own covenant. Of course, this should be considered a living document that can be expanded as the group matures in their expectations for Christ-like teaching and leading.

Reflect and react

Collaborate with another student or ministry partner to design a scenario in which you recruit someone to fill a hypothetical position in a local church. Create two scripts. In the first, write dialogue in which the recruiter violates the principles laid out in this chapter. In the second, write dialogue in which the recruiter portrays recruitment done well.

The What: The Activities That Help Us with *The Why*.

Taylor assists us in the discussion of transitioning from *The Why* to *The What*:

> God has entrusted the teacher with the responsibility of caring for their souls (class members) and feeding them spiritually, so they can grow up to be big boys and girls in Christ. God never intended for them to sit in a class all of their lives and never experience the joy and fulfillment of getting out on their own and standing on their own two spiritual feet. If they are incapable of service, then the teacher cannot consider his ministry to these people a complete success.[140]

So what does this process look like that yields mature disciples who are ready to take the lead in the mentoring of new disciples?

Growing Leaders One Week at a Time

One Sunday morning as I was greeting my group members as they arrived for Bible study, I had young man about half my age ask me if we could talk. I could tell that he was troubled, so I suggested that we step outside. During the ten minutes we were together, the man tearfully described a recent visit to his doctor. He detailed some health issues and explained the ultimate revelation that he had spots on his lungs. The magnitude of his fear was palpable, and my full attention was riveted on my friend. As the minutes went by, I had a fleeting thought that the class was waiting for me to start. But I dismissed the concern because I had trained the leaders to perform their duties as if I weren't there.

But what if I had not coached others to take care of the numerous responsibilities? The activities and duties would have gone undone by me and my wife, or I would have had to cut short my ministry to a brother in desperate need in order to serve the entire group.

Check Table 1 for a list of things that need to be done every time you gather. While some of the items listed could be done by anyone, some group members will have an affinity for specific duties. The important thing is that these entry-level activities do not require special recruitment or training. However, each task is important and those who participate can have the sense of making a contribution.

Table 1: Developing leadership through participation: entry-level responsibilities

- Room set up
- Snacks set up

- Greet visitors
- Fill out visitor's slip
- Record attendance
- Collect/record prayer requests
- Open class with announcements, welcome visitors, and prayer

Some group members will come with prior experience, be more energetic, and will make it known that they can take on more challenging and time-consuming responsibilities. Table 2 contains a list of seven of responsibilities that require greater discernment and spiritual maturity.

Table 2: A higher level of responsibilities for more experienced and mature participants

- Call and follow up with visitors
- Call missing members
- Plan socials events
- Prayer chain for group emergencies in between meetings
- Ministry of specific needs
- Assist the teacher in teaching the lesson in view of having his own class
- Care group leader that oversees care for a subset of the class

What This Might Look Like in Your New Ministry

Frequently, young pastors have asked, "How I can motivate my existing teachers and leaders to approach our Bible study program with fresh enthusiasm for teaching God's Word, for reaching unbelievers, and for developing new leaders?" As I have explored various options with them, in some cases this change was simply not going to happen without the pastor modeling it for his people. My solution: start your own class made up of participants who do not currently attend Bible study. To the best of your ability, do this is a way that that does not conflict with others, such as moving into a room that is currently in use or poach group members from other groups. Next, set some goals such as the following:

- Goal one: In six weeks I will not have any responsibility related to the class other than praying for our group members and preparing the lesson.
- Goal two: In six months I will have trained a substitute teacher with whom I share the teaching responsibility.
- Goal three: In one year I will turn the class over to its new leaders and begin a new group.
- Goal four: In two years I will have two stand-alone Bible study groups, and I will turn my attention to meeting regularly with the current and future teachers of new groups.

Braddy has described the successful process of growing and multiplying leaders through weekly Bible study in his list of Six Marks of a Healthy Group:[141]

1. Growing: One mark of a healthy group is numerical growth.
2. Sending: Healthy groups regularly release people to serve, a catch and release mindset.
3. Engaging: Healthy groups engage people in active learning. (See below.)
4. Depending: Healthy groups have learned not to be prideful about their accomplishments, but rather serve in the Lord's strength.
5. Including: A healthy group is outwardly focused yet has the ability to keep an eye on its group members.
6. Serving: Healthy groups are involved in ministries both inside and outside the church.

The How: Engage Your Learners!

With over thirty years' experience of teaching Sunday School in three different locations, this author has discovered that the key to seeing this change happen is the short, but powerful word, *engage*. Content that is taught with the use of techniques that offer the opportunity for Bible study participants to engage with God's Word, with the instructor, and with his/her classmates is more likely to take hold in the believer's mind and heart than instructional approaches in which the participants remain passive. Students learn more when they actively engage with the content than when they sit, listen, take notes, and watch. This chapter will reflect briefly on the challenges and barriers to more effective teaching that exist in nearly every church and steps you and your teachers/leaders can take to engaging your members in life-changing Bible study.

Here's a brief outline that most teachers used while preparing his/her lesson:

- **Connection:** Begin with a "hook" that connects the learners' prior experiences with the content.
- **Context:** Select important aspects of the cultural, historical, or geographical setting of the lesson.
- **Context in the book:** Clarify how the passage is tied to the overall flow/theme of the book.
- **Content:** The major focus of that day's lesson–what is God saying to us in His Word?
- **Comprehension:** Take time to measure the students' understanding.
- **Conviction:** What are aspects of my life about which the Lord is speaking to me?
- **Challenge for application:** How might I think, feel, or respond differently this week based on this lesson?

Engage through Active Learning Techniques (ALTs)

As previously stated, adult learners stay focused better when they are actively involved in the lesson as opposed to listening passively to a lecture. Merely asking, "Does anyone have any questions?" does not count as discussion or participation. Teachers need to be challenged to plan intentionally to design participation opportunities in their lesson plans. This is not to say that any lecture is a poor second to active learning. What needs to take place is a balance between the teacher presenting the information that he/she has researched prior to class with episodes in which the class members interact with the teacher, the Scripture, and each other. A teacher who is new to this approach might set a goal of making use of two ALTs each lesson, placing new ones at different places in the lesson each week. As both the teacher and the class become used to the new expectations, the number of ALTs per lesson could increase to three or four activities each week. An ALT can take as little time as it takes for class members to show their responses after considering a question and giving it a "thumbs up" or a "thumbs down." Fifteen seconds! Yount explains the dynamic energy generated when learners are engaged in his description of class interaction:

> We build relationships with individuals, teacher to learner, and encourage relationships among learners as well. As we interact, we learn from one another and teach one another. One learner's answer raised a question for another. A third learner's question caused several others to think in different ways. A matrix of relationships generates multidirectional, multilayered teaching.[142]

Here are a few Active Learning Techniques along with a suggestion of where each might work best: (No one would do all of these in one lesson. But this does demonstrate how the activities can occur at different times in the lesson).[143]

Before the class begins: The teacher prepares five statements that connect with the theme or topic of the lesson. As each member enters, he/she is given one of the statements and asked to consider a brief response. As the room fills up, class members are encouraged to interact with other students who have a different statement. Each reads his statement to the other and then shares his reaction to the statement. (Technique: *Tea Party*)

Review: How many of you encountered a situation this week that reminded you of the lesson theme from last Sunday's lesson? Raise your hand. (Technique: *Polling*)

Connect: This week's lesson involves the concept of *forgiveness.* I want you to think for a few moments about a time when you chose to forgive someone who had offended you. (Pause thirty seconds.) Now, I want you to turn to the person next to you and briefly describe the decision that you made. (Pause sixty seconds.) Thanks for participating. Who will share what you and your partner discussed with the entire class? (Technique: *Think-Pair-Share*)

Context: These events influenced the culture and political environment in our passage today. I am going to put you into two teams, and I would like for you to place these events in chronological order beginning with the one that occurred first. The team that finishes first gets first run at the box of doughnuts that I brought for snack today. (Technique: *Get It Straight*)

Content: Please take a look at the first five verses in our passage today, and while you read them, I want you to look for the identity and description of the group that Jesus is addressing. Begin reading. (Pause for one minute.) When you have made the identification, please look up so I will know that you are ready to answer. Who can help us identify the characters? (Discuss.) Now that we know who the players are, please continue reading and look for information about how they responded to Jesus' teachings. Please look up when you completed the entire passage and have an answer. (Technique: *Read with a Purpose*)

Check for comprehension: I placed three cards in your seat. I am going to ask you two important questions about the lesson and for each question I would like for you to hold up one of the cards that indicates your level of understanding. *Red* means, "Stop. I am not ready to move on"; *yellow* means, "I'm not sure. I need to examine this some more"; *green* means, "I got the concept and I'm ready to move on." (Technique: *Stoplight: checking for levels of understanding*)

Confirm conviction: Using one of the note cards that we just used in the comprehension check, I would like for you to reflect on the most important issue confronting your life this week in regards to this study. I would like you to write a statement about what you think the Holy Spirit is asking you to change and how you plan to respond. This will be between you and the Lord, and I will not call of you or ask to read your card. (Technique: *Writing for Understanding*)

Challenge for application: This week the Lord wants to impact people around you. Using one of the Post-it® Notes, write down what you can do this week as a response to today's lesson. After you have written on one or more notes, I want you to come up and place your note under one of the four categories I have written on the whiteboard: Home, Community, Work, the Mall. (Technique: *Post-it Note Response*)

Research and create

Working with a team of experienced teachers, craft a lesson plan that illustrates the team's understanding of the 7 Cs represented above. Select a passage that is familiar to the group but one in which a discussion of the historical context and the biblical context would be important to an effective lesson plan. Look for places in the plan to include engagement activities. At your earliest opportunity, test-drive the new lesson plan.

Moving Forward in Pursuit of Excellence

Gather a group of teachers together—as many as are willing to participate. Begin a serious dialogue about how teachers influence their students to fall more in love with God's Word and make it a real and vibrant part of their lives. This discussion should include an awareness of the differences within the class, such as backgrounds, biblical knowledge, personalities, and learning styles. From this discussion the group fashions a philosophy about Sunday school teaching and learning.

1. Lay out the basic motivations for what you are organizing. Parr lists three motives:
    - The lost will be reached. Teachers and group members work together to share the gospel within the boundaries of their Bible study and beyond the walls of the church in the community.
    - Lives will be changed. As discussed throughout this chapter, God's Word is powerful, and people are transformed as they are exposed to it.
    - Leaders will be sent. A consistent encounter with God through the study of His Word will lead many participants out of the class into ministry.[144]

2. Work together to select a suitable curriculum resource that will support a commitment to study God's Word in a systematic way. (LifeWay Christian Resources have a variety of excellent resources.)
3. Initiate a discussion on *Active Learning Techniques* and find ways to share lesson plans and tips about successful teaching episodes with each other. Many teachers would profit from getting together weekly or monthly to reflect on effective ways to involve adults in the teaching/learning process. Some teachers would likewise enjoy using social media for immediate sharing of ideas.
4. Remember the goal is for your teachers to say about their classmates, "You accepted it not as the word of men, but for what it really is, the word of God, which also performs its work in you who believe" (1 Thessalonians 2:13).

Respond to a case study

Mark had been at the two-year-old church plant for three months as lead pastor. His bivocational position had kept him consumed with sermon prep and financial planning and his to-do list full. But because he had a conviction for training lay people to lead Bible study, the importance of the community groups was never far from his mind.

Since he was not currently committed to one particular group, he determined he would do two things to collect some firsthand information about the vitality of the eight adult groups that had formed as subsets of the young church. First, he would have two casual lunch meetings with three or four of community group leaders attending each meal. At the two "focus group" style get-together, Mark planned to ask a series of open-ended questions and try to mentally record data about the health of the Bible study groups the church called community groups. Second, over the next two months he hoped to attend each group and make some observations for himself. From the lunch meetings, attended by six of the leaders, he heard the following:

- Four of the six groups were near capacity each week.
- Five reported adding no new members during Mark's tenure.
- All of the leaders commented that they had received no training, only a job description.
- Two leaders said their attendees expressed interest in drilling deeper into Scripture.
- All of the leaders expressed reservations about their members growing as disciples.

During the weeks that followed Mark made it to all of the community groups. Here are some of the notes that he took:

- All of the leaders were following the prescribed

outline that was generated by the staff based on the Sunday sermon.

- Half of the group leaders conducted nearly the entire session without deviating from the script.
- Few attendees in most of the groups used their Bibles.
- Mark's sermon was referenced much more often that he was comfortable with.

As Mark reflected on his observations, he noticed a couple of positives but overall he had grave concerns about the long-term health of the congregation. He needed a strategy to rejuvenate these Bible study groups and their leaders.

- Highlight what you believe to be the major issues in the scenario.
- What do you believe to be important but secondary concerns for Mark?
- Evaluate how Mark conducted his assessment of the community groups and related Bible study.
- What do you think Mark needs to undertake first? Why?

11
SUPERVISING THE CHURCH STAFF
Ken Coley

"What was I thinking when I encouraged the church to call this guy to be part of the staff?" James asked himself over and over. As senior pastor, James was responsible for the oversight of the other three staff members and their job performances. Two out of three might be considered a high batting average in baseball, but not so for this responsibility. There were no points of crises that James could point to related to this staff member, but an overall pattern of ineffectiveness that was nagging at him and creating drag on the forward momentum of the church. "What if" kept coming to his mind. What if things continued to unravel to the extent that the personnel committee started to blame James for the overall lack of achievement? Where had he gone wrong and how could he turn things around?

Many pastors have soared in ministry when their preaching, their vision-casting, and their commitment to their flock were being admired. These attributes of pastoral leadership have one thing in common: each involves personal leadership of self. Unfortunately, a crucial dimension causes some to run aground.

My first teaching job was in Williamsburg, Virginia, at a school located on the beautiful Colonial Parkway. Nestled among the lovely dogwoods and magnolias along this picturesque drive was the Yorktown Naval Weapons Station, where US ships delivered and loaded various secret munitions. The parkway ends at Yorktown, the site of the final engagement of the Revolutionary War. Situated at the mouth of the York River, the town has a prominent bridge that connects the mainland to a peninsula across the river. The bridge is unusual because it does not open like a drawbridge, but two sections of the bridge rotate on giant columns to create an opening for large ships to pass through. After returning home from school one afternoon, I observed a major traffic backup in this small community and learned that the unthinkable had occurred–one of the naval destroyers had collided with the bridge and had knocked off one section from the mechanism that allowed it to close. Unfortunately, many commuters from the other side of the bridge had to drive nearly one hundred miles up to Richmond and back again to get to and from work for weeks while the bridge was being repaired. The military's decision was not made public at the time, but everyone assumed that the captain of the ship lost his commission. His crew, because of poor training or lax supervision, had failed to carry out their assigned tasks.

I share this story to illustrate the most significant responsibility that the helmsman has after correctly setting the course of the ship. That responsibility is to train the crew and to monitor their performances. The helmsman is ultimately responsible for how effectively each crew member carries out his or her assigned tasks. It is at this point that the leader has the greatest influence on the organization's success in reaching its prescribed destination. The helmsman may not be able to carry out the specifics of each crew member's job, but the helmsman must understand the relationship each member's performance has to the whole and be able to provide the necessary training and resources to help each one be successful. How this training and monitoring is carried out is vital to the health and vitality of the entire community.

> In Greek the word is *episkopos*, made of the roots for *over* and *view* or *look*. We get *Episcopal* from the word, and it's translated as *bishop*. The Latinate word is *supervisor*, from *super* (over) and *videre* (to see). The English word is *overseer*. All three words mean basically the same thing: watching over someone.[145]

In the above illustration, the bridge was eventually repaired and life returned to normal for all those inconvenienced by the accident. However, in the execution of daily ministerial duties in a local church, the church's crew is responsible for the destiny of far greater cargo—the souls of God's children. Let's examine three biblical pictures that relate to the pastor as overseer of his staff.

Biblical Pictures of Supervision
Equipper of the Saints

The supervisor believes that God has gifted each staff member with special talents that need to be developed. *Growth* is the key word in the relationship; conducting performance evaluations provides the staff member with the opportunity to learn and grow.[146]

The apostle Paul challenged the church leaders at Ephesus to build the body of Christ as they equipped each member to perform some ministry for the advancement of the kingdom. This exhortation applies to leaders of a church staff today: "for the training of the saints in the work of ministry, to build up the body of Christ, until we all reach unity in the faith and in the knowledge of God's Son, growing into a mature man with a stature measured by Christ's fullness" (Ephesians 4:12–13). The Greek word that gives us our word, *prepare* can also be translated as "equip." This word in Paul's day was used to describe the activity of mending nets. (We find this same word used in Matthew 4:21 to describe the work of James and John when Jesus called them to join Him.) Paul presents the leaders with the responsibility to adequately equip God's people so they can actively and effectively participate in serving. The result is powerful–the body is unified and mature, and it is able to strive for the fullness of Christ.

Good Shepherd

The overseer should see himself as God's "under-shepherd" while overseeing the sheep in his care. *Trust* is the key word in the relationship.

The sheep respond to the suggestions and directions of the leader because there has been a spirit of trust established through the care and concern that has been shown to each sheep.

Proverbs 27:23 provides pastors with another exhortation: "Know well the condition of your flock, and pay attention to your herds." The shepherds in Solomon's day were expected to be diligent, compassionate, and caring while supervising the flock. A literal translation for the word *condition* is "face." To respond in this way requires the overseer to spend the necessary time to focus on each person under his care to understand each person's unique needs, personal struggles, and maturity level. I have always found that the most challenging aspect of leading people is the mysterious process of discovering what motivates or demotivates them. To do so, the pastor indeed must "pay attention" to identify what inspires each staff member to do more than is required. The parable of the good shepherd spoken by Jesus presents a beautiful picture of the relationship that results when a supervisor is attentive and caring: "The one who enters by the door is the shepherd of the sheep. The doorkeeper opens it for him, and the sheep hear his voice. He calls his own sheep by name and leads them out. When he has brought all his own outside, he goes ahead of them. The sheep follow him because they recognize his voice. They will never follow a stranger; instead they will run away from him, because they don't recognize the voice of strangers" (John 10:2–5). This picture of Jesus as the Good Shepherd whom believers respond to reveals the heart of a leader who has spent the time with His flock that is necessary to be known by them. The result is that the sheep respond to His voice and follow. It is well known that shepherds lead sheep; they do not drive them. It is also well known that if shepherds spend time with their sheep, they will smell like them.

Steward

A third picture from Scripture is that of *steward*—one to whom God has entrusted a special responsibility. In his letter to the Ephesians, Paul wrote of the life-changing assignment the Lord gave to him: "you have heard, haven't you, about the administration of God's grace that He gave to me for you?" (Ephesians 3:2).

The supervisor believes that he has been given a responsibility from the Lord to care for the needs of the staff. *Service* is the key word in the relationship. The steward serves both the Master and those entrusted to him. Each staff member should be viewed as a part of the leader's stewardship: for some reason, this individual has been assigned to you. It may not be apparent at first. It could be that the individual is not really called into ministry. But caring for the individual staff member is a part of the overseer's responsibility.

Recite and rehearse

Describe the three biblical pictures related to being an overseer presented in this chapter.

Which one do you find to be the most inspiring? Explain your choice.

Can you think of other biblical pictures or passages that enhance your understanding?

How are You at Connecting the Dots?

A significant dimension of leadership of people in general and your staff in specific is the pastor's ability to connect the dots, first in his own ministry and then in his communications with everyone else. In administration and management, the more formal term is *alignment*. Most of us know what it means to drive a car that is "out of alignment" and immediately recall the rough ride this problem produces. So too, when the written documents of the church, the activities of various departments, and the expectations of staff members' performances are not in sync, the pastor and the staff are in for a bumpy trip. Think through the relationships and points of intersection that should exist in the following:

- The church's overall mission and vision statements.
- The pastor's philosophy about leading others.
- The segments of the surrounding community the ministry is called to reach.
- The goals that are unique to a specific subset of the ministry.
- The duties and responsibilities outlined in each pastor's job description.
- The expectations of the leader of that ministry.
- The evaluation of the leader of that ministry.

Did you recognize that the items above are listed from the broadest ministry concept to specific ones? Having thought about the overall connections among these aspects of church life, can you quickly identify the frustrations and conflict that arise when the leader fails to articulate how these things align? Or if a staff member willfully disregards the direction of the overall church program? The expression, "the wheels come off the cart," applies in those cases.

Potential Points of Breakdown in the Teamwork of the Staff

Let's switch metaphors and continue to examine the importance of alignment as it relates to supervision and teamwork. Have you ever been white water rafting? I have enjoyed several adventures on rivers rated Class IV and Class V. In such risky rafting trips the guide that is assigned to a group's raft takes time to rehearse the importance of following his commands, the responsibility that each participant has, and the critical importance of teamwork. Absent these things, folks fall out of the raft or the entire raft can capsize. As the "hold harmless" documents that you must sign indicate, "Participants may be injured or die during this activity." A church might be viewed as an even larger raft that experiences periods of great turbulence. The pastor and his staff must all agree on where the ministry is headed, how to row in unison, and how to respond in the rapids of daily ministry. Here are some potential dysfunctions that may occur:

When the River Guide Is at Fault

- The pastor is uncertain or capricious about the overall direction of the church. For example, periods of demanding emphasis on evangelism or discipleship or international missions without coherent coordination. (Clarifying of mission/vision)

- The pastor's leadership style and approaches to developing church leaders is at odds with a staff leader. For example, the pastor wishes to organize the church around Sunday school Bible study as opposed to cell groups preferred by the discipleship pastor. (Building unity around philosophy of ministry)
- The pastor fails to communicate his expectations or outcomes for individual ministries. For example, the pastor does not articulate to the youth minister that a steady increase in numbers in attendance is the primary goal. (Establishing clear job descriptions and expectations)
- The evaluation process is not clear or the agreed upon procedure is not followed. (For example, the leader of the children's program is given a low evaluation because there is no parenting class offered, even though the expectation was never mentioned.) (Designing performance review process)

When the Paddler in the Raft Fails to Respond

- The individual leader of a ministry wants to go his own way. For example, the worship leader consistently selects a style of music that the pastor does not like. (Conflict with mission statement)
- The staff member gets discouraged and stops paddling. For example, the finance committee alters the budget line item for a particular ministry. (Loss of commitment to the ministry)
- The staff member puts his own safety (dig your feet underneath the side of the raft and just hang on!) ahead of the wellbeing of the entire

group. (Loss of spiritual courage)

Do you find yourself in a raft that is constantly being slowed by staff members who are not fulfilling their duties or responding to your commands in the middle of a long stretch of rapids? Perhaps you need to take a closer at the process of overseeing your staff that can lead to more harmonious teamwork and greater productivity for the kingdom.

Reflect and react

Develop an illustration of alignment for a hypothetical church plant. Write a brief statement for each category that demonstrates your understanding of "connecting the dots."

Include mission statement, core values, goal for _____ministry, performance objective for the leader of that ministry, and assessment measure for that leader.

The Process Leading to the Performance Review

After solidifying a biblical perspective regarding your responsibility as the overseer of your staff and identifying the importance of "connecting the dots" in your ministry, the next step in clarify with your staff members the core values that will guide the development of the process. I recommend the following:

- Growth: The review process will focus on the growth of the staff member.
- Transparency: Each phase of the process will be agreed upon by all involved.
- Authentic: The expectations will be clearly tied to things that matter in ministry.
- Measurable: The assessments will be designed so that the outcomes can be measured.
- Obtainable: The goals will be realistic and reachable.

As stated above, transparency is a hallmark of trusting relationships. The process must be developed with the full participation of the pastor and the staff member. If there is a leader in the church that has expertise or experience in conducting performance reviews, then it may prove helpful to involve that individual. Without question, each facet of the review must be directly related to the minister's job description. (See "Sources of Objectives" in Figure 1.) Anthony and Estep list the following questions that can guide the design of the process.

Who establishes the criteria for the review? The participants could be limited to the pastor and the staff member, but others, such as church members or denominational consultants, could be asked to participate.

How are the criteria stated? Are the statements considered outcomes with objective measures? (See the sidebar below that suggest terminologies for rating systems.)

How are the criteria communicated? Who gets to see the individual staff member's performance criteria? Are they printed in a staff handbook? Job description?[147]

Bacher and Cooper-White affirm this approach to oversight and performance review. "A key to effective performance appraisal is to evaluate in reference to established goals (ideally in writing) that have been mutually agreed on by the parties. Such an approach helps avoid purely subjective evaluations by a supervisor that may be based on whim or rather capricious views of what her or his subordinate should be doing."[148]

A significant stumbling block for many pastors and individual staff members is the matter of intermediate updates prior to an annual performance review. Determining how often to meet and what the purpose of the update is to be should be part of the planning process. "A key component of effective supervision is a mutual commitment to frequent interaction and communication. Depending upon the work setting and work styles of staff members, this may range from daily face-to-face interaction to infrequent in-person consultation."[149]

The language of the assessment standards is very important. Rush points out, "When setting performance standards the supervisor and employee should set both *preferred performance standards* and *minimum performance standards*."[150] This highlights the need for a rubric that acknowledges an ideal goal but also includes a range of acceptable performance.

Brown describes three different approaches to rating systems:

> *Comparative ratings.* These ratings require supervisors to compare individual staff members with a certain population of ministers. The rating values often used are *Excellent, Above Average,* or *Good; Average, Below Average,* or *Fair; Poor;* and *Unsatisfactory.* A

comparative scale does not indicate whether the staff member's performance is acceptable or unacceptable in a particular church, and thus it provides no clear basis for determining the staff member's total worth to the church's ministry.

Frequency ratings. Frequency ratings call for descriptions of employee performance that assign a quantitative rating to each behavior. These schemes provide such classifications as *Always*, *Usually*, *Seldom*, or *Never*, or similar ones. Another form is *Consistently*, *Occasionally*, and *Seldom*.

Criterion-referenced ratings. These ratings compare employee performance against a standard of excellence that all ministers should strive for and can achieve. This type of scheme usually includes words like *Acceptable* or *Competent*, *Satisfactory*, *Needs Improvement*, *Unacceptable*, and *Unsatisfactory*. These words suggest that performance criteria for staff members are not dependent on comparisons between them. Potentially, every staff member can achieve excellence. Staff members must be evaluated against standards of performance expected by the church.[151]

Mentoring Relationships

The term we now use for leaders in mentoring relationships came about in ancient Greece because of a father's love and concern for his son. Before Ulysses, the warrior, set sail for the Trojan War, he recruited a trusted friend, an older man he had known since childhood, to watch over the training of his son, Telemachus. The trusted friend's name was Mentor. The impact of that arrangement would not be evident until Ulysses returned some twenty years later and the three would stand together to fight off the angry band of suitors that had gathered in their home in pursuit of his lovely wife, Penelope. When called on, Telemachus was prepared to perform as a man at his father's side.

In light of this legend, my story is much less dramatic and somewhat ironic. My son was God's instrument to teach me about leadership development. My battlefield was my backyard, and my foe was the tall grass that rose up against my family every week. How ironic that I thought I was teaching my son, when it was he who trained me. My training began when Scott was four years old and asked if he could help with the yard work. I purchased a toy lawn mower that made bubbles when it was pushed, but his interest quickly waned when he discovered that he was not actually cutting any grass when he followed along beside me. The next week, he came over to get between the engine and me and reached up for the handle. "I want to help, Dad," my son announced. We proceeded to try to guide the mower together, stumbling along in ninety-five-degree heat. It was slow going, but I did not want to extinguish his desire to learn. After a few more trips down and back, he tired of the project and left to play.

The next summer, his reach was higher and his limbs were stronger. This time he announced that he was ready to do it by himself. After grabbing the handle of the mower, which was now just slightly over his head, he gave his dad a push with one hand and started across the yard. Yes, he was holding on while the engine pulled the big mower; unfortunately, not much grass was being cut because the front wheels were not touching the ground. I watched as the boy and machine traversed the yard a few times, and I calmed his mother's fears about her son losing a foot during this exercise. Once again, he tired and needed to rest after a few passes. His first solo flight was not a success by anyone's standards—I had to retrace his steps over the uneven spots. However, he kept coming back, and at age seven, he took over one hot afternoon and cut a good portion of the grass while I stood in the shade and watched. With the exception of a little bit of weaving (he could barely see over the top of the handle), the blades were cut straight, all four wheels touched the ground, and the job was well done. The next summer, he cut half the yard while I drank lemonade and watched the baseball game with one eye and my new assistant with the other. (His mom kept a closer watch out the kitchen window.) At age nine, five years into the process, my son cut the entire backyard while I did other chores.

When Scott turned eleven, I spent two hundred dollars on a small, self-propelled mower—the best two hundred dollars I ever spent. We made an agreement. He would cut our yard, front and back, whenever it needed to be cut, without expecting any money from his parents. In return, I would pay for the mower and the gas and he could cut the neighbors' lawns and pocket all the money that he earned. Soon he was mowing three lawns in addition to ours, and I no longer had to concern myself with cutting grass. I left home for a business trip when Scott was fourteen, and he said I did not have to worry about the lawn—he would take care of it. When I returned, he had cut it in a new diagonal design after raising the base to allow for a taller cut so the grass would not burn in the summer heat. At age sixteen, he fussed at me one afternoon when he returned home from baseball practice and saw me behind the mower.

He claimed, "Dad, that's my job."

What had happened over the period of twelve years? You might be cheering and laughing as you conclude that I got out of performing a never-ending task that is despised by most. But actually, I gave up an activity that I enjoy and shared it with my son, because he wanted to participate in something meaningful with his dad. After a period of supervision and coaching, my son took complete responsibility and ownership of the project and learned to accomplish the task more quickly and effectively than I could do it. His dad had meticulously mentored him to perform his task (and future tasks) in a spirit of excellence and creativity.

In his ground breading discussion on mentoring, Blanchard describes how a pastor can inspire staff members to invest their full reservoir of creativity and energy, while serving both the senior pastor and congregation faithfully. We are all familiar with the high energy leader who prides himself on 'hiring the right person and then turning him loose to do ministry.' Making use of Blanchard's model, the reader should consider how he can avoid the pitfalls of that approach and apply Blanchard's four critical steps in developing leaders:[152]

1. *Direction.* The first stage involves the careful training of the inexperienced mentee. Basically, the leader is actually doing the ministry through the trainee. This process can take the form of regular meetings to discuss step-by-step activities, the demonstration of necessary steps by the teacher, or the side-by-side execution of the tasks. As is discussed by the authors and Blanchard, the extent of the supervision depends on variables, such as the level of maturity and experience the mentee brings to the relationship, the critical nature of the projects that need to be completed, and the length of time the student requires to gain confidence and skill in the new area of training.

2. *Coaching.* The next step takes place when the mentee's confidence and competence grows. At this point, the leader steps off the court and

begins to observe the performance, making specific corrections as necessary. The student makes suggestions and the two work together; the project is a joint venture. The coach's primary responsibilities are affirmation and redirection.

A *Recipe for Disaster*

A senior pastor remarked to the new youth minister, "I'm so glad you're here to relieve me of all responsibility for the young people of the parish. Check in once in a while and don't surprise us with wild crazy programs. I'll run some interference for you with the church council, especially when it comes to budget, but for the most part, from now on you're on your own!"[153]

---

3. *Support.* The first two steps may take as long as a year, depending on the progress of the follower and the sophistication of the new task. At this point, he is ready for the third step in the relationship. A significant milestone occurs as the leader turns over more responsibility to the follower; *the follower begins to set the agenda and prioritizes what needs to be done.* He knows what needs to be accomplished and primarily needs to know that the mentor is there to provide emotional support, encouragement, affirmation, and correction, if necessary. The coach now becomes a cheerleader.

4. *Delegation.* The final step is turning over the project or activity to the new leader. Even though reporting continues and the mentor maintains interest in the mentee, the task now belongs to the latter. Unfortunately, the act of turning over a ministry or responsibility all too often happens first before any guiding and training are done. The usual result, in this case, is a "train wreck" that brings about the dismissal of an employee who began with great enthusiasm for the task but was given no training or guidance. Another difficulty can occur at this point.

The mentor can be unwilling to let go of the activity that the follower was trained for, and he can insist on continuing to micromanage the project and the trainee. The result from this behavior can be that the follower will not feel trusted or adequate to do the job and may mean that, though well trained, he will leave the organization in pursuit of a yard of his own to cut and to take care of.

Delegating: But They Think I Am Dumping on Them!

Are you reluctant to let go and allow your co-laborers to own a piece of the ministry? Perhaps you have the perspective that others don't desire the responsibility, when in fact, many followers genuinely do. It could be that your staff members long for opportunities that have the following characteristics:

Challenging. People grow when they are stretched to develop new skills. More importantly, they expand in their faith as they encounter hurdles that cannot be overcome in their own strength. Consider the blunt, unattractive truth of the following recruitment notice for the Pony Express that was printed in a California newspaper in the 1800s:

> WANTED:
> Young, skinny, wiry fellows not over 18.
> Must be expert riders willing to risk daily.
> Orphans preferred.

The simple fact is this: The Pony Express never experienced a shortage of riders!

Significant. People are motivated to accomplish tasks that they view as significant in kingdom work. If just anyone can do the work, then let someone else do it. Administrators who are effective recruiters emphasize the importance of the project, describe it in terms of its eternal significance, and connect it to the overall goals of the school. Here is another recruitment advertisement allegedly from a London newspaper:

> Men wanted for hazardous journey: small wages, bitter cold, long months of complete darkness, constant danger, safe return doubtful. Honor and recognition in case of success.

Countless men responded to Ernest Shackleton's ad for men to accompany him to the Arctic Circle. They were looking for significance.

Personalized. People need to be challenged to learn new tasks that they are uniquely qualified for. When discussing a new opportunity with someone you are mentoring, point out the mentee's gifts or abilities that make him capable of performing at a new level and that will encourage the mentee to consider how God wants to use those gifts in this situation.

Knowing Peter's strength of personality and courage, Jesus singled out one disciple and made a bold statement: "on this rock I will build My church" (Matthew 16:18).

But I Love Doing the Work Myself.

What skills or gifts do you bring to ministry that might be considered ways in which you have a special impact? This task or responsibility is where the leader leaves his imprint on the culture of the organization. This task or activity need not be delegated or given away to a subordinate. In ministry, the special influence of a pastor might be doing pulpit ministry or officiating at events such as weddings and funerals. For a youth minister, it might be teaching the weekly Bible study or planning the annual youth retreat. For a discipleship pastor, the significant role of selecting the curriculum resource to be used in an upcoming study. But I want to encourage you to consider sharing these opportunities with others in order to provide them with special events to stretch their faith and for you to demonstrate your trust in their abilities.

John Maxwell, in *Developing the Leaders Around You*, structures the process in these five steps:
Step I: Model–the trainee watches the entire process.
Step II: Mentor–the trainee receives instruction

while participating in the process.
Step III: Monitor–the trainee performs the task and the leader watches and corrects as needed.
Step IV: Motivate–the leader removes himself once the trainee knows how to perform the task, but is there for encouragement.
Step V: Multiply–the new leader is free to begin to develop other trainees.[154]

A Biblical Model for Mentoring

One of the most significant transfers of power in the history of humankind would take place in the coming years. The Lord had raised up Moses and equipped him in both ordinary and extraordinary ways. But his days of leadership would one day come to an end.

The Lord had special plans for Joshua, the man He had chosen, and He gave specific instructions for Moses to mentor his replacement. One especially interesting moment occurred after Moses sent Joshua into battle against a mighty foe that was attacking Israel. Following the Israelite victory, the Lord gave precise instructions to the aging leader: "The Lord then said to Moses, "Write this down on a scroll as a reminder and recite it to Joshua: I will completely blot out the memory of Amalek under heaven" (Exodus 17:14). The verb *recite* here can be translated "place in the ears of," and it helps paint a vivid picture of the mentoring relationship between

Moses and Joshua. It also indicates the importance the Lord placed on the message. The significance of this message may be lost on a modern reader, but it certainly would not have been on Joshua. Deuteronomy 25:18 explains to the Israelites what Amalek had done: "They met you along the way and attacked all your stragglers from behind when you were tired and weary. They did not fear God." No doubt the Lord's solemn promise would encourage the heart of the young commander in the future when he would face the enemy again. How about in your administration? Has the Lord led you to prepare a younger educator for future challenges? I believe a part of the stewardship of every leader is that he must constantly look for opportunities to recite in the presence of others—to download to their mental iPods—what the Lord has been doing in the ministry and to share with them the vision for the future.

Here are some additional steps and activities suggested in the relationship of Moses and Joshua:

- **Formally establish the relationship at the proper time**. "He took Joshua, had him stand before Eleazar the priest and the entire community, laid his hands on him, and commissioned him, as the Lord had spoken through Moses" (Numbers 27:22–23).
- **Start early with the opportunity for training**. Numbers 11:28 gives the following description: "Joshua son of Nun, assistant to Moses since his youth."
- **Take your understudy with you so that he can observe and learn.** "So Moses arose with his assistant Joshua and went up the mountain of God" (Exodus 24:13).
- **Provide time for private consultation**. "The Lord spoke with Moses face to face, just as a man speaks with his friend. Then Moses would

return to the camp, but his assistant, the young man Joshua son of Nun, would not leave the inside of the tent" (Exodus 33:11).

- **Correct your understudy in an appropriate but direct way when he needs correction**. Joshua asked Moses to restrain two men who were prophesying in the camp. Moses responded, "Are you jealous on my account? If only all the Lord's people were prophets and the Lord would place His Spirit on them!" (Numbers 11:29).
- **Formally introduce the future leader at the proper time.** In a special ceremony in the sight of all Israel, Moses encouraged and challenged his replacement. He went on to point Joshua to the Lord, not to himself. In addition, Moses reassured Joshua of God's protection and faithfulness (Deuteronomy 31:7–8).

Have some ideas already? Whether you're having coffee with a visitor who is new to the church, conducting a difficult conference with a couple who needs counseling, preparing for a leadership meeting, or developing a meaningful write-up for a lay leader's evaluation–wherever you go and whatever you're doing–be on the lookout for information to put in the ears of the future leaders that God has called you to develop.

Research and create

With the four levels of Personalized Leadership in mind, write a brief description of four different staff members, with each description depicting a minister at each of the four levels.

Include in your description the methods and the

process that the overseer will be using for a staff member at that level of maturity. Once you have written your four descriptions, share them with an experienced leader in that particular area of ministry and ask for his evaluation of your application.

Schedule for Success

Are you a victim of "tyranny of the urgent"? The word *tyranny* comes from a Latin term that means "tyrant." This is also the root word in the name of the most famous and feared dinosaur, *Tyrannosaurus rex* (literally, "the king tyrant lizard"). That might be a fitting metaphor for most administrators as they try to manage their schedules while being pursued by a tyrant lizard! Most pastors readily agree that staying connected to the core ministries of the church, observing some of the activities, and discussing each staff member's progress are vitally important. However, the sad truth is that few leaders actually budget time that is needed to execute an appropriate level of supervision for every minister who God has assigned to them.

As the agreed upon process unfolds, the staff member's performance may not be acceptable; simply put, the job isn't getting done. The pastor should begin immediately to document his concerns in general as well as including specific details about events or conversations. "Such file notes should be dated, cite issues addressed, and document a plan of action whose aim is to enable the supervisee's improvement."[155]

Prayerful consideration should be given to how soon a "corrective action" conference needs to take place. It is my counsel that sooner is always better than later. In his discussion on the process leading to termination, Zigarelli references Proverbs 19:11 and concludes, "the Bible instructs that the prevailing attitude throughout the decision-making process must be one of patience and forgiveness."[156]

Berkley addresses poor performance in this way:

> We avoid heartache by providing immediate feedback regarding inferior work. If our initial feedback doesn't bring about the desired change, we need to offer more. Eventually we may have to say, "in spite of my repeated expressions of concern, you are making the same mistakes again and again. If this continues, it may lead to the loss of your job." Yes, this creates insecurity, but ultimately honesty is in everyone's best interest.[157]

Following the conference, the supervisor should put in writing what was discussed and the recommendations for change that were agreed upon. Such a document should be signed by the staff member with space provided for his/her comments regarding this situation and the accuracy of the conference summary. The follow-up documentation is important for a number of reasons. First, the staff member may have been emotionally upset by the conference and not been able to process the details that were discussed. Second, future expectations for change will be based on accurate understanding of the problem and related solutions. Third, the pastor/supervisor may need this documentation as evidence of his efforts should accusations be made against him in the future or should legal action occur.

Most pastors readily agree with the overall themes in this chapter regarding patience and encouragement in the face of ineffective staff members. However, some may be at a loss for just how to proceed and uncertain about the options that are available. Here is a dozen to consider:

Prior to Dismissal: Options for Discipline of Employees

1. Verbal warning–note in the administrator's file.
2. Written warning–signed by the employee.
3. Suspension with pay–take time away to reflect on areas that need improvement.
4. Suspension without pay–like #3, but with more sting.
5. Probation–with clearly defined objectives and a periodic evaluation.
6. Counseling–suggest 50/50 payment so that employee shares in the investment.
7. Training or a workshop–ask for a summary of valuable new concepts.
8. Research and writing–agree upon a topic that speaks directly to an area of weakness.
9. Biblical study and writing–reflection on God's Word brings conviction and change.
10. Poor performance review–the finality of an annual review can bring clarity.

11. Freezing or lowering of salary–this approach is attention-grabbing for some.
12. Accountability team–a group of qualified leaders can reduce the stress between the pastor and employee, and hopefully introduce new approaches.

If the best decision is for termination, there are several cautions and considerations. As the pastor prepares for the conference in which the staff member will be dismissed, it is vital that he review the decision with an attorney who is familiar with federal and state law as well as recent rulings in employment law. Part of the review with the attorney should include applicable sections of the church's by-laws, staff handbooks, and employee contracts, if one has been used. I also recommend that the pastor rehearse with legal counsel what will be stated at the conference as well as what should not be stated. Finally, it is advisable to develop a letter of recommendation (approved by the attorney) to present to the terminated employee. This can be done with the explanation, "Should you list me as a reference, here's what I will share." Doing so reduces the potential for accusations of defamation down the road.

> For some readers of this text, this chapter may be the most challenging. Chaffee summarizes the responsibility this way, "Nowhere is a leader's maturity so tested as in the arena of employee relations. The spirit of the relations contributes to staff and volunteer morale, satisfaction, and effectiveness. Those without experience as employer best approach the task with care, respect, and humility."[158] As a skillful

overseer/guide/mentor, the pastor blesses his staff as he equips each minister in serving Christ and the local body of believers.

Respond to a case study

What was supposed to be a ten-minute conversation with a young couple new to the church had morphed into nearly an hour. The initial request was to discuss a recommendation that the couple had regarding the church's children's ministry. Since the director was out of town, the pastor agreed to meet with them. Perhaps that was his first mistake. The second mistake was appearing receptive to their idea regarding their child's classroom in general and the program's biblical content in particular.

The pastor was having difficulty focusing as the couple charged forward with stories about other churches they had attended, books they had read, and conferences they had attended. His mind drifted to some occasional snapshots in his mind's eye of brief visits he had made through the wing of the building that housed all the children's classes, from infants through grade five.

So far the discussion topics had covered some suggestions regarding changing the layout in the room, updating the furniture, and reducing the class size. The lack of emphasis on Scripture memory came next. Trying to recall from his sporadic walks—praying, singing, group work—he wished he had made some notes so he could more accurately describe his own encounters. His overall impression was favorable, but his recollections were too fuzzy to be of much help.

When the topic of legal issues came up, the pastor's attention snapped back to the present. The couple described in detail how easy it was each week to pick of their child—too easy, as a matter of fact. Apparently no effort was being made to verify family members at the point of drop off or at the time of departure. The pastor did recall sending some information about related legal matters to his ministry directors, but what, if any, follow-through may have occurred was unknown to him.

His overall impression was that the couple respected the children's ministry director and was willing to tolerate a period of growth and improvement. But just how long was uncertain. The meeting wrapped up on a positive note; he would be meeting with his director the next day.

But just how he was going to proceed was not clear to him. Changes how to take place—in his leadership and supervision of the staff, first and foremost.

1. What are the primary issues in this case study?
2. Looking back, what are some steps that should have taken place in the pastor's supervisory role of his staff member? Clarify who is responsible for each of the issues you listed in question 1.
3. What specific plan or approach do you recommend as the pastor prepares for his meeting with his staff member the next day? What emotional tone do you recommend given the information presented in the case study?

12
PROTECTING THROUGH RISK MANAGEMENT
Greg Lawson

Larry had been the senior pastor of his rural church for over ten years, but his upcoming appointment was a first for him—a meeting with a young couple threatening legal action relating to an incident in the church nursery during worship two days ago. His church was used to handling problems in simple ways and had never given much thought to concerns like incorporation, arbitration, and other legal matters. He had to admit his blood ran cold when he first heard their complaint. He was determined to listen carefully to what they had to say, but beyond that, he was at a loss for a plan of action.

The apostle Paul warned Timothy regarding unique challenges that disciples of Christ would confront in the last days: "Difficult times will come in the last days. For people will be lovers of self, lovers of money, boastful, proud, blasphemers, disobedient to parents, ungrateful, unholy, unloving, irreconcilable, slanderers, without self-control, brutal, without love for what is good, traitors, reckless, conceited, lovers of pleasure rather than lovers of God, holding to the form of godliness but denying its power. Avoid these people!" (2 Timothy 3:1–5). While Christ-followers must reject the sins mentioned by the apostle, it is imperative that pastors know how to address the challenges presented by ministry in our contemporary culture. Ministry involves difficulty. It can be tough, and it remains a challenge even in the best of circumstances. Both biblically and historically, ministry has taken place in changing societal and cultural contexts. Paul Wegner indicates, "shifts in marriage and family have taken place over the past fifty years."[159] If the Lord Jesus Christ delays His return for another fifty years, it is inevitable that additional changes take place. The purpose of this chapter is not to provide legal counsel but to introduce the reader to key issues related to risk management in a church or nonprofit environment. Competent legal counsel licensed to practice law in the appropriate jurisdiction should be consulted.

Christ-followers understand that government is ordained by God as a divine institution. Just as God ordained the institutions of church and family, He ordained government. In Romans 13, the apostle Paul makes it clear that believers are to be in subjection to the governing authorities, and no authority exists apart from the sovereignty of God. Romans 13:1 states, "Everyone must submit to the governing authorities, for there is no authority except from God, and those that exist are instituted by God." A proper understanding of legal issues and risk management means that even when Christ-followers disagree with the government or legal decisions, it must be acknowledged that government remains a divinely ordained institution. Christian attorney and leader in the Peacemaker movement, Ken Sande, warns the church about the difficult issues related to ministry in a contemporary context. Addressing similar challenges to those Paul warned Timothy about, Sande indicates that there are certain hard facts about the legal system, which need to be understood as foundational for a risk management strategy:

1. The church is not immune to being sued. The First Amendment provides only limited protection: it gives us the freedom to believe what we want, but it does not give the freedom to take any and all action that we want.
2. The doctrine of "charitable immunity" has been totally abandoned in most states and is of limited scope in others.
3. The legal climate in the United States has changed dramatically in the past few decades. Forty years ago, actions against the church were usually for reinstatement; today they generally involve tort actions seeking large sums of money.
4. American preoccupation with individualism, a diminished respect for authority, and the acceptance of relative morality have infiltrated the church. As a result, many people, including Christians, have a general antagonism toward concepts of accountability, responsibility, and discipline.
5. A church can be sued for virtually any reason, even if in reality it has done nothing wrong or illegal. Once an action is filed against it, the church will be compelled to defend itself or lose by default judgment.
6. It often costs plaintiffs little money to sue a church. Many, if not most, cases against churches are taken by attorneys on a "contingency fee" basis, meaning that the plaintiff pays no attorney fees unless he or she wins the case.
7. The direct legal cost of defending against a lawsuit is costly and will run into thousands of dollars.
8. Awards for actual damages can easily exceed $100,000 and $1,000,000 awards have become commonplace. Punitive damages awards can be even higher and may be awarded when an intentional act caused an injury or when extreme carelessness contributed to it.

9. Lawsuits also cause major disruptions to a church and usually demand a great deal of time, energy, and attention from key leaders, thus taking them away from important ministry responsibilities. Lawsuits can also attract damaging publicity and even divide a congregation when members take sides or disagree as to how the suit is being handled.
10. Insurance will not necessarily cover all of the costs and damages that may be imposed upon a church.
11. Sande concludes by saying that it is not good enough to do things so well that you will merely prevail in a lawsuit; you must do them so well that you will prevent lawsuits from ever being filed.[160]

Even the most faithful ministers and ministries of the gospel will never be able to be removed completely from all risks in ministry. James Cobble and Richard Hammar provide appropriate advice: "Following Jesus includes risk, both personally and corporately. Risk taking, however, is only half of the story. Caring and thoughtful service to God is also manifested in avoiding certain risks and attempting to reduce others."[161] With this in mind, it is important to remember the words of Jesus in Matthew 10:16: "Look, I am sending you out like sheep among wolves. Therefore be as shrewd as serpents and as harmless as doves." God's wisdom serves as a necessary foundation to address risk management. The purpose of this chapter is to assist the minister in reducing and eliminating risk in ministry as well as following the instruction of Jesus to be wise and harmless even when ministry takes place in difficult circumstances. Bob Welch indicates, "Risk management is the scheme the prudent administrator takes to foresee dangers in the environment of the church or organization and the actions taken to prevent them or address the consequences in case they occur."[162] The following areas addressed in this chapter should be considered in the development of a comprehensive risk management strategy.

Alternatives to Litigation

Observers of the American legal system could determine that if the legal system isn't completely broken then it may be on life support. Multiple millions of lawsuits are filed in the United States each year. While some plaintiffs and attorneys have strong legal grounds for filing a lawsuit, many other lawsuits are frivolous in nature. As indicated by Sande and other legal experts, no longer is the church immune from being sued. While a church or Christian organization may have no option other than having to defend a lawsuit, every effort should be made to investigate and ultimately implement alternatives to litigation.

The question of whether or not to go to court should require a great deal of soul searching on the part of the believer. Buzzard examines four principles that will help Christians determine whether or not to assert their legal rights. They are:

1. What are your motives? Why you do something should be considered on an equal plane with what you do. Often your participation in the legal process will depend upon an objective and sincere assessment of your purpose or underlying motive.
2. Do your responsibilities or your positions of authority cause you to assert rights on behalf of people you may be accountable to? In

some cases, you may be expected to go to bat for someone who has entrusted you with certain duties–your church, your employee, your local government.

3. On what law are you relying? Do you want to assert your legal rights because you feel justified by Scripture, by culture, or by legislation? A comparison of God's character with man's laws should help you decide.
4. What responsibilities to others are involved? When you are the defendant in a legal case or when you are being sued, you should consider your obligations to your family and as steward over the property God has entrusted to you (1 Timothy 5:8).[163]

In addition to the strong questions raised by Buzzard, Bill Caldwell examined critical issues to be considered when a church may have to go to court. He writes that there are "times when the church may be required to go to court to resolve the problem which exists. There are several considerations the church must make when this happens."[164] The considerations are:

1. Stewardship–What is the responsibility of the church from a stewardship standpoint? The church must analyze the situation from the perspective of the wise and proper use of its resources.
2. Safety–The responsibility of the church to provide adequate safety precautions is sometimes overlooked and may result in a court case. The church must not hide behind any spiritual excuse when its negligence concerning the safety of its members and guests is involved.
3. Fraud–In the case of a company that has demonstrated outright fraud, the case may have to be settled in court. The church may have

a responsibility to keep it from happening to others who might be treated in a similar manner.

4. Public relations–Going to court should always be the last resort. It will be embarrassing and difficult and may have a negative effect on the image of the church in the community.[165]

Apostle Paul's Legal Advice

While the questions and issues related to risk management are of the utmost importance, to better understand alternatives to litigation, pastors should develop an understanding of 1 Corinthians 6. In this chapter, Paul instructs the church at Corinth that if a legal issue arises among believers, the dispute must not be taken to unbelievers to resolve, but rather wise believers should resolve the dispute. Paul presents the argument that a believer is better off being cheated or wronged than prevailing in a lawsuit against a fellow believer with the decision being made by non-believers or believers. With this biblical admonition in mind, it becomes important to examine alternatives to litigation. These alternatives must always be based on biblical principles. J. Warren Kniskern addresses the goal of alternatives to litigation. He writes, "The primary goal of conflict resolution among Christians is to promote forgiveness and reconciliation between those who formerly loved each other but are now, unfortunately, divided."[166] Both mediation and arbitration provide significant alternatives to litigation, which can be implemented within a biblical framework.

Mediation functions as a process where one or more impartial people provide counsel to help people resolve a matter in conflict or dispute.

It should be noted that the process of mediation can take place from either a Christian or non-Christian perspective. When the parties desire Christian mediation, the truth of Scripture becomes the foundation for decision-making. With the Bible as the standard, the primary objective of Christian mediation is God being honored and glorified in the process. If the parties to the conflict desire that God is glorified in the process, then the Holy Spirit may work in the lives of the believers to accomplish what they could never accomplish on their own. Godly counsel should be considered but the parties to the dispute are ultimately responsible for resolving their differences. Mediation is normally voluntary in nature and not legally binding. Reconciliation that honors God is always a priority of Christian mediation. The glory of God and the reconciliation of believers remains the key focus of each of the Christian alternatives to litigation.

While an arbitration process can accomplish the same objectives as mediation, such as reconciliation and glorifying God, a higher legal standard is involved. In mediation, the parties come together and decide the outcome of the conflict. In arbitration you give up this approach and designated arbiters make the decision. Arbitration normally comes about as a result of a contractual obligation. Since a contract is involved, absent fraud or a violation of public policy, the courts generally uphold an arbitration decision. Legal obligations become a primary focus of the arbitration process. Parties to arbitration may have a right to have an attorney present. As a result of the arbitration contract, the parties are unable to appeal the decision to a court of law unless fraud is involved. Arbitration decisions become binding upon the parties and enforceable by the court system. As a legal process, arbitration can save time and economic resources. With Christian arbitration as the focus, the objective remains to establish the truth of Scripture and glorify God in the process.

Christian organizations and nonprofits should consider arbitration, particularly in dealing with employee related issues. An arbitration clause needs to become a part of ministry-related employment contracts. Churches, Christian schools, and Christian nonprofits can benefit from including an arbitration clause. This means that if an issue arises between the organization and the employee, the matter would be resolved through arbitration and not through a costly and drawn-out court process. If yearly employment contracts are the norm, then the employee should be asked to sign the arbitration agreement on a yearly basis.

Also, a church should consider providing an arbitration clause consistent with 1 Corinthians 6 as part of a requirement for church membership. The arbitration clause could be included as a part of a formal application for church membership. (Role of church membership and risk management is discussed in the next section of this chapter). When the prospective member signs the arbitration statement, he or she agrees in advance to not sue other church members or the church as a legal entity based on the principles found in 1 Corinthians 6. When a conflict arises, the issues should be resolved based on the foundation of the Word of God. Churches have both the freedom and obligation to decide whom the arbitrators will be in advance. An example would be arbitrators approved by Peacemaker Ministries. No matter who is selected, the arbitrators should have a high level of Christian character and display godly wisdom. As previously noted, these agreements are normally upheld by the courts, based on neutral principles of contract law.

Recite and rehearse

What is the potential damage when a congregation refuses to follow the biblical guidelines in 1 Corinthians 6? To what extent should we legally protect our "rights" as Christians? Is the ministry of the Holy Spirit hindered in the life of a believer when the believer refuses to deal with conflict biblically?

Church Membership and Risk Management

As a member of a seminary faculty, local church lead pastor, and licensed attorney, I view our eroding culture from a multifaceted perspective. It is easy to look at the state of our country and be discouraged, but all hope is not lost. First and foremost, we must acknowledge that God remains sovereign. He rules and reigns and is still in the business of changing lives. Furthermore, the Bible, God's Word, remains true and is just as applicable to our culture as it was to each previous generation. The rapidly developing changes in American society have not taken God by surprise. Using the Bible as the standard, we can prepare to engage our culture. As previously stated, Jesus instructed His disciples to be "shrewd as serpents and harmless as doves" (Matthew 10:16). In order to do so, pastors of local church congregations must proactively address the issues we currently face or may be forced to confront in the future. The following foundational principles are key:

- The Bible is inerrant and infallible and the church's standard for faith and practice. Anything less is a foundation of sinking sand.
- We must be ready to follow Peter and the other apostles' declaration found in Acts 5:29: "We must obey God rather than men."

Assuming these foundational principles are in place, church leaders should address the paramount issue of church membership. Leeman indicates that the local church is sometimes treated "like a club to join—or not."[167] A tight membership policy minimizes some of the legal challenges churches could face in the future. The covenant nature of church membership must be emphasized, but there should also be recognition of the contractual obligations between the local church and its members. From a risk management perspective, the strongest approach to church membership includes a yearly commitment to the covenant and contractual obligations inherent in church membership. With this approach each church member recommits each year to the acceptance of the church's statement of faith, constitution, bylaws, and administrative policies. Members are asked to agree in writing to these principles based on the legal concept of informed consent. Simply stated, informed consent takes place when information is presented and an adult, normally by a signature, acknowledges agreement to the statements or information presented. It remains important that each of the written documents involved in church membership be established based on a biblical foundation and provide a clear and easy-to-understand explanation of the key provisions. The concept of informed consent cannot take place unless an understanding takes place regarding the matter being considered.

A church's statement of faith, constitution, and bylaws must include the biblical and theological foundation for doctrine and living the Christian life. These documents are essential components of a comprehensive risk-management strategy. It should be noted that most churches have unique administrative structures and a distinct ecclesiology. In some churches it is difficult to amend or make changes to a church's constitution or bylaws. A simpler solution may be to adopt policies that address these critical issues. Relevant topics that church bylaws or policies should address related to risk management include, but are not limited to, marriage, human sexuality, arbitration, church discipline, and use of facilities.

The human sexuality policy must have a biblical foundation with a focus on God's gift of sexuality. While the positive nature of the biblical concept of sexuality is emphasized, the rationale for prohibited sexual activity must also be examined. This includes multiple issues such as pornography, homosexuality, and gender identity issues. Issues of the mind and heart related to sexuality must not be neglected. With the biblical standard being clearly stated, the human sexuality statement should remain positive, adequately explaining the biblical concept of human sexuality.

An examination of church discipline as a risk-management issue is addressed later in this chapter. As it relates to church membership, a church discipline statement needs to be a part of the church membership process. Regarding a church discipline statement, members agree in advance that if a church discipline issue should arise, they will voluntarily consent to the process of church discipline. Church members need to be aware that the foundation of church discipline is based on the holiness of God, purity of His church, and restoration of the believer.

The use of church facilities and all ministries related to the church need to be restricted to activities consistent with the church's statement of faith, constitution, bylaws, and policy statements. Policies need to be developed and implemented that protect both the pastor and church from having to perform and support weddings inconsistent with the church's statement of faith. While evangelism and outreach are important components of the mission of the church, the church as a legal entity may find it necessary to limit the leasing or renting of church facilities to the general public. Church leaders need godly wisdom to address the unique challenges posed by the contemporary culture. Even with the possible restriction of the use of church facilities, Christ followers should always be challenged to fulfill the Great Commission by taking the gospel outside the church facilities. Brad Dacus suggests the following policies related to marriage and the use of premises for weddings:

Clergy Policies on Marriage

1. Only duly ordained clergy shall officiate at marriage ceremonies conducted on church property.
2. Clergy employed by the church shall be subject to dismissal and/or loss of ordination for officiating a marriage ceremony inconsistent with the definition of marriage in the statement of faith.

Applicants for Marriage

1. Applicants wishing to have a ceremony performed by a member of the clergy employed by the church or to use the church facilities for a ceremony must be entering into a marriage within the definition of marriage in the statement of faith.
2. Applicants shall receive __ hours of required premarital counseling by

clergy or counselors employed by the church or other persons who, in the sole opinion of the pastoral staff of the church, have appropriate training, experience, and spiritual understanding to provide such counseling.

Use of Premises for Weddings

1. Any marriage performed on church premises shall be officiated by a member of the clergy employed by or approved by this church.
2. Clergy officiating marriage ceremonies on church premises, whether or not employed by the church, shall affirm their agreement with the statement of faith and shall conduct themselves in a manner that is consistent therewith.
3. The clergy assigned by the church to implement the procedures contained in this marriage policy may, in the minister's sole discretion, decline to make church facilities available for, and/or decline to officiate at, a ceremony when, in the pastor's judgment, there are significant concerns that one or both of the applicants may not be qualified to enter into the sacred bond of marriage for doctrinal, moral, or legal reasons.[168]

Dacus correctly asserts that at times it becomes appropriate to have an overlap between a church's bylaws and adopted policy statements.[169] He also draws a critical distinction between church bylaws and policy statements, "Policy statements apply to a wider audience than church bylaws and can usually be changed more quickly; thus additional issues are addressed in this format."[170] It is necessary to understand the importance of both bylaws and policy statements as well as the critical distinctions.

A strong biblical witness must take place through each believer and ministry of the church consistent with Jesus' instructions in Matthew 5:16: "In the same way, let your light so shine before men, so that they may see your good works and give glory to your Father in heaven." Even if a church is not ready to move to signing a yearly recommitment covenant for ongoing membership in the church, leadership should consider adopting the key provisions discussed in this section to mitigate the risks of current cultural challenges.

Reflect and react

How specific should you be in dealing with contemporary social issues in a church's constitution, bylaws, or policy and procedures? How do you determine which social issues are a primary or secondary issue? What about the argument sometimes made that Christ followers should only be concerned about sharing the gospel?

Contract Law

A contract involves a promise or set of promises performed according to mutual agreement and if breached violates a duty recognized by law. It remains important for ministers to make sure they do not become personally liable for a contract they sign involving a church or ministry. According to Cobble and Hammar, pastors generally will not be personally liable if the following conditions are met:

1. The contract was authorized by appropriate church action in accordance with the church's governing documents.
2. The pastor is authorized to sign the contract on the basis of either the church's governing documents or by action of the church board.
3. The identity of the employing church is disclosed in the contract.
4. The pastor signs in a representative capacity, such as "Pastor John Smith, President" or "Pastor John Smith, authorized agent."[171]

As a matter of practical wisdom, a pastor should refrain from signing contracts related to the church unless it is absolutely essential. If it's absolutely necessary for the pastor to sign the contract, he must be authorized to sign the contract and sign only in a representative capacity.

Risk Management and Church Discipline

Church discipline is a biblical concept. For a thorough discussion of the biblical and theological foundation of church discipline see Chapter 4. It is absolutely essential because of the following key reasons: the holiness of God, purity of His church, and the restoration of the believer. An objective of church discipline remains to bring repentance and restoration to the person who has sinned. Leeman states that "many texts in the New Testament point to the practice of church discipline."[172] This list is not exhaustive but includes: Matthew 18:15–17, Galatians 6:1–10, 1 Timothy 5:19–22, 1 Corinthians 5, and Acts 5:1–11. An educational process should take place in a church regarding issues related to church discipline.

A pastor needs to understand the legal issues to be addressed, regarding the issue of church discipline. This is another instance where the admonition of Jesus found in Matthew 10:16 must be followed, which says, "Behold I send you out as sheep in the midst of wolves. Therefore, be wise as serpents and harmless as doves." If a church is going to engage in church discipline, it becomes imperative that the exact process be specifically outlined in the churches by-laws and/or governing documents. There should never be a question about how this process takes place. Although the vast majority of Baptist churches never require a formal written application for membership, churches that use these applications are on a stronger legal foundation, especially if they require prospective members to sign a statement indicating that they have read and understand the church's governing documents and understand that the church practices church discipline if necessary. This reinforces the legal concept of informed consent because the member is made aware that church discipline is practiced and consents to acceptance of this issue. To reinforce this process from a legal perspective, the membership application also should state that all disputes will be mediated according to the principles of Christian conciliation.

Once the church discipline process begins, it is essential that the leadership involved reduce the risk of defamation by limiting both oral and written statements that could lead to a future cause of action. Appropriate information must be provided in the governing documents regarding who will be involved in the disciplinary process, particularly in the advance stages of church discipline. Also, these documents should indicate to what extent the person undergoing discipline can be involved in the life of the church while the disciplinary process takes place. This might include whether or not the person involved can participate in regular church activities and communion. Other matters of concern to be addressed relate to how the church handles situations where the person refuses to submit to church discipline and what happens if the member attempts to join a new church or engage in another ministry without submitting to church discipline. Also, information should be provided as to how the church corporately and individual members should relate to the person undergoing discipline. While not establishing precedent in all jurisdictions, it should be noted that the Oklahoma Supreme Court case of *Guinn v. The Church of Christ of Collinsville* had the effect, according to Wayne House, to determine that the Church of Christ could not "legally discipline its members according to the Scriptures."[173] In view of the changing nature of court decisions and the establishment of legal precedent, it is always important to consult a competent local attorney to help determine the law in the appropriate jurisdiction.

Throughout this process it is important to remember the reasons for church discipline, such as the holiness of God, the purity of His church and the restoration of the believer. Christ followers should pray that repentance and restoration take place in the life of the believer undergoing church discipline and for God to be glorified in the process. When a person functions in a leadership role related to church discipline, it should be approached in a spirit of humility, remembering the admonition of Galatians 6:1: "Brethren, if a man is overtaken in any trespass, you who are spiritual restore such a one in a spirit of gentleness, considering yourself lest you also be tempted." Humility and a proper understanding of God's grace should be foundational in the life of any leader who provides assistance for anyone undergoing church discipline.

Research and create

How do you determine how much information to provide a congregation in a church discipline matter? Would you give a different response if the person is in a position of leadership in the church? Is there a "statute of limitations" on when a situation occurs and church discipline takes place?

Reducing the Risk of Defamation

The Bible gives clear instruction concerning the use and abuse of the tongue. Proverbs 10:19 states, "When there are many words, sin is unavoidable, but the one who controls his lips is wise" (HCSB). James 1:19–20 says, "My dearly loved brothers, understand this: Everyone must be quick to hear, slow to speak, and slow to anger, for man's anger does not accomplish God's righteousness" (HCSB). James 3:8 states, "but no man can tame the tongue. It is a restless evil, full of deadly poison" (HCSB). Failure to tame the tongue not only has spiritual but potential legal ramifications as well.

A pastor can find himself in trouble by making certain oral (referred to as *slander*) or written statements (referred to as *libel*). The legal concept is known as *defamation*. Defamation consists of the following elements:

1. Oral or written statements about another person,
2. that are false,
3. that are "published" (that is, communicated to a sufficient number of other persons to affect the other person's reputation), and
4. that injure the other person's reputation.[174]

Hammer and Cobble provide two illustrations where the court found defamation in a religious context: "A minister publicly stated that a member of his congregation had a vile spirit and utter disrespect for leadership and declared that another member had associated himself with a pastor who under the role of a minister of Jesus, is one of Satan's choicest tools."[175] Also, "A Roman Catholic Archbishop was found guilty of defaming a priest by publicly referring to him as an 'irresponsible and insane' person who was 'morally blind' and 'disobedient to the laws of the church.' "[176] In each of these cases there would have been a better outcome if the biblical admonition to tame the tongue was followed.

There are legal defenses to defamation. The primary defense is "truth," which means that the defendant has to prove the truth of the statement. It must be noted, however, that even if the statement is true, the defendant may be liable for another tort (civil wrong or action), which is the invasion of the right to privacy. This could take place in a ministry context though a public disclosure of private facts about a person. Truth is not a defense to the tort of the public disclosure of private facts. The pastor may not have to worry about these torts if he takes to heart Ephesians 4:29, which says, "No foul language is to come from your mouth, but only what is good for building up someone in need, so that it gives grace to those who hear" (HCSB). While the truth must be spoken in love, every effort should be made to reduce or eliminate words defamatory in nature.

Incorporation

An ongoing issue faced by many churches is whether or not to incorporate. A corporation is a legal entity in and of itself. In other words, it is a legal entity separate and distinct from the members or shareholders who formed the corporation. If a church is not incorporated, it is known as an unincorporated association, which means, in theory, that each member could become legally responsible for the actions and liabilities of the church or other members of the congregation who act representing the church.

There are several advantages of incorporation. The primary advantage relates to the issue of limited liability. This means that there is a shield or protection of the personal assets of individual members of the corporation. While this point alone may be a sufficient ground to incorporate, it must be noted that, even with incorporation, individual church members may be liable for negligent deeds or financially liable for their individual actions.

Opponents to incorporation assert that incorporation allows the state to become involved in the internal affairs of the church, even related to biblical and theological issues. At this point there is no evidence to validate this claim. In some states an incorporated church may have to file an annual form to report that the corporation is still in existence. Other arguments against incorporation include the time and costs involved in both setting up and maintaining a corporation. In most states, there is not a legal requirement that mandates you have to have an attorney incorporate the church (but even if an attorney is used, the cost should still be minimal).

In many states the incorporation process takes place through the Secretary of State's office. Hopkins and Middlebrook assert, "It is rare for a state to require the filing of a constitution or a set of bylaws as part of the process of forming the organization."[177] Incorporators generally file Articles of Incorporation with the official governmental office. For example, in North Carolina, Articles of Incorporation include the following:

1. Corporate name.
2. Designation as a Charitable or Religious Corporation.
3. Designation of the Registered Office and Agent.
4. Incorporator: The name and address of each incorporator must be indicated.
5. Members: Members are not required in NC, but if a corporation is going to have members it must be stated in the Articles.
6. Provisions for Distribution of assets.
7. Designation of a Principal Office.[178]

Once the Articles of Incorporation have been approved by the Secretary of State's office, the church needs to schedule an organizational meeting. A temporary moderator should be selected, one who serves until a moderator can be elected for the newly formed incorporated church. Careful notes of the meeting should be kept by a person appointed by the moderator until a church clerk or other officers are selected. The filed copy of the Articles of Incorporation can then be adopted.

Another important issue to deal with is the election of the directors of the new corporation. The directors can be the original incorporators or the deacons, elders, trustees, or whomever the church may designate. Next, the church should approve the constitution and bylaws, vote to receive the members from the previous unincorporated association church, and elect whatever officers, teachers, and committees that have been previously functioning. Next, bank accounts should be opened under the new corporate name, and all legal documents, such as deeds and loans, should be changed to include the new name. Once all of the assets and liabilities of the unincorporated association are transferred to the incorporated church, then it is proper to make a motion to dissolve the unincorporated association. At this point, the church can legally function as an incorporated church.[179] It must be noted that the process of incorporating a church may vary from state to state, so it may be necessary to consult a local attorney to assist in the process.

Gifts, Wills, and Estates

A pastor should have a basic understanding of gifts, wills, and estate planning. The establishment of a legally enforceable will is normally a simple process, as long as the person has the mental ability and intent to establish a will. With limited exceptions, wills have to be in writing. If a person dies without making a will, he is said to have died intestate. In this case, the state has a clearly defined legal procedure that functions as a will and determines how the assets and liabilities are to be divided.[180]

While gifts, wills, and estates can contribute greatly to the financial foundation for a ministry, the pastor has to reduce the risk of undue influence. The pastor crosses a moral, ethical, and legal line when he exercises undue influence to the point of control over the mind of another or where the control or persuasion destroys the ability of the person to make a clear, uninhibited decision.[181] Undue influence can be proven from the unique situation and circumstances surrounding a gift.[182] The following situation should be analyzed to determine if undue influence has taken place:

1. Whether the gift was the product of hasty action.
2. Whether the gift was concealed from others.
3. Whether the person or organization benefited by the gift was active in securing it.
4. Whether the gift was consistent or inconsistent with prior declarations and planning of the donor.
5. Whether the gift was reasonable rather than unnatural in view of the donor's circumstances, attitudes, and family.
6. The donor's age, physical condition, and mental health.
7. Whether a confidential relationship existed between the donor and the recipient of the gift.
8. Whether the donor has independent advice.
9. Undue influence must normally be proven by clear and convincing evidence, which is a much higher legal standard than a preponderance of the evidence.[183]

While it is illegal, immoral, and unethical for a pastor to exert undue influence over a person making a gift, pastors have a mandate to educate the flock regarding the principles of biblical stewardship. This involves much more than basic teaching on the importance of faithful giving and tithing. Through estate planning a Christ follower can continue to impact the kingdom of God, long after he or she has died. The ultimate disposition of assets should be seen as one of the most important decisions that a person makes during his or her lifetime.

Privileged Clergy Communication

Privileged clergy communication remains one area of protection that pastors have enjoyed for many years. The roots of this privilege go back to the time of the church fathers and have developed over a period of several hundred years as part of the English common law.[184] Hammar indicates, "Every state has a law making certain communications to clergy 'privileged.' This generally means that neither the minister nor the 'penitent' can be forced to testify in court (or in a deposition or certain other legal proceedings) about the contents of the communication."[185] Most state statutes require an expectation of privacy between the parties involved with the clergy, relating to the person or persons in a professional capacity.

One of the issues in the area of privileged communication is the question of who may assert the privilege. Since this privilege exists as a rule of evidence, only the person who made the communication and the pastor to whom it was made may claim the privilege.[186] If an independent third party overhears or becomes a part of the confidential communication, the privilege may be declared to be null and void. Because of this possibility, a pastor should establish privacy safeguards and conduct counseling in a professional environment.

One key area where the concept of the privileged clergy communication does not apply is in the mandatory reporting of child abuse. Pastors are normally mandatory reporters of child abuse. The protection of children should always be a priority for both the church and pastor. The next section of this chapter addresses the importance of protecting the children.

Protecting the Children

Since September 11, 2001, the United States of America has been engaged in an all-out war against terrorism. On a different front, a battle has been raging in many of the churches and places of worship across America. The battle in the "church war" involves much more than land or physical resources. It is a direct challenge to the integrity of the church. If the pastors fail to vigorously confront this issue, there will be no winners, only losers. At stake is one the most valuable assets any society or culture has to offer. At issue is the "child" and his or her survival in the institutional church. This war is winnable but requires an aggressive course of action on the part of every pastor and congregation.

In recent years international attention has been focused on the sexual abuse crisis facing the Catholic Church. Allegations have been made against a large number of priests related to the sexual molestation of numerous children. Glover asserts that "there are no 'absolute' statistics on the number of children molested every day in the United States, Canada, or any other country."[187] While it is not possible to determine the exact number of children harmed, it is an alarming crisis. In many of these cases, it appears that the supervisors often looked the other way and either covered up or failed to deal with the allegations. This growing problem and the media scrutiny that followed became so severe that leaders of the Catholic Church had national and international meetings to deal with this ongoing crisis. Anyone who has been following this difficult issue soon realizes that this is not just a "Catholic" issue. Million dollar judgments have been established against Baptists and other Christian denominations and independent churches as well.

Addressing the child sexual abuse issue in Southern Baptist churches, a noted expert remarked that most churches aren't doing anything to "minimize the risk of a minor being sexually touched, abused, or otherwise physically injured while involved in child care, day care, or church-related activities."[188] Also, "only a minority of churches have studied the issue, approved policies and procedures to minimize risk and followed through to implement the protective policies and when you consider that a simple incident of child molestation can devastate a church, one must question why so few churches have dealt with the subject."[189] The protection of children remains an essential issue that every church and religious organization must confront.

So few Southern Baptist churches have addressed these issues because of the mistaken belief that child sexual abuse is something they will never face or that no one related to their congregations could stoop to such depths of sin and depravity. Hammer, Klipowicz, and Cobble in their manual, *Reducing the Risk of Child Sexual Abuse in Your Church*, indicate that the typical stereotype of molesters being strangers wearing trench coats or dirty old men is not accurate.[190] While no one profile fits all types of abusers, Hammar and his coauthors assert that the following information should be considered:

1. Over eighty percent of the time the abuser is someone known to the victim.
2. Most abuses take place within the context of an ongoing relationship.
3. The usual offender is between the ages of twenty and thirty.
4. Twenty percent of sex offenders begin their activity before the ages of eighteen.
5. Child abusers often are married and have children.[191]

While it is uncomfortable to think about, Hammar reports that the most likely assailants include Sunday school teachers, nursery or preschool workers, teachers in a church-operated school, camp counselors, clergy, and concerned adults who volunteer in the transportation ministry of the church.[192]

The ongoing problem related to child sexual abuse in the church has led many churches and denominational entities to suggest a formal application process for both paid staff and volunteer workers. The Baptist State Convention of North Carolina in the *Church Policy Manual Guidebook* suggest that the application and accompanying process should include the following information:

1. Personal Information: Name (and prior names), address, prior addresses.
2. Ministry Information: Areas of interest, gifts, talents, etc. The applicant should indicate their prior church history and ministry involvement, perhaps a five-year history.
3. References: References should be required for paid staff positions, and perhaps for volunteers who have been in the community for less than five years. References should be from persons unrelated to the applicant, and emphasis should be put on references who have had some knowledge of the applicant's work with preschoolers, children, and teens.
4. Procedures: The packet should include a statement of church policy concerning the care and guidelines for ministering to preschoolers, children, and teens.
5. Statement: A place for volunteers and staff to sign a document stating that they have read the procedures and agree to observe the

safeguards.

6. Reference and background checks must take place.[193]

For a church to protect itself against a charge of negligent hiring, particularly as it relates to a paid staff member, the following seven key policies in the screening process should be considered:

1. Job description and qualifications
2. An application process
3. References which are checked
4. Criminal and other background checks
5. Thorough interview process
6. Final approval authority
7. Probationary employment–related to non-ministerial staff[194]

Churches must also become aware of another major issue in the area of protecting children and youth, which comes under the general heading of negligent supervision. This involves a failure to exercise reasonable care in the supervision of church workers and church activities.[195] The experts have stressed that the following ideas need to be implemented in order to reduce the risk of negligent supervision:

1. Use a team approach, which is known as the two-adult rule. This rule says that two adult supervisors should be present during any church activity.
2. Obtain parental permission before children are involved in church sponsored programs or activities.
3. Discuss suspicious behavior immediately.

4. Discuss potential criminal sanctions with youth workers.
5. Install windows on classroom doors.
6. Provide adequate personnel.
7. Use extra care and supervision with overnight activities.
8. Use a church nursery identification procedure.
9. Adopt an appropriate children and youth worker's policy statement.[196]

Other considerations involve avoiding ultra-hazardous activities. If extra precautions in regard to supervision, planning, training, and equipment are considered, then activities such as boating, swimming, and hayrides may be enjoyed. Also, church leadership should mandate that appropriate permission slips and release forms be utilized. Ken Sande writes regarding this important issue:

1. A permission slip is a form parents or guardians sign to give permission for a child to participate in a particular activity. Although it is not a complete release from liability, it can help to reduce liability by assuring that the parent or guardian is aware of the child's activities that present unusual hazards. The permission slip should specifically describe these hazards and indicate that the parent is aware of them and consents to the child's participation in the activity anyway.
2. A medical release slip is a form parents or guardians sign to allow others to authorize medical treatment for a child. Such slips should be used on any activities that are away from home where a caretaker may have to deal with a medical problem in the parent's absence.
3. Many states place different limitations on the use of permission slips and release forms, so you should consult with a local attorney to determine what would be acceptable in your state.[197]

With regard to medical release statements, information must be provided regarding the unique medical needs of a child, such as food or other allergies. In all of these areas, the health, safety, and protection of the children and youth should be the primary objective.

Davidson and Lawson place an emphasis on the importance of expert opinions to review safety and security policies, as well as evaluate insurance requirements with regard to protecting the children. Plans need to be updated and reviewed on a scheduled basis. The following practical areas should be evaluated by church leadership:

- Specific check-in and check-out procedures required for all children attending any program offered at the church. These procedures must be followed for every child in attendance, including the children of any staff or employees.
- Handbooks in place with detailed guidelines and procedures for parents, staff, and volunteers that include comprehensive emergency plans for fire, tornado, earthquake, lock down, as well as disciple, child restroom guidelines, and a strategy to handle reports of child abuse.
- The church must meet the state fire codes, and the building must be inspected by the fire marshal on a regular basis. Place emergency exit instructions in each classroom, and schedule maintenance tests for fire and carbon monoxide alarms.
- Playground equipment should be maintained with scheduled maintenance. These areas need to be located within a fenced area and provide protective material for the fall zones around equipment.
- A first aid kit should be available for each classroom. Workers should be trained in first aid and CPR.
- Equipment and furniture maintained in good condition and have a

schedule for regular maintenance.

- Infant classrooms should have fire-safe cribs that meet Consumer Product Safety guidelines. All cribs should be positioned away from blinds and cords. See the Consumer Product Safety Commission website (http://www.cpsc.gov) for updated guidelines.
- Age-appropriate toys and furniture should be in each classroom. The toys should be checked regularly for choking hazards and to ensure they are not broken. Each classroom should have antibacterial disinfectant provided, and all toys must be cleaned after each use.
- Changing tables must have safety straps and be stocked with wax paper, non-latex gloves, and antibacterial disinfectant.
- Avoid overnight activities unless absolutely necessary. Make sure that all precautions are taken into account and adequate supervision is maintained.
- Constantly monitor all areas where children and youth are involved. This includes restrooms.
- Cover all electrical outlets with safety plugs. There should be no cords hanging down from any appliances (such as TVs or CD players)–children could pull the appliance off of the surface by the cord.
- Maintain adequate lighting both inside and outside facilities as well as playground.
- Establish a zero tolerance policy for anyone who has abused a child.
- Develop a policy regarding restrictions of teenagers' involvement with children.[198]

Many churches and Christian schools have difficulty setting these types of plans in place. Church members and parents are comfortable in familiar surroundings and trust the people they have worshiped with for many years. They also want to be able to welcome newcomers and visitors with open arms. It is the responsibility of church leadership to see the big picture and protect all of their children by providing a safe and secure place to learn about the love of God and His Word. A key aspect of a Great Commission ministry involves passing the faith on to the next generation. Both the church and the family share a great responsibility to nurture, train, and protect its children and youth. No matter what it takes, every effort must be made to ensure that the protection of the children remains a central focus of the ministry of the church.[199]

Final Words of Encouragement

As contemporary society and culture evolves, the issue of risk management continues to remain a major ministry focus. Yes, ministry involves difficulty and remains a challenge even in the best of circumstances. Even in the midst of challenges, the good news is that the power of the gospel will always prevail. From a perspective of victory, each church must move toward the development and implementation of a comprehensive plan of risk management.

Respond to a case study

This is your friend. I'm now in my fifth year of ministry at Your Blessed Baptist Church in Pit, Alabama. Our growth has leveled off in the church, but it remains a blessing and honor to pastor this fellowship. Pit, Alabama, is an old-fashioned, family values kind of community. Yet, I can see that times are a changing. We see greater evidence of families in turmoil. Ongoing changes in family structure are inevitable. While we want to share God's gift of salvation and minister to everyone, I've often wondered how to address the issue if a couple whose lifestyle I biblically disagree with ask me to marry them? Our church facilities are normally open to anyone willing to pay a $100 fee and reserve the date on the church calendar.

1. Should we be proactive in addressing these issues?
2. What might need to change? Should our constitution and bylaws, policies and procedures be reviewed?
3. Could the church lose its tax-exempt status?

13

DESIGNING BUDGETS AND FINANCIAL REPORTS

Greg Lawson

It's hard to believe my name is on the church sign as pastor, Reverend Lonely Pasteur. Time flies when you're having fun. Six months have passed since becoming pastor at Your Blessed Baptist Church in Pit, Alabama. The church finances are interesting. The deacons informed me that I should only worry about the spiritual issues such as preaching and ministry. I'm convinced that the deacons are really unaware of what's happening as well. The church finances are handled by only one person. Now eighty years of age, Ms. Louise Benedict has been in charge of the church's finances for the past fifty years. Ms. Benedict is trusted by the church and a woman who can do it all. She educates the Finance Committee on what the line items should be in the budget. Ms. Benedict is a selfless servant. She hasn't taken a vacation in twenty years. Our beloved treasurer collects the money from the offering plates each Sunday, takes the money home, counts the money, then makes the deposit on Monday at our local bank. She is also faithful to pay all the bills, reconcile the bank statements, and manage all of the accounts. It is easier for the work to be performed at her home since she doesn't know how to use a computer.

Some members complain that they never receive an end-of-the-year charitable giving statement. Ms. Benedict believes that it is their job to keep up with their own personal giving. Also, our beloved treasurer is a conservative woman who tightly manages our spending. No spending takes place unless she believes it's for the good of the church. Ms. Benedict reminds members of what happened to the couple in Acts 5 that were killed over issues related to money. This appears to be Ms. Benedict's favorite Bible story and church members have learned to never question what she does. This is my first church to pastor. I don't know if this is the normal way for church finances to be handled. In my short six months of being pastor, I've learned not to question the wisdom of Ms. Benedict, especially if I want to get paid. Again, I'm seeking your counsel. Are there any changes in how the finances should be handled at Your Blessed Baptist Church? Should I accept what the deacons indicated and just mind my own business? Any constructive advice would be appreciated.

God is creator and worthy of worship and praise. While disregarded or ridiculed by the materialistic philosophy of the contemporary culture, in actuality God is the Creator who spoke everything into existence and owns everything. James writes in 1:16–17, "Don't be deceived, my dearly loved brothers. Every generous act and every perfect gift is from above, coming down from the Father of lights; with Him there is no variation or shadow cast by turning." The psalmist declared in Psalm 24:1, "The earth and everything in it, the world and its inhabitants, belong to the Lord; for He laid its foundation on the seas and established it on the rivers." With a proper perspective of God as Creator and owner of everything, it becomes necessary to understand God's perspective on issues related to possessions and finances.

It is estimated that as many as 2,350 verses in Scripture deal with money and possessions.[200] John MacArthur, addressing how important the issues of money and possessions are to God, writes, "Sixteen of Christ's thirty-eight parables speak about how people should handle earthly treasure. In fact, our Lord taught more about such stewardship (one out of every ten verses in the gospels) than about heaven and hell combined."[201] It is evident from the totality of Scripture related to finances that God desires His followers to understand this subject from His point of view. Issues related to finances comprise a major part of the spiritual growth necessary for the Christ follower to grow in disciple making and the sanctification process.

As money and material possessions reflect areas of spiritual growth and discipleship in a Christ follower's life, it must be acknowledged that money and possessions fulfill many objectives in God's economy. Tangible assets should be used to meet human needs and, in the process, give God glory. Money functions to finance God's earthly ministry through the lives of believers. God has promised to provide for His children, as stated in Philippians 4:19, "And my God will supply all your needs according to His riches in glory in Christ Jesus." While spiritual needs are always a primary focus in Scripture, many believers mistakenly believe that finances are not spiritual in nature. A proper understanding of the character and nature of God acknowledges God as both Creator and Provider. With this concept in mind, the believer can rely on God with the assurance that however God wills He always provides. This is one way God helps believers sense His direction for their lives. In the life of the believer, this may mean a need for increasing faith and reliance on God, not only as Savior but provider as well.

Central to God's plan of economy is a proper understanding of the biblical concept of stewardship. Since God is to be recognized as Creator, Owner, and Provider, Christ followers become stewards of God-given resources. What is *stewardship*? Ron Blue writes, "Stewardship is the use of God-given resources for the accomplishment of God-giving goals."[202] Blue goes on to add that "this view of stewardship acknowledges God's ownership over my possessions and His direction of my use of them."[203] As faithful stewards, Christ followers must display God given wisdom and discernment in dealing with finances. Roebert reminds his readers about God's provision and His expectation of stewardship in all areas of believers' lives, "He has given us health, strength, our time, our education, our financial resources, our specific talents and so much more. He expects us to use all wisely. He will reward us accordingly."[204] The concept of stewardship remains a critical area where many disciples of Christ may have to give an account regarding how financial issues were handled throughout life as the believer's life is evaluated at the judgment seat of Christ (2 Corinthians 5:10; 1 Corinthians 3:10–15). Based on the foundational concepts of stewardship and accountability, this chapter examines practical ways to handle God's money, budgets and financial reports, debt and ministry development, and tax issues for the pastor.

Recite and rehearse

Why does the Bible spend so much time on money and finances? How should a Christ follower look at finances differently than a nonbeliever? Do questions and concerns about finances always point back to heart issues? Select one Scripture passage related to this topic and commit it to memory.

Practical Ways to Handle God's Money

God is an advocate of order, not disorder. All issues related to finances in a local church or nonprofit ministry should be handled according to the apostle Paul's command in 1 Corinthians 14:40 related to the exercise of spiritual gifts: "But everything must be done decently and in order." Earlier in the same chapter (v. 33), Paul stated that "God is not a God of disorder but of peace." Biblical principles of stewardship and accountability must govern all areas of the financial ministry of the church or nonprofit organization.

Acknowledging that accountability is a biblical principle, and the concept of accountability runs throughout the Bible. Rollie Dimos reminds his readers, "In practical terms, without accountability, human nature tends to drive us to the dividing line between right and wrong, where we encounter the gray areas of life ... Accountability and transparency of financial operations aren't meant to constrain leaders; instead, they are meant to protect leaders and the reputations of their organizations."[205] A key illustration of financial accountability is found in 2 Corinthians 8 as the apostle Paul gives instruction regarding the collection for the Jerusalem Christians. Paul commends the generosity of the Macedonians while presenting the same challenge to the Corinthians. Jesus' example of a life of sacrificial giving is the standard for all believers and churches to follow.

In Paul's instructions for the administration of the collection in 2 Corinthians 8, he establishes principles of financial accountability, transparency, and responsibility. Titus appears to have a leadership role in overseeing at least part of the collection. Paul desired that those involved in this process be above reproach in dealing with this important ministry to the Jerusalem Christians. No one person was to handle the important ministry by himself, thus establishing principles of accountability, transparency, and responsibility. Paul addresses these issues in 2 Corinthians 8:20–21: "We are taking this precaution so no one can criticize us about this large sum administered by us. For we are making provision for what is right, not only before the Lord but also before men." Paul realized that God was the ultimate Judge, but it was important to be above reproach in dealings with financial matters of the church. With the same standard in mind, biblical principles of responsibility and accountability must be foundational in dealing with financial issues related to life and ministry. The following guidelines should be considered as ministers practically deal with finances in church and nonprofit organizations:

1. Guard your integrity and be above reproach when it comes to money. Exceed expectations and be an "open book" with regard to finances.
2. As a pastor, give careful attention to stewardship related issues but limit your direct contact with money. Allow trusted people to directly handle money. In other words, have a hands-off approach with regard to the direct handling of money.
3. Always follow the principle of two. One person should never be alone with money in any stage of the process. Establish separation of duties.
4. Avoid check-writing authority and, if possible, require two signatures on checks.
5. Make sure any expense you take is a legitimate and documented expense. Expenses should be approved in advance and authorized by a budget or other equivalent policies. Establish some kind of a purchase order system.
6. Never replace a legitimate business expense with a personal expenditure for the purpose of reimbursement. Also, never use a ministry

credit card for personal reasons. Again, make sure all expenses are authorized and approved by the appropriate person or entity.

7. Maintain accountability with someone on your leadership team or a person who works with finances in the administrative structure. In an environment where volunteers perform many of the financial functions, make an extra effort to maintain accountability with a church treasurer or chairperson of a financial related committee.
8. In dealing with finances, always establish a paper trail.
9. With regard to personal finances, develop an attitude of gratitude and never one of entitlement.
10. Pastors do not deserve nor should expect special treatment with regard to finances.
11. Review financial reports and documents in a timely manner.
12. Establish appropriate safety procedures and develop a pathway for online giving to receive contributions 24/7.
13. Inventory ministry-related assets.
14. Evaluate insurance needs on an ongoing basis.
15. Establish financial procedures to reduce the possibility of embezzlement and prevent fraud, waste, and abuse. It must be noted that transparency and accountability are key to address each of these areas.

While the previously stated guidelines are not exhaustive in nature, they provide key suggestions for consideration. As stewards of the finances God has provided, each minister has a biblical obligation to be a faithful model and, most of all, to be above reproach in every area related to finances.

Reflect and react

Discuss the importance of the principle of two as the concept relates to church finances. Explain the necessity of the separation of duties as applied to church finances. What guidelines should be established to reduce or eliminate the possibility of fraud, waste, and abuse?

Budgeting and Financial Reports

Pastors may struggle with the concept of budgeting. Possibly based on past negative experiences, many pastors see the budgetary process as something to be feared rather than a challenge to be embraced. Some pastors mistakenly believe budgets serve no other purpose than restricting salaries or limiting biblically-based ministry in the church.

A budget functions as an operational tool that establishes financial guidelines related to the allocation of resources within an organization or other legal entity. Budgets become an important element of a planning process. While a planning process can be directed toward short, intermediate, or long-term goals, the budgeting process tends to be utilized in all of the life cycles of the organization.

Sound budgeting practices contribute to a solid foundation for financial integrity and accountability. There are many benefits to budgeting for a nonprofit organization. The advantages of budgeting far outweigh any possible disadvantages. The budgeting process benefits a church or nonprofit Christian organization in the following ways:

1. An intentional budgeting process should cause the organization to carefully examine which priorities are consistent with the mission and vision of the organization.
2. A completed budgetary process communicates the mission and vision of the organization by establishing priorities.
3. A sound process of budgeting should encourage widespread participation involving individuals from all facets of ministry and congregational life.
4. Budgets should be structured in such a way to check progress and engage in ongoing evaluation in multiple areas of ministry and congregational life.
5. A budget provides a format to put faith into action.

Church and nonprofit budgeting normally follows a twelve-month calendar in either a yearly or fiscal format. According to Jack Henry, a budget must do several key things:

1. Set goals.
2. Establish priorities for each of them.
3. Estimate your income.
4. Estimate your expenses
5. "Balance the Budget" or get the projected expenses equal to or lower than the projected income.[206]

It must be noted that the key elements referenced by Henry would have application in both Christian and secular organizations.

Church and nonprofit budgets tend to fall into two broad categories: line-item and zero-based or ministry-action budgeting. It should be noted that both philosophically and practically these two approaches to budgeting may overlap at times. Both approaches to budgeting have merit and have become effective tools in Christian and nonprofit organizations.

Line-item budgeting remains the simplest and easiest approach, particularly for smaller congregations or organizations. In line-item budgeting, expenditures are organized into categories and then those categories have an assigned place in the budget reflected by a line item. In organizations that utilize line-item budgeting, a tendency exists to approach the budgeting process with one basic question, "What did we do last year?" When this becomes the only consideration, the organization defaults into accepting the status quo instead of careful consideration of what might be God's direction in a particular area. While the line-item approach to budgeting is an easier approach to establish and maintain, it is imperative that organizations continue to address the critical issues related to the organization and establish priorities for ministry.

Zero-based or ministry-action budgeting, in theory, takes a completely different approach to the budgeting process. When ministry action budgeting is utilized, you never begin or end the budgetary process with the question, "What did we do last year?" In ministry-action budgeting, you begin the budgeting process each year with a clean slate. Henry states, "The only way to insure that your budget truly reflects your current needs and priorities is to consider every budget item on its own merit each year, a technique called 'Zero-Based Budgeting.' "[207] With a zero-based or ministry-action budgeting approach, every budget item or ministry is on the table for evaluation each time a budget is developed. As a result of the evaluation process in ministry-action budgeting, major changes could take place in the organization, resulting in the elimination of budget items, which are inconsistent with the mission, vision, or values of the church or organization. Ministry effectiveness becomes a key issue in the evaluation process related to ministry-action budgeting. Johnson indicates advantages of ministry-based budgeting:

> In this approach emphasis is placed on the fullest participation of people possible. The process involves more people than traditional budgeting by requiring a larger budget development team and extensive use of church leaders and organizations. Emphasis is also given to priorities in planning. Church entities must discover needs for ministries and project solutions. In all stages, priorities are to be determined.[208]

Even with a ministry-action or zero-based approach to budgeting, certain items remain a part of the budget from year to year. Welch reminds his readers that not every budget item is evaluated each year and "items such as debt, utilities, salary, insurance, and so forth are carried forward as required portions of the budget with little or no modification each year."[209] When budget items of this nature are carried over from year to year, then the more traditional line-item budgeting practices contribute to the budgeting process by examining what happened during the past year. Even when this dual approach to budgeting takes place, the establishment of priorities and the practice of biblical stewardship should always be the norm.

Johnson indicates that as priorities in the organization are determined, the following steps in ministry-based budgeting should take place:

1. Analyze ministries.
2. Propose ministry actions.
3. Evaluate ministry actions.
4. Prepare the budget.
5. Present the budget to the congregation.
6. Promote the budget.
7. Report on ministry progress.
8. Review and evaluate.[210]

If the principles of ministry-based budgeting are carefully followed, the organization engages in ongoing evaluation related to perceived effectiveness and consistent with the mission and vision of the organization. The result of the process should be a unified church establishing priorities to be engaged in kingdom ministry.

After a budget has been prepared and implemented, it becomes necessary to report the progress taking place. Normally, people want to know the following items about the church's finances, according to Marvin Owen:

1. What we started with.
2. What we received.
3. What it is intended for (designated and undesignated).
4. What we spent.
5. Where it went.
6. What we have left.
7. How we are doing.[211]

Owen goes on to state that budget and financial reports should be prepared, processed, and presented with the following goals in mind: make it clear, make it correct, make it complete, make it concise, and make it compelling.[212] When this takes place, the report should be prepared in such a way that it is easy to understand for the average layperson and nonprofessional. Consistent with the apostle Paul's principles of financial accountability in 2 Corinthians 8, budgets and financial reports should reflect sound financial principles and be representative of stewardship that gives glory to God.

Debt and Ministry Expansion

One of the most difficult issues faced by ministers individually and the church corporately revolves around the issue of debt. Does the Bible address the issue or concept of debt? If so, what does the Bible have to say? How should the biblical principles be applied to contemporary ministry? It must be noted that Christ followers may disagree on both the interpretation and application regarding a biblical understanding of debt. In the Torah, God provided foundational principles regarding lending and debt. Leviticus 25:25–38 addressed the issue of lending as it related to poor, destitute, struggling Israelites. If one Israelite provided assistance in the form of a loan to a needy or destitute Israelite, he was not to accept interest as part of providing assistance to the fellow Israelite. This mandate is clearly stated in 25:36–37: "Do not profit or take interest from him, but fear your God and let your brother live among you. You are not to lend him your silver with interest or sell him your food for profit." In this context, lending was permitted but the charging of interest or profiting was strictly prohibited.

Moses focused on covenant obedience in Deuteronomy 28. Acknowledging and accepting God's gracious blessings of obedience meant that the Israelites were not to borrow: "The Lord will open for you His abundant storehouse, the sky, to give your land rain in its season and to bless all the work of your hands. You will lend to many nations, but you will not borrow" (v. 12). The theme of the Israelite's being a lending people, but not a borrowing people, was continued later in the same chapter: "The foreign resident among you will rise higher and higher above you, while you sink lower and lower. He will lend to you, but you won't lend to him. He will be the head, and you will be the tail" (vv. 43–44). God made it clear that His covenant people were to be lenders and not borrowers. Borrowing was perceived to be a curse and never a blessing for God's people.

While the New Testament focuses on the importance of finances and possessions, the issue of financial debt receives either little or no consideration. One New Testament verse has generated debate both for advocates of going into debt and those opposing borrowing. Romans 13:8 states, "Do not owe anyone anything, except to love one another, for the one who loves another has fulfilled the law." While this verse is in the context of a Christ follower's obligation to pay taxes, the broader context points to a concept reminding the believer of a debt which can never be repaid, the debt of love. Based on the foundation of the Great Commandments of loving God and loving your neighbor, Romans 13:10 states, "Love does no wrong to a neighbor. Love, therefore, is the fulfillment of the law." The Christ follower should have the focus in his or her life to "love one another" (13:8). While a case cannot be made in these particular verses for establishing a prohibition against borrowing, it must be noted that financial integrity remains a key aspect of Christian growth and discipleship and a Christian is to fulfill his or her obligations.

Christians may honestly debate the issue of debt, but one biblical admonition remains crystal clear, which is that the borrower is servant to the lender. Proverbs 22:7 indicates, "The rich rule over the poor, and the borrower is a slave to the lender." When a person, church, or non-profit organization engages in borrowing, the person or entity places themselves in a subservient relationship. In other words, the lender is in charge, in control, and remains the ruling authority in the relationship. This can never be perceived as positive, only negative. In essence, the borrower is in a servant, slave-type of relationship with the lender.

The issue of church debt has become a matter of controversy among many believers. Again, godly people argue both sides of the issue. Arguments made for going into debt to finance church debt and ministry expansion, include, but are not limited to, the following:

1. Debt may be appropriate if it is limited in nature.
2. Debt may be considered if it poses no harm to the ministry or reputation of the church.
3. The issue is not debt but paying your obligations in a timely manner.
4. The reasonableness of debt is the key issue based on the totality of the circumstances.
5. The motivation for going into debt remains the primary factor to consider.
6. Debt is okay if the financial structure of the church and economy is stable.
7. Reaching people for Christ and kingdom expansion are always appropriate reasons to go into debt.
8. Since God allowed the Israelites to lend, it must be okay to borrow.

Opponents of debt tend either totally prohibit debt or restrict the use of debt based on the following reasons:

1. In God's economy, money should not be an issue.
2. Relying on a loan to provide instead of the promise of God constitutes a lack of faith in the character and nature of God.
3. The Bible either restricts or strongly discourages debt.
4. Where God wills, God always provides.
5. Going into debt may mean getting out of the will and timing of God.
6. There is an absence of examples in Scripture of God instructing His church or individual believers to borrow.
7. Interest paid for a church loan becomes wasted money for kingdom purposes.
8. Going into debt reflects compromise and the church should maintain a higher standard than the world.
9. Debt always presumes on the future.
10. Only God, not man, knows the future.
11. Changes in individual lives and the economy can negatively impact a church in debt.

Another important issue to be considered related to the issue of debt in the local church relates to what extent the church corporately should provide an example for individual church members to follow. How can church leadership challenge members to get out of debt if the church is always in debt? Larry Burkett points out that teachers, deacons, and elders are held to a higher standard in Scripture (cf. James 3 and 1 Timothy 3) and as a result, "Since each of these is under the authority of the Church, shouldn't we assume that the Church is held to an even higher standard?"[213] When a pastor who is opposed to church debt finds himself in a ministry environment that encourages debt, prayerful consideration of the situation needs to take place. If God provides the freedom for the pastor to remain in the church with debt, then opportunities may become available to promote a debt-free model. Berg and Burgess reflect on the situation, "After all, how will a ministry ever become financially free if there is no one to pray, to model, and encourage debt-free ministry?"[214] Debt-free living should be held as a goal to be achieved both for the individual believer and the church corporately.

Pastors can develop expertise in how to provide counsel related to debt-free living. A starting point will be to provide wisdom, counsel and assistance in helping individuals and families get out of debt. Whether the philosophy and approach of Dave Ramsey, Ron Blue, Crown Financial Ministry, or other credible sources are considered, the following concerns need to be addressed to help someone get out of debt:

1. Acknowledge God's sovereignty and ownership of everything in the believer's life.
2. Commit to God's leadership and direction to help get out of debt.
3. Recognize that as believers we are stewards of the resources God has provided.
4. If you are a couple or family with children, work on getting each person on board for the goal of debt reduction.
5. Establish a budget.
6. Continue biblical giving.
7. Determine to not have any new indebtedness.
8. Adopt a simple lifestyle and stop any unnecessary spending.
9. Establish a procedure to pay off debt, such as paying off the smallest

debt first and then when the debt is paid rolling that money into the next debt. (Ramsey, Snowball Effect).

10. Set up an emergency fund.
11. Once some stability returns, begin to accumulate three to four months of living expenses.
12. Eliminate investing until you are out of debt.
13. Sell any items you do not need.
14. Evaluate food and automobile costs.
15. Look for other ways to save money, such as moving to term life insurance and increasing your insurance deductibles.
16. Throughout the process continue to reinforce positive goals for debt reduction.

Psalm 37:21 clearly mandates an obligation to repay debts, "The wicked man borrows and does not repay, but the righteous one is gracious and giving." Christ followers must understand the necessity of financial integrity. Principles of accountability, responsibility, and transparency should guide all areas of finances. Finances provide a key area for Christian growth and development and most of all for God to be glorified.

Research and create

Is going into debt biblical? Does the answer to this question change when addressed to the church corporately or to individual believers? How does ministry debt impact kingdom ministry?

Taxation

Being involved in God's ministry is a blessing, yet always a challenge. Many pastors have limited training in areas of business and finance. Art Rainer states, "The minister's financial package is one of the most misunderstood concepts in ministry finance."[215] This is especially true in the area of ministerial taxation. The issue of taxation has both biblical and contemporary implications to be considered.

Jesus was clear regarding the Christians responsibility in the area of taxation. When questioned by the Pharisees and the Herodians about whether or not it was lawful to pay taxes to Caesar, Jesus clearly stated that you are to render to Caesar the things that are Caesar's and to God the things that are God's (Matthew 22:21). The apostle Paul also issues a mandate about this civic duty: "Therefore, you must submit, not only because of wrath, but also because of your conscience. And for this reason you pay taxes, since the authorities are God's public servants, continually attending to these tasks. Pay your obligations to everyone: taxes to those you owe taxes, tolls to those you owe tolls, respect to those you owe respect, and honor to those you owe honor" (Romans 13:5–7). For the Christ follower the payment of taxes remains a biblical mandate.

Since being subject to the government in the area of taxation remains a biblical command, it becomes important that each pastor understand his unique standing in the tax code. A major issue to be evaluated revolves around whether or not a taxpayer functions as a pastor for tax purposes. Guidestone Financial Resources of the Southern Baptist Convention stipulates that the following factors must be considered consistent with IRS regulations guidelines and relevant case law and that according to the IRS:

> Ministers are individuals who are duly ordained, commissioned or licensed by a religious body constituting a church or church denomination. They are given the authority to conduct religious worship, perform sacerdotal functions and administer ordinances or sacraments according to the tenets and practices of that church or denomination. If a church or denomination ordains some ministers and licenses or commissions others, anyone licensed or commissioned must be able to perform substantially all the religious functions of an ordained minister to be treated as a minister for Social Security. (See *IRS Publication* 517.)[216]

When a person can address the previous points in the affirmative, he is considered a minister for tax purposes and may be eligible for a housing allowance. When recognized as a minister for tax purposes, then the taxpayer finds himself placed in a dual tax status. This dual tax status recognizes the pastor as an employee for income tax purposes but self-employed for social security. Being self-employed for social security and Medicare means that the pastor is responsible for paying the full amount of social security and not the one-half amount of the traditional employee. As a result of this issue, churches are encouraged to provide their pastors social security offset by paying half of the social security payments. This offset becomes taxable income for the taxpayer, but in reality becomes a net gain in income. Also, it must be noted that pastors are not subject to traditional withholding rules although many pastors still have their churches withhold taxes. If the taxes are not withheld, then the pastor must personally file the appropriate withholding documents. Each year a pastor should receive a Form W-2 reporting taxable income and never a Form 1099. Employees receive a W-2, not a 1099.

The issue of whether or not to remain in the social security and Medicare systems presents a difficult issue for many ministers. A pastor may opt out of the social security system by filing IRS Form 4361 by the due date of the pastor's tax return for the second year with four hundred dollars or more of ministerial income.[217] To claim the exemption from the social security system, you must comply with the following requirements:

1. File Form 4361 within the limited time period.
2. Further, the exemption is available only to pastors who are opposed on the basis of religious considerations to the acceptance of benefits under the social security program (or any other public insurance system that provides retirement or medical benefits).
3. A pastor's opposition must be to accepting benefits under Social Security (or any other public insurance program). Economic, or any other non-religious considerations, are not a valid basis for the exemption, nor is opposition to paying the self-employment tax.
4. An exemption from self-employment taxes applies only to ministerial services.[218]

According to B. J. Worth, before the year 1968 ministerial services performed by ministers were exempt from social security unless the minister had filed a certificate expressing a desire to be covered by social security. If a pastor has already paid into the social security system and is vested, they remain vested, even if they opt out of social security for ministerial earnings.[219] Considering the issue of exemption from social security, the bottom line remains that the decision to opt out of social security and Medicare must be based on conscientious grounds and never to make a political statement or for personal economic gain.

One of the greatest tax savings available to pastors is what is known as the housing allowance. The housing allowance becomes an exclusion from income for federal income tax purposes. A housing allowance is available to a pastor who owns his own home, rents a home, or lives in a church-owned parsonage.

For a housing allowance to be valid, it should be in writing and approved by either the congregation or governing board, depending on the polity of the church. Also, the housing allowance must be established in advance and can never be applied retroactively. Many churches establish the practice of adopting a safety clause that allows the housing allowance to continue from year to year if the church fails to take the appropriate action. B. J. Worth indicates that the following expenses may be considered in computing the housing allowance:

1. Rent or principal payments, cost of buying a home, and down payments.
2. Real estate taxes and mortgage interest for the home. These expenses are deductible *again* as itemized deductions. It is a double deduction, but it is allowable by the IRS.
3. Insurance on the home and/or contents.
4. Improvements, repairs, and upkeep of the home and/or contents. Such as a new roof, room addition, carpet, garage, patio, fence, appliance repair, etc.
5. Furnishings and appliances: dish washer, vacuum, TV, VCR, DVD, stereo, piano, computer (personal use), washer, dryer, beds, small kitchen appliances, cookware, dishes, sewing machine, garage door opener, lawnmower, hedge trimmer, etc.
6. Decorator items: drapes, throw rugs, pictures, knick-knacks, painting,

wallpapering, bedspreads, sheets, towels, etc.

7. Utilities: heat, electric, nonbusiness telephone, water, sewer charge, garbage removal, cable TV, nonbusiness Internet access, etc.
8. Miscellaneous: anything that maintains the home and its contents that you have not included in repairs or decorator items.[220]

Even though the preceding list seems to indicate that almost anything could be included in a housing allowance, there are still several limitations to be considered. According to Busby, Martin, and Drunen, the following limitations are placed on the housing allowance, "The cash housing allowance excludable for income tax purposes is the lowest of (1) reasonable compensation, (2) the fair rental value of the furnished home, plus utilities, (3) actual housing expenses paid from current ministerial income, or (4) the amount properly and officially designated."[221] In a majority of cases, the fair rental limitation becomes the norm for determining the housing allowance.

Another way for the pastor to enjoy substantial tax savings is through the proper development of an accountable reimbursement plan. If this type of plan is not used, then many of the business related reimbursements that a church normally provides to the pastor must be considered as income and included on the pastor's W-2. Busby places an emphasis on the importance of an accountable expense reimbursement plan being provided to all pastors. He writes, "An ideal policy provides for full reimbursement of all professional expenses. Alternately, the plan should provide for reimbursements up to a specified annual limit."[222] Busby goes on to add, "If an expense limit is set, use one limit for all business and professional expenses."[223] It is important to remember that whenever an accountable reimbursement plan is utilized, the principle use of it or loss of it will apply. If this principle is not followed, then the plan should be considered to be non-accountable and subject to taxation.

Ministerial expenses placed in an accountable reimbursement plan should be seen as serving a business purpose. Guidestone Financial Resources provides a framework for an accountable reimbursement plan, including examples of appropriate business expenses for the pastor:

1. The church will reimburse only reasonable ministry-related business expenses incurred by a pastor or employee. Subject to budget limitations, these expenses will include:
    - Business use of automobile, up to the current IRS standard mileage rate
    - Business travel away from home: transportation, lodging and meals on overnight trips
    - Convention, conference and workshop expenses
    - Continuing education expenses
    - Subscriptions, books and tapes, if related to ministry or employment
    - Entertainment/hospitality expenses, if business connection requirement is met
2. The pastor or employee will account for each allowable expense in writing at least every sixty days. Documentation will include the amount, date, place, business purpose, and business relationship of any person entertained for each expense. A receipt will accompany the documentation.
3. The minister or employee will return advances that exceed actual business expenses within 120 days.
4. Under this accountable arrangement, the church will not report

reimbursed amounts as taxable income on the pastor's or employee's W-The pastor or employee should not report reimbursed amounts as income on his federal income tax return.[224]

Business expenses are a necessary part of doing ministry in the contemporary culture. A properly structured accountable reimbursement plan provides a tool for the church or nonprofit organization to assume responsibility for the financial cost of doing ministry. Also, the business related expenses that are reimbursed do not become taxable income for the pastor. This should be considered a "win-win" situation for both the church and pastor.

Respond to a Case Study

This is your friend Rev. Lonely Pasteur. I'm now in my third year as Pastor of Your Blessed Baptist Church in Pitt, Alabama. We have faced our challenges but are thankful that worship attendance has increased from one hundred to two hundred on a weekly basis. The budget has increased from $200,000 to $300,000 per year. Part of the increase in attendance is due to our after-school programs and ministry to economically disadvantaged neighborhoods. Each Sunday we have fifty children and youth who attend as a direct result of our outreach efforts. Pastoral and administrative salaries account for

50 percent of the budget. Currently, we do not have any debt. To reach more people for Christ, our outreach committee has determined that we need a family life center, which would be foundational for current ministry and future growth. We just spent the last $50,000 in savings for a specially designed bus for our senior adult ministry. Attending the state fair is one of the favorite activities in Pitt, Alabama. Now the senior adults can ride in comfort. Building costs are low in Pitt compared to other parts of the country. The Building and Grounds committee reported that a nice family life center would cost $2 million. A smaller, scaled-down version could be built for $1 million. As pastor, I would like to see this building completed. I have a few members who believe that going into debt is not biblical. This issue was never addressed in seminary. I only want to reach and disciple people for Christ. I need your counsel. Please advise me about the biblical and practical issues on both sides of this issue. Should we build at Your Blessed Baptist Church?

1. What do you believe is the single most important issue in this scenario? Explain your response.
2. List what you believe are contributing or minor issues that must be dealt with.

3. What are alternatives to responding to this dilemma?
4. If you were called as a consultant to Your Blessed Baptist Church, what would be the first steps in your Action Plan?

14
INSPIRING CONGREGATIONAL WORSHIP
John Boozer

Sugarland Baptist Church (SBC) of Nashville has depended on the piano to help lead worship for the past thirty years. The pianist, Aunt Geraldine, had occupied the piano bench since she was a teenager. She was religiously committed to playing from the 1956 Baptist Hymnal and bristled when anyone suggested a new approach. Reverend Branson, the new pastor, was deeply concerned by the lack of numerical growth and enlisted the advice of a church growth consultant he knew that attended a large church in Brentwood to attend one Sunday and give him some advice. To the young pastor's horror, the consultant had one piece of advice: get rid of Aunt Geraldine!

Leaders Make Mistakes

The mistakes churches leaders make when they seek change can be devastating to a congregation. Most of these missteps can be attributed to the fact that people and organizations resist change. Suzanne Madsen in her blog *The Liquid Planner* gives wonderful insight as to why people resist change: "People resist change because they believe they will lose something of value, or fear they will not be able to adapt to the new ways."[225] However, when changes in worship are founded on sound biblical principles, are communicated well with the congregation and its leadership, and are done in an orderly process, the church can change, grow, and flourish. These changes can happen without discarding those things a congregation values, including unity in fellowship and worship.

One has only to go back to the last inauguration of President Obama to be reminded that men falter. The world watched as Chief Justice John Roberts and President Barack Obama made a mistake in saying the words to the Inaugural Oath. The oath is just thirty-five words and both men, without doubt, practiced them many times. Sometimes it is easy to make mistakes even on seemingly easy tasks. Musicians know this all too well. Although people have sung it most of their lives, hearing seasoned veterans trip over the words of the National Anthem is all too familiar.

What Went Wrong?

Church leaders can also make mistakes while attempting to build upon the successes they have already achieved. To some pastors, changing musical styles is a logical step to growing a larger church. The Church Growth movement's advice was the use of a secular and entertainment-influenced style of music would attract a larger segment of the population and therefore cause the local church to grow. Present-day leaders in rejuvenating slumping churches advise these churches to think carefully about the possibility of making this change before implementing a plan.[226]

The Southern Baptist Convention's Sugarland Baptist Church's first mistake was to take at face value the claims by a church growth consultant that a change in musical style is key in growing SBC into a larger church. The second mistake was to assume the musical style of some larger churches was the reason these churches grew. The fact is, many churches that have contemporary worship styles started as new church plants and, therefore, did not have to go through a change to become the church it is.

According to Richard Watson, one reason for further complicating mistakes is what he calls *egocentric bias*. The idea here is that we usually think we are right and nothing will change our minds.[227] This brings to mind the often-quoted saying, "Don't confuse me with the facts." Everyone on a team (or church staff) thinks they know what should be done and spends most of their time making sure the opinions of others (for instance, the congregation) aren't heard. Throw in some alpha-personality behavior and you wind up with "the perfect storm."[228]

Confirmation bias is another cause of things quickly going from good to bad. In short, some leaders subconsciously seek out facts and opinions that strengthen their existing opinions. Information that does not support their plans is ignored. Empirical research could be an excellent tool to overcome this unfounded information.

Empirical research is one of the best ways to find out what is true by means of direct and indirect observation and recorded experience. The data gathered can be analyzed quantitatively or qualitatively. While using this research method in analyzing over 576 of the most evangelistic churches in America, Thom Rainer found a wealth of information. As it relates to worship style, he discovered that although music can be an effective evangelistic tool, there was no single music or worship style predominated these growing churches.[229]

The pastoral leadership team often makes mistakes in its efforts to bring change. However, by following biblical principles of unity, introducing new songs that are theologically and musically rich to the church, and making changes to the musical style incrementally, future pastoral leaders can make changes in worship and still allow a church to grow and flourish.

Maintaining Fellowship

There are biblical principles that guide churches in the act of worship. Scripture teaches that the church should maintain fellowship and unity even while it sings "new songs unto the Lord."

> "To a true child of God, the invisible bond that unites all believers to Christ is far more tender, and lasting, and precious; and, as we come to recognize and realize that we are all dwelling in one sphere of life in Him, we learn to look on every believer as our brother, in a sense that is infinitely higher than all human relationships. This is the one and only way to bring disciples permanently together. All other plans for promoting the unity of the Church have failed."
>
> –A.T. Pierson

From the Psalms, Jesus' teachings, and in Paul's letters the church is taught to love each other and to live in unity. There is no doubt SBC became divided, and the conflict was the result over the issue of worship style. However, a church whose goal is to reach a community for Christ and be recognized in the community as followers of Christ, according to the biblical principles, should display unity and love to that community Psalm 133:1–3 teaches about the attributes of unity when it says:

> Behold, how good and pleasant it is for brothers to dwell in unity! It is like the precious oil on the head, running down on the beard, on the beard of Aaron, running down on the collar of his robes! It is like the dew of Hermon, which falls on the mountains of Zion! For there the LORD has commanded the blessing, life forevermore. (ESV)

In addition to commenting on the sweet nature of unity, the psalmist speaks of two significant aspects of the result of unity.

The reference to the sweet nature of unity "good and pleasant" is used in other places in Scripture to describe what He gives or the worship He receives from His people.[230] Many scholars see this verse as referring to the spiritual unity of the Jewish people coming together to worship God during the celebration of the feasts in Jerusalem. However, this also refers to the unity of the Jewish and Gentile peoples being united by their faith in Jesus.

This "goodness and pleasantness" (33:2) is also illustrated in two additional ways. Unity is compared to the consecrating act of "the precious oil" being poured on Aaron's head. Because of the fact this was "precious oil" indicates it was special oil used for anointing purposes; therefore, this blessing is referring to a consecrating effect it can have on a church.

The second way is how refreshing this unity can be to the fellowship of the church. The illustration of the dew coming down from Mount Hermon is significant because this mountain is the highest point in Israel and is always snow covered. The snow-capped peaks are the cause of refreshing dew forming at the foot of a mountain that is an area, which is traditionally dry. Additionally, the melted snow flows to the mountains of Zion (Psalm 2:6) and seeps through the limestone and forms springs, which eventually becomes the source of the Jordon River, which is in turn the source of most of Israel's water supply.

Jesus also teaches the congregation should love each other when He says:

> A new commandment I give to you, that you love one another, even as I have loved you, that you also love one another. By this all men will know that you are My disciples, if you have love for one another. (John 13:35 ESV)

The love His disciples display for each other is a witness that they are, indeed, followers of Christ. Moreover, Jesus included the words, "as I have loved you," which indicates the love the disciples have for each other should be a sacrificial love, just as Jesus had loved them. In the context of worship music and musical styles, this seems to indicate Christians should be willing to show grace toward the musical preferences of other believers. Donald Hustad says:

> Christians have an added incentive to show grace, because of God's grace extended to them; none of us measures up to God's expectations, yet He accepts us. It is not for us to judge the worship or

musical practices of other cultures, even when our own aesthetic sensibilities are offended.[231]

Paul insisted the church not have divisions but "agree" in matters as part of the early church. He admonishes:

> Now I exhort you, brethren, by the name of our Lord Jesus Christ, that you all agree and that there be no divisions among you, but that you be made complete in the same mind and in the same judgment. (1 Corinthians 1:10)

Although the divisions Paul spoke of were probably doctrinal issues, it is indicated these issues were destructive to the unity of the early church and that they needed to be "made complete," which is a verb form that was sometimes used in setting a broken bone. Although the issues then were not about musical style, this passage does seem to indicate there was an issue that divided the congregation similarly to the divisions music style have caused in today's congregations. Finding a style of worship expression that can help unify a congregation would be a lesson today's churches might take from 1 Corinthians 1:10.

Sing a New Song

The term "new song" is mentioned no less than nine times in the Bible. We are commanded to *sing* "new songs" five times. Several times God *gave* individuals a "new song." And in Revelation, John indicates two instances where a "new song" *will be sung* (Revelation 5:9, 14:3).

Throughout the church's history there have been seasons when new songs and styles of music have been introduced. These have coincided with times of spiritual renewal. According to Hustad, "Invariably these revival periods have been graced and supported by a flowering of Christian song, which quickly became very popular."[232] This new music borrowed poetic and music style from secular forms of the day.

Along with periods of new worship songs, there were understandably conflicts concerning the music. The new songs lost identity with the established church music, and many traditional congregation members felt they were "losing something of value."[233] Therefore, it is no surprise there were clashes between the established church and the renewal movement. Although some new movements brought with them higher artistic forms, such as Martin Luther's hymns, new expressions were usually expressions of the popular cultural and tended to influence the church for a period of time.

Recite and rehearse

Psalm 133:1–3 could be motivational and useful in your future ministry. Read it several times with the view toward memorizing all three verses. Meditate on its meaning for corporate worship today.

> "While we should never say that popular music is out of place in Christian expression, we must protest when shallowness is the chief preference. The gospel is heavy and it is deep. The question is: How can CCM (or the modern worship movement) point beyond shallowness toward deeper engagement with deepening content?"
> –Harold Best[234]

The psalmist urges us to "Sing to Him a new song" in Psalm 33:3. This psalm encourages the church to sing a song meant to give a new expression of the worshipper's continued and fresh experiences with God. It is apparent the song is to be sung by a congregation because it addresses, "O you righteous one" and is accompanied by an assortment of instruments.

Many new songs used in worship come from personal experiences of salvation or deliverance from terrible circumstances. This is the case with Psalm 40. This psalm is a reflection of God's deliverance in Psalm 39. David cried to God and "the Lord heard my cry" (v. 1). Because David was saved from a pit of destruction, this experience caused David to have a new song to sing because of the fresh experience of God's grace. Such experiences in contemporary life are natural opportunities to write and sing new songs of testimony.

Another reason to write new songs is because of the great things God is doing in our lives. In 1976 during the keynote address at Urbanna,[235]

Edmund Clowney told a crowd of seventeen thousand college student delegates:

> Ladies and gentlemen, it is my privilege to announce our international anthem: "Declare His glory among the nations, His wondrous works among the nations." We are called to doxological evangelism. When the people of God sing His praises, then the nations listen.[236]

According to the International Music Director of Operation Mobilization, Frank Fortunato, Clowney began the redefining of evangelism itself as an act of worship. When someone says, "Let me tell you how great God is and the great thing He has done for you through Jesus," such sharing is evangelism using a worship vocabulary. In 2000 Barney Ford said: "Urbana 2000 is about worship–all in response to God's initiative and great love: 'Because He first loved us.' "[237]

New songs are written to praise God for how He triumphed in the lives of Christians. These new songs are written using the "heart language" of the individual. Additionally, the songwriter uses his or her "heart music." To expect a modern Christian to write in a literary style of another era, or use music unfamiliar with his or her experiences, would make this expression less than authentic. New worship songs are written as a reaction to God's work in an individual's life.

Pastors are on firm biblical grounds in encouraging the church to sing "new songs." However, the process some use divides the congregation and create disunity. The next section of this chapter will explore ways to promote unified worship where God's people are:

- preserving what is considered valuable worship expressions,
- promoting unity in the fellowship,
- discovering new songs to sing to the Lord, while
- making changes incrementally.

Developing Unified Worship

Although a church's current music style may be contemporary, blended, or traditional, this style may not reflect the music that best communicates to its congregation or community. However, changing the current worship style too abruptly will usually create conflict. In fact, *change* is rarely taken well in most circumstances. As discussed earlier, most people are resistant to change because they believe they will lose something of value or fear they will not be able to adapt to the new ways. This resistance to change may be eased while assuring the congregation it will keep valuable expressions of worship, promoting unity, discovering appropriate new songs, and making changes incrementally.

Preserving What Is Considered Valuable Worship Expressions

Every culture has its own "heart language," and sometimes within a culture there are dialects and regional accents unique to other segments of this culture. International church planters know this well and seek to minister to the culture where they live with that culture's heart language. Every culture also has its own "heart music." According to Robin Harris, "heart music" is like a mother tongue for expressing your heart, and it affects how you worship.[238] In fact, every church has a style of music that can be considered as *their* "heart music." This "heart music" is a something this church highly values.

Church leadership should begin ministering to a congregation by discovering and then celebrating those things a church already values. Discovering the songs that are valued should be determined through a survey. In this way the congregation can celebrate the songs they value most. These songs can then be featured by using them during worship and by telling the stories that led to them being written.

When surveying the congregation, make sure all age groups from youth through senior adults are included. It is important to formulate a way to determine which group voted for which songs. Taking the survey during small group meetings and color-coding the surveys given to each age group can help accomplish this.

I would suggest revealing one song per week over as many as ten weeks during worship, including several of the favorite youth and college choruses. Before singing the song with the congregation, tell the story behind the song, making sure the story does not last more than three minutes.[239] This activity will help each generation understand and appreciate each other's worship expression beyond just the style of music.

Promoting Unity during the Change Process

No one likes to have any change "imposed" on him or her. It's far better to draw people into the story by making them active participants. Church leaders who only see the strategic side of a change will not be able to bring their congregations with them. One of the best approaches is to address the real concern, "What's in it for me?"[240]

I am reminded of a conference of worship leaders where the speaker shared a conversation he had with the senior adults at his church. His church was on the cusp of changing some of their approaches to ministry, and he was speaking to an influential group. He asked the group, "How many of you have children or grandchildren who live in other places in the country who do not attend worship and are not involved in the local church?" Immediately, hands went up all across the room.

He then asked, "How many of you wish a church where your family members live would start an innovative ministry that would attract your family and therefore involve them in those churches?" Again, hands went up all across the room.

He then said, "There are grandparents all across America who have children and grandchildren living right here in our community. They wish we would do the same thing here." He could see the heads nodding in their understanding of the unreached people in their own city. This conversation was the turning point for the group in this church because they had a clearer understanding of why change needed to happen. The senior adults were now invested in seeing that change happened in this church.

Leadership should be sure to give people as much clarity as possible and communicate the impact to those who are affected. They should walk in their shoes, listen to their fears and concerns, and make them part of the process to unify worship.

Reflect and react

Think back to your most meaningful times of corporate worship, especially the portions of the service involving music. Describe the environment, the participation of others, the biblical nature of the experience, and your own personal spiritual takeaways.

Discovering New Songs to Sing to the Lord

Both Ephesians 5:19 and Colossians 3:16 mention the use of psalms, hymns, and spirituals songs. Some scholars have sought to define these as individual "appropriate" songs of worship, whereas other scholars take these passages to indicate an all-inclusive list. In other words, whatever songs you sing should be used for teaching and instructing each other, and the songs should be sung with "thankfulness in your heart to God," no matter the style.

Although there may be a lot of latitude available for the style of music to be used, Donald Hustad suggests six evangelical standards that should apply to a worship song:

1. It should express and communicate the gospel in text and music languages that are richly understandable by the culture for which it is intended.
2. It should be a worthy "sacrifice of praise." It should be "their best"—their best performance of the most meaningful text and music that is shared by most of those present. It should be offered in love, humility, gratitude, and grace, without arrogance or shame in comparing it to the offering of other persons in the same culture or in other cultures.
3. It should express and enhance the best Christian theology of each particular culture or subculture, supporting all tenets of that faith in proper balance.
4. It should express and support all the activities related to the group's beliefs with due consideration to the musical needs of each.
5. It should speak from the whole person to the whole person, carefully balancing the physical, intellectual, and emotional, while avoiding the sentimental.
6. It should be genuinely creative, shunning the hackneyed (clichéd) and trite, as well as the elitist and obscure.[241]

Therefore, whatever music is chosen for a congregation, the above list puts a heavy burden on the pastor and the worship leaders to choose appropriate music within the culture of their church and community.

If a church is seeking to do more contemporary music for worship, seeking "new songs" with the above guidelines will result in music and text that would be appropriate. However, the change of style should be done incrementally and with discretion.

Making Changes Incrementally

There is a unique balance between pushing the worship envelope with a congregation and allowing the church to feel comfortable with the changes the church is making. Allowing the congregation to feel comfortable while introducing new songs has the added benefit of developing a multigenerational church that can worship together. A church that is singing "new songs" to the Lord and displaying unity would be scripturally sound. One must conclude that there is a way for the church to sing new songs, but do so in a way that maintains the unity in the fellowship.

I have often given my "rubber band sermon" to my students about how to accomplish incremental change in a worship setting. The rubber band sermon starts with me passing out standard four-inch rubber bands. I ask my students to imagine a large cardboard box about the size copy paper comes in when delivered to an office, roughly a sixty-inch perimeter. I then ask them to tell me whether they could stretch their rubber bands around the box. Their answer is always no.

I explain to the students that because of the molecular structure of a rubber band, once it is stretched and then allowed to relax, may look like it did before it was stretched, but it is not. Stretching uncoils the kinks and tangles in the molecules, which do not return to their original positions when unstretched. This is called "hysteresis." Each time the rubber band is stretched and then relaxed, the rubber band changes a little each time. Eventually, the rubber band will be flexible enough to fit around the box.

The rubber band is similar to a congregation who is stretched to try some music or style that is new one Sunday and then is allowed to go back to the same type of music and style of the previous week. The congregation may look the same, but it has actually changed. Through a careful process of stretching the congregation and letting them go back to where they are comfortable, allows them to become more flexible.

Tom Kraeuter recalls the words of a worship leader who was relating the change process in his church. He says:

> I asked Richard Webb what he would tell another leader who was about to embark on a worship transition. He replied, "I'd tell them that it will take time and patience." He went on to say that he witnessed situations where "the whole process never really sank into the DNA of the congregation because sufficient time was not allowed for people to own the change."[242]

I am quick to warn my students that if they try to force the issue and put the rubber band all the way around the box immediately, the rubber band would snap in half, be destroyed, and the resulting snap-back would hurt the student. Although, they may immediately force a church into a style of music they are not used to, there will be a "snap-back" and the effort to have the church embrace a new worship experience would be destroyed. Leadership always gets hurt in the "snap-back."

The same principle is in effect when you see someone making balloon animals; he always stretches the balloons before blowing them up. He does this so his work does not "blow up" in his face.

So it is in making changes in congregational music. After a new innovation is tried, the church should return to the familiar the next week. After a few weeks, the same small innovation can be used, as long as you let the church go back to its original state. Eventually, the new innovation can be used in worship and the congregation will hardly notice it as being unusual. But their worship experience will have changed.

Contemporary worship is generally more spontaneous than traditional-style services. Moving a congregation to be more spontaneous would be an appropriate step in moving slowly toward a more contemporary style of service. An effective way to do this is to move directly from one hymn into another hymn without telling the congregation. My suggestion would be to sing all three stanzas of "Grace Greater Than All Our Sin" followed immediately by the first stanza only of "Amazing Grace." For a congregation not used to such spontaneity, the experience will be refreshing. The worship leader will no doubt get many positive comments about it as he leaves church that Sunday.

A word of caution here: it is important that your music team, the pianist, and the organist have practiced this thoroughly before the service. As is usually the case, those things that seem the most spontaneous have been the most rehearsed.

After letting the congregation relax for a few weeks, the worship leader can do the same thing but with different hymns. Care should be given to select two hymns that are in the same key and are based on similar themes. Most traditional congregations know the first stanza to between thirty and fifty hymns. As long as the hymns and the transition are rehearsed well with the choir and the music team, it will be successful. After repeating this process several more times and slowly decreasing the time between occurrences, this spontaneity may become comfortable experience.

Special events in a church are also excellent times to introduce innovations for worship, such as new music, new instruments, and new technology. The worship leader is given two times per year, Christmas and Easter, that are prime times to introduce new concepts to a church that will enhance the programs and expose the congregation these new styles and worship aids.

A church not used to the use of media presentations during worship can watch a DVD presentation available for their musical presentation. Most music companies are now providing "stem tracks" to accompany seasonal musicals. These accompany tracks are played through a computer and have the option of turning off certain tracks when played "live" during the performance with the rest of the recorded music. The offers an opportunity for musicians who might become part of the church's worship team to play in church and add a "live" feeling to the music. The church becomes used to seeing rhythm instruments playing in church.

The next step is to have the rhythm instrument accompany the choir or ensembles during featured music about once a month. The frequency should increase after six months to once every three weeks. This interval should shorten over a two-year process until they are playing every Sunday. During this process the instruments can play softly during the hymns after about a year. This incremental introduction of the use of rhythm instruments helps the musicians get used to playing during worship as well and taking on this responsibility.

The use of media during worship can be almost as upsetting to many traditional churches and drastically changing the worship style. However, the use of screens and media presentations gradually by using them for special events and conferences will allow the congregation to "warm up" to their use and eventual acceptance.

The introduction of new worship songs to a church is another challenge for the worship pastor. There is an example of this being done, and it was probably the best instance of a "new song" being accepted by congregations across America. At one time "How Great Thou Art" was a new song. The only place church members heard that song was during Billy Graham Crusades as it was sung by the crusade choir or as a solo by

George Beverly Shea. America loved this song but couldn't sing it because the song wasn't published in hymnals until years later. At that time there was no media presentation for song lyrics. If it wasn't in your church's hymnal, your church didn't sing it. By the time the church got to sing the song, it was so beloved and congregations sang the great hymn with no hesitation.[243]

Research and create

Using the content and coaching from this chapter, create a chart of worship qualities, characteristics, and ingredients. Enlist three classmates and together, using your chart, attend five unique churches and rate each one using the categories in your chart. Come together and aggregate your data and analyze your results.

The likelihood of the same process above happening in our culture today is unlikely. As soon as a new song is written and published, it is available to be put on screens the next Sunday. And sadly, in too many cases, this is exactly what happens. All too often, churches are asked to sing songs they have never heard on a weekly basis. Congregations don't know the melody or how it fits with the text and find it difficult to sing. Many churches become "audience congregations" that wind up just watching and not participating in worship. Having a congregation participate in singing new songs takes careful selection, planning, and introduction strategy.

"How Great Thou Art" owes its successful introduction to more than just the exposure it got from the Billy Graham Crusades. First, it is a deeply theological song with rich texts that honor God with "awesome wonder." In addition to the text, it has a singable melody that is reminiscent of a folk song. In fact, it was first sung to a Swedish folk tune before it was sung in German and Russian. The tune we know today is a Russian folk tune. Choosing new songs to introduce to a congregation should have these same qualities: it is easy to sing and it has a theologically sound text.

The next task is to expose the song to a congregation so that, by the time they are asked to sing it, they feel that they already know it. The easiest way is to provide multiple opportunities for them to hear the song. Some worship pastors have a rule of thumb that the congregation should get at least eight "touches" of a new song before they are asked to sing it. Ways this may be accomplished include:

- The choir can sing it as a featured song.
- The praise team can play it as prelude music.
- The song can be performed as a prelude or an offertory.
- The music can be put on a continuous loop that is played throughout the church campus during the week and before worship.
- Soloist can sing it.

The goal is to have the congregation feel they know the song before they are asked to sing it. This way you will never have to interrupt worship by saying, "I'd like to teach you a song this morning."

Congregations do resist change in worship style and music. One reason is that they feel that they will lose something of value. The other compelling reason is that they are not sure they will be able to handle what the change means. By keeping those elements of worship that the congregation values while making changes incrementally, so that the people can easily handle the change, worship leaders can make these changes and still keep unity in the fellowship of the church.

Respond to a case study

Suburban Baptist Church (SBC) is located in one of the fastest growing suburban communities in the southeastern United States. Since becoming the pastor of SBC, Dr. Joe had led the church in steady growth for over two years. There was a great spirit in the church. The church had grown to three worship services and two Sunday schools.

When Dr. Joe arrived at SBC, the worship style of the church would have been considered very traditional with only hymns accompanied by the piano and organ. During the one-year tenure of one minister of music, the worship style had changed to more of a blended style with both hymns and contemporary worship songs being used. Sunday morning worship included a large adult choir, the use of both the piano and organ, and a thriving orchestra. However, Dr. Joe was convinced from what he had heard church growth consultants claim that the worship style at SBC needed to be updated to a more contemporary style in order for the church to grow. So with intention, the pastor led the music search team to seek a worship leader who used a high-energy style. The new worship leader quickly transformed worship to a service led primarily by a worship band. The orchestra was informed they were no longer needed. Hymns were replaced by a steady diet of contemporary worship songs, many of which were unfamiliar to a large segment of the congregation.

A segment of the church loved the new style and embraced the new contemporary worship music. Traditionalists in the congregation reacted negatively to the change. In reaction to this conflict, two distinct worship services evolved. One service used strictly contemporary music and the other only traditional music. Although this was an effort to put at ease the conflict, it had the result of more deeply distinguishing the contemporary crowd and the traditionalists. The radical shift in worship style, coupled with a lack of communication leading up to the changes, developed a great feeling of distrust and suspicion of the pastor and other leaders in the church.

The resulting divisive spirit at the church contributed

to the pastor and the new worship leader taking a large portion of the congregation to start a new church plant not far from SBC. However, the division within the remaining congregation continued to exist in the church. Congregation members had chosen sides. This division and conflict still contributes a negative undertone more than a decade later.

Questions to Guide Your Critique

1. Identify what you believe to be the one central issue that caused the divisive spirit and the eventual church split. In addition, list points you believe to be minor or contributing factors.
2. Recalling key points in chapter 9, "Leading Conflict Resolution," outline a five-point plan for managing change in a church conflict like this.
3. Now review this chapter and integrate specific, music-related steps that need to be considered to avoid the explosion that took place in Suburban Baptist Church.

15

LEADING IN UNCERTAIN TIMES

Ken Coley

Eric unpacked his notebook and handouts from the conference he attended over the last three days. He had heard and taken notes on messages by veteran pastors who appeared to be talking directly to him. He admitted to himself, hoping no one would know, that he was feeling overwhelmed by the multifaceted changes that he felt he needed in his pastoral leadership in order to be successful. He wanted to continue improving in his study and sermon delivery, while being a loving shepherd to his vibrant congregation, many whom he had cared deeply for and many he knew hardly at all. As he sorted the notes he had taken, Eric viewed them as scattered puzzle pieces in search of a unifying picture. He was anxious to spend time alone with God and His word, looking for a composite picture of the pastoral leader he was committed to becoming.

Young pastors in the 21st century are called to navigate swirling winds and turbulent seas. In some cases, they minister to and preach to five generations each Sunday, including saints who have been serving that congregation longer than the senior pastor has been alive. Some are faced with rapidly growing communities; others have communities that are unexpectedly changing in their demographic make-up or declining each year. The needs are multi-layered and often desperate—struggling economic conditions, drug abuse, caring for elderly parents, and marital strains, just to name a few. All this against the backdrop of a culture that is often committed to showing indifference to the Gospel at best and hostility at worse.

The Apostle Paul selected an apt metaphor for the leadership skill needed in these uncertain waters with an ever-changing seascape in I Corinthians 12:28, the helmsman concept behind the word that the apostle Paul selected when he discussed the *gift of administration.* In Paul's day, when his readers encountered the Greek word *kybernetes* (a form of *kybernesis*, used in 1 Corinthians 12:28), they connected it with the ordinary use of that word—a *helmsman*, or a *pilot* of a ship—because of their familiarity with sea travel. Effectively leading and managing a group of believers is analogous to steering a ship. It requires the skillful leadership of someone at the helm, someone who is charged with keeping the ship on course and ensuring the safety of all the passengers and the cargo. Through discussing this concept with many leaders and educators, I realized that the word the Holy Spirit had inspired Paul to write provides a compelling picture for twenty-first-century ministry leaders. In this word picture is a powerful metaphor capturing the challenges and crises that are standard fare for those called to ministry. As the church leader, you are the helmsman, and the church staff and other lay leaders are your crew. But another important dimension of the metaphor is that the helmsman is neither the owner of the vessel nor the captain of the ship. In the case of the church, these roles belong to Jesus, and He calls pastors to be His helmsmen. That's a New Testament portrait. Here's one from the Old Testament.

A Powerful Old Testament Picture of Pastoral Leadership

Smith paints an intriguing and inspirational picture from the leadership of Ezra for today's church leaders.[244] Drawing from a careful analysis of Ezra chapters 8–10 and Nehemiah 8, Smith describes the significant leadership behaviors of Ezra as he courageously carried out God's instructions for the restoration of authentic worship. Ezra prayed for the identification of the men God had called, and he recruited and trained them for specific roles. After Ezra articulated God's expectations and standards, the leader-priest boldly supervised, assessed, and disciplined those under his care. Working alongside Governor Nehemiah, Ezra continued his equipping ministry, detailed in Nehemiah 8, by modeling the proclamation of God's Word. See Figure 1 for a comparison of Ezra's leadership behaviors with a 21st century implementation by a senior pastor in his local church.

Figure 1: Comparison of Ezra's leadership behaviors with a Senior Pastor today.

Ezra's Leadership Behaviors	**Leadership Behaviors for Senior Pastors**
Recruiting and Training Leaders (Ezra 8)	
Pray for future leaders	• Pray for potential Sunday school leaders
Select and train a group of recruiters	• Choose Sunday school leaders as recruiters • Direct recruiters to potential leaders • Use spiritual gift inventories or interest surveys to find potential leaders • Stay involved and aware of the recruiting process.
Recruit specific roles with clear expectations	• Define specific roles of leadership in Sunday school • Lay out clear (written) guidelines that leaders can commit to and understand • Hold and attend regular training sessions • Offer resources to leaders for personal development • Provide leaders with training in Christian doctrine and discipleship
Holding Leaders to God's Standards (Ezra 9–10)	
Teach God's standards for living	• Faithfully teach and preach God's Word • Make the standards of Christian living clear to leaders through covenants and training opportunities
Respond to sin with a call for confession and repentance	• Encourage fallen leaders to pursue repentance and obedience to God

Work with leaders to fairly adjudicate cases of sin and broken standards	• Select a group of mature Sunday school leaders to develop clear standards and disciplinary measures • Select a group who can serve as an accountability team to investigate allegations and execute disciplinary actions
Personally Teaching God's Word (Nehemiah 8)	
Proclaim God's Word publicly to all people	• Faithfully teach and preach God's Word • Utilize expository preaching principles
Encourage leaders to explain and apply God's Word in small groups.	• Use the pulpit and the influence of the pastor to encourage Sunday school leaders and involvement in Sunday school • Serve as a champion and cheerleader of Sunday school
Teach the Scriptures in small groups	• Take part in a Sunday school class and small groups • Lead a Sunday school class

Drawing from some of the chapter headings in this text, *Entrusted to the Faithful*, it is instructive to take a closer look at the pastoral leadership of Ezra the priest.

Ezra as Shepherd: He knew the presence of God and modeled submission for his followers.

God positioned Ezra the priest to step to the forefront of breath taking change–leading thousands of refugees from captivity back to a place none of them had ever known, but a place of significance in which most had longed to resettle. Clearly it would not be possible as a result of human endeavors. From the first verses of his instruction, Ezra was associated with the phrase, "the hand of God was on him" (Ezra 7:6). In verse 9 it is stated, "The gracious hand of his God was on Him," and in verse 27 his testimony was, "I was strengthened by the Lord my God."

As their guide in an arduous and dangerous journey, Ezra called his people together early on to beseech the Lord for His protection. The thrilling narrative reads: "I proclaimed a fast by the Ahava River, so that we might humble ourselves before our God and ask Him for a safe journey for us, our children, and all our possessions" (8:21). This courageous leader had taken an almost unthinkable step of faith. He had chosen to forego the king's protection! The account continues, "I did this because I was ashamed to ask the king for infantry and cavalry to protect us from enemies during the journey, since we had told him, 'The hand of God is gracious to all who seek Him, but His great anger is against all who abandon Him'" (8:22). As we learn in verse 23, God granted Ezra' request. McConville provides additional detail related to his faith and bravery: "Verses 8-9 relate crisply that Ezra and his companions completed the arduous journey from Babylon in quick time...The journey was undertaken at the hottest time of the year, along a route which though well-trodden and avoiding the desert, was not without it risks from banditry."[245] McConville continues, "A caravan so richly laden yet so undefended would surely be easy prey for the bandits who haunted the route...Ezra is well aware that real dangers lie ahead and that the circumstances require, first of all, uncompromising faith."[246]

Ezra as Faithful Preacher of God's Word: He committed himself to knowing Scripture.

God called as the leader of the second wave of Israelites returning from exile a priest who was "skilled in the law of Moses..." (7:6). In addition, we learn that Ezra "had determined in his heart to study the law of the Lord, obey it, and teach its statutes and ordinances in Israel" (7:10). Regarding Ezra's training, McConville points out, "Ezra was no mere passive inheritor of the past. He had made himself highly competent in the area of his responsibility. The word translated *skilled* has at its root the idea of speed. He was so conversant with his material that he could make considered judgments rapidly."[247] But for all of us who spend significant amounts of time in academic pursuits and scholarly research, it is paramount to note that Ezra coupled his scholarship with a determination to obey the law. He knew he must live it out.

> This is what lies behind Ezra's readiness to leave his, probably comfortable, situation in Babylon for the perils of an arduous journey and the uncertainties of life in the small, ill- defended community in Judea: a desire that the people of God should walk with God. Such a desire also underlies the words "all that he asked" (7:6).[248]

The biblical evidence to support the effectiveness of Ezra's preaching of the word can be clearly seen in his followers' reactions in 10:1—public prayer and confession of the nation's sin and his presentation of the Law of Moses in Nehemiah 8:1-6. In both cases large numbers of men, women, and children responded with all-consuming spiritual, emotional, and practical commitments.

Recite and Rehearse

Return to your notes and observations about shepherding and preaching in chapters one and two of this text. Compare the key ideas in those chapters to the main leadership points found in the narrative in Ezra 7 and 8.

Ezra as Recruiter: He identified and recruited capable leaders to share in the work.

Ezra 8:15 could be overlooked in the larger narrative of the enormous caravan gathering on the outskirts of town, preparing to depart and not look back. Ezra determined that he needed to check for the presence of Levites among his fellow travelers. He found none! Determining this significant deficiency, Ezra asked his leaders to search for "ministers for the house of our God" (8:17). The next verse cannot be disregarded by today's leaders who feel like they are struggling alone. In verse 18 the narrative reads, "Since the gracious hand of our God was on us..." God supplied a direct descendent of Levi son of Israel, along with 38 other ministers. In addition, 220 temple servants "who had been appointed by David and the leaders for the work of the Levites" (8:20).

Recall from chapter 10 of this textbook that the word *recruit* is based on the concept "to grow again." Ezra knew he could not possibly service all the needs of his followers nor maintain the worship center and its accoutrements. His entourage of leaders had "to grow again." Williamson's perspective on this significant hurdle for Ezra can serve as encouragement to young pastors today struggling with the task of recruitment: "There can have been little to attract recruits to Ezra's group of returning exiles. Those with a pioneering spirit or strong feeling for the land of Israel would have gone long before, and, although history is silent as to detail, it does not seem probable that reports from those in the land to others of their families in Babylon would have been very encouraging."[249] But come they did. God provided Ezra's needs and He will assist you in recruitment of leaders today.

Ezra as Faithful Steward: He oversaw resources with diligence and integrity.

This Old Testament narrative offers today's leaders a dynamic contrast of faith in the dimension of God's protection and human diligence in the dimension of stewardship of the resources that belong to God. Ezra 8:24-30 describe the leader's meticulous oversight regarding the gold, silver, and other articles that had been contributed for the house of God by the king, his counselors, his leaders, and all the Israelites who were present (8:25). The amounts and weight are staggering. Ezra viewed his responsibility with seriousness. Here is his charge to those he appointed: "You are holy to the Lord, and the articles are holy. The silver and gold are a freewill offering to the Lord God of your fathers. Guard them carefully until you weigh them out in the chambers of the Lord's house before the leading priests, Levites, and heads of the Israelite families in Jerusalem" (8:28-29). Referring to the contrast between faith and human industriousness in chapter 8, Southwell explains, "His faith was, however, matched by his shrewdness, for he took no risks with bad book-keeping (24-30, 34). The treasure, of enormous value, belonged to the Lord, and all of it had to be accounted for. Ezra was aware that he was steward, not master, of all his company conveyed."[250]

Williamson agrees:

> "God's grace and human effort thus go hand in hand...Such a text reminds us of the necessary truths of the sovereignty of God and man's inability to save himself apart from grace. Alongside that, however, we see, as is in this chapter, the developing emphasis on he equally necessary theme that God's grace is operative through human channels, a theme which reaches its definitive climax in the incarnation itself (John 1:14).[251]

Breneman challenges today's pastors to follow Ezra's administrative approach.

"Following Ezra's example, Christian leaders should delegate

> responsibility. Ezra carefully chose the people to whom he gave responsibility. It may seem exaggerated to have taken such precautions with the money...However, to do things carefully, with decisions and transactions documented in writing, is a sign of wisdom rather than a lack of confidence. It protects everyone. Many present-day scandals could be avoided if Christian leaders would learn from Ezra."[252]

Perhaps in our contemporary culture this focus on elaborate resources for religious practice and the use of time and human resources to take care of these items may seem to be misplaced values. "This sort of concern for external beautification can strike the modern reader as at best irrelevant and at worst misplaced. It is, however indispensable to the proper restoration of the exiles." I can hear the discussions that take place in contemporary ministries—*we don't need a finance committee, or an audit, or a business meeting. So-in-so's wife is a bookkeeper. She can keep all the records.* (Notice 8:34—once they arrived, "Everything was verified by number and weight, and the total weight was recorded at that time.") McConville argues from Ezra's perspective, and hopefully ours:

> For Israel, the Temple, with its adornments, was the place above all others in which God' praises should be sung, and its rituals were correct accompaniments to prayer and penitence...Proper attention to prescribed ritual, therefore, was part of obedience, scarcely separable in the Israelite mind from ethical requirements. Ezra's arrangements for these huge offerings, then, was no frustrating delay, but time well spent, perhaps even prompted by the period so recently spent in prayer.[253]

Reflect and React

Evaluate your congregation's approach to stewardship of the contributions to your ministry? Do you perceive the same meticulous record keeping and accountability exercised by Ezra? Review your notes from chapter 13 on Designing Budgets and Financial Reports. In light of Ezra's stewardship what changes need to be made in your ministry?

Ezra as Change Agent: He identified the need for change and led through the related conflict to a new order.

Many pastors today have identified the need for change in their ministries or individuals within their churches, but these ministers are at a loss for how to proceed. Review this statement from chapter 8, Leading Change Management: "I teach ministry leaders the principle, to the degree that a congregation believes there is a crisis, the congregation or group empowers the leader to make a change." Let's test this principle out on Ezra 9 and 10 as we examine the malignant cancer his people are involved with: Israel's intermarriage with pagans.

This dramatic scene unfolds after the caravan of returnees and their leader had only been in Jerusalem approximately 4-5 months.[254] Ezra is confronted by the news that Hebrew inhabitants of Jerusalem had intermarried with the inhabitants of surrounding nations who habituated detestable practices clearly forbidden in the Mosaic Law (Deut 7:1-6). To make matters worse, "the leaders and officials have taken the lead in this unfaithfulness" (9:2).

Is there a more dramatic display of spiritual leadership in all of Scripture apart from that of Christ? Notice Ezra's behavior and words that reflect his deep spiritual pain: "I tore my tunic and robe, pulled out some of the hair from my head and beard, and sat down devastated" (9:3). "I sat devastated until the evening offering" (9:4). "I got up from my humiliation, with my tunic and robe torn" (9:5). "Then I fell on my knees and spread out my hands to the Lord my God" (9:5).

What was the people's reaction to Ezra's intense demonstration of remorse and repentance? Chapter 10 tells us that an extremely large assembly of men, women, and children gathered around him, and they, too, wept bitterly (10:1). A remarkable event took place at this gathering. A leader of one of the families stepped up, confessed openly the sin of the people, and proposed a covenant to send away all the foreign wives and children (10:2-3). But even more amazing was Shecaniah's insistence to Ezra: "Get up, for this matter is your responsibility, and we support you. Be strong and take action" (10:4). What an incredible picture of leadership in our day. As the pastor comes before the flock, communicates his brokenness before the Lord, and articulates the will of the Lord, and not his own, people will respond.

Ezra as Instrument to Carry Out Discipline

Now that the leaders and the people were firmly behind him and ready for change, the grave task of discipline fell to Ezra. But he secured their support (10:5). Breneman points out that his decision to go alone in verse six and continue in prayer and fasting "shows that his weeping and mourning outside was not just superficial or a 'show' to produce an effect on people. He was sincerely mourning for the returned exiles who had so soon forgotten why they were punished; now they again were unfaithful to God."[255] The leader's heart was right and his people saw this.

Next, Ezra circulated a proclamation that all the exiles would gather in order to receive the instruction uniformly. They would be reminded of God's standard, have the violations clarified, and be called to repentance. Then they would be required to turn from their sin and separate themselves from the foreign wives and children. In verse 11 *separate* is *herem*, which refers to putting something "under the ban."[256] The decision to honor God and separate from unfaithful practices were made quickly and had immediate buy-in from the people (10:12). Wisely, though, the execution of the discipline was carried out over a period of three months by discerning judges who examined each situation individually.[257] A quote from McConville concludes this section:

> The whole is a striking picture of the nature of influence. Ezra was not the only Old Testament leader to exercise a quiet but powerful ministry. The prophet Ezekiel had actually been struck dumb by God, if only temporarily (Ezek 3:26), and was obliged to portray visually Judah's coming doom through his own suffering (4:4). Both men remind us forcefully that real leadership cannot be a detached

thing, but must be fully engaged. It was the godliness and commitment of Ezra, testifying more powerfully than any harangue to the reality of God, of right and wrong and of judgment, which brought others to repentance.[258]

Research and reate

Research the crisis caused by the marriage of Israelite men to foreign wives in Ezra 9 and Nehemiah 13. Compare and contrast your findings with the re-definition of marriage and family in our own day. In what ways are the two situations similar? In what ways different?

Ezra as Teacher Trainer: He selected and trained others to teach small groups.

Ezra had a prominent role in the proclamation of the word at the occasion of the celebration of the completion of the wall of Jerusalem as recorded in Nehemiah 8. As Smith notes in Figure 1, the Levites had been trained to step in to instruct the people in smaller groups. Breneman points out some in attendance had lost their ability to understand Hebrew because of their time in Babylon. The Levites had the task of making sure that the Scriptures were understood that day.[259] The phrases "translating and giving the meaning" (HCSB) can also be translated as "making it clear" or "to break up" (as in paragraph by paragraph).[260] But the teaching by others in smaller units did not end at that event. "On the second day, the family leaders of all the people, along with the priests and Levites, assembled before Ezra the scribe to study the words of the law" (8:13). Regarding the inclusion of these new teachers-in-training, Williamson writes, "Perhaps more than anything else, Ezra's importance lies in the fact that he put the Bible of his day into the hands of the laity; it was no longer the exclusive preserve of the 'professionals'."[261]

Ezra as Worship Leader: He participated in worship and celebration with his people.

At the occasion of the dedication of the wall of Jerusalem, Ezra was given a prominent role in the worship and celebration. Nehemiah 12 lays out the formation of two massive processions that would lead all the city in a day of thanksgiving and joyful dedication. The line-up of singers and musicians is described in chapter 12, including the names of some of the family leaders and some of the trumpet players (32-35)—at the head of the procession, "Ezra the scribe went in front of them" (12:36).

Final Charge

Do you believe the Lord has called you to be the helmsman of a ministry and oversee the safe passage of a crew and passengers? He wants you to take hold of the helm with courage, conviction, and commitment because the winds and the currents will demand your very best. But by now you have probably discovered that your leadership is insufficient. You must look to Jesus as your Captain and have confidence that He desires to provide your every need. Have you sensed a call to be a modern-day Ezra—leading in a time of extraordinary uncertainty and cultural upheaval? As the Lord did in his day, He still does today. He will strengthen you as you fulfill your duties in pastoral leadership. The authors of these chapters exhort you to remain true to your call because we have entrusted these things to the faithful.

Respond to a case study

As Eric read the Scriptural passages in Ezra and Nehemiah, he made notes comparing the challenges that the leaders faced in the changing times in the biblical context as opposed to his own. Here are some of his notes:

Preaching: Sometimes borrowing outlines from other pastors that he picked up online.

Change Agent: He was attempting to change the

culture and establish new routines by planning new activities and signaling to folks that these events would be the common practice in the future.

Finances: He was fairly certain that some federal regulations regarding tax documents were not being filed with the government on time. In addition, he and a two staff members were deciding which bills to pay as money was available, regardless of whether or not the contributions were 'designated' for special projects.

Sexual immorality: He wondered how Ezra needed to be told in chapter 9 about the marriages to pagan wives. Eric knew stuff related to immoral practices that he had not preached about nor dealt with. It was just so difficult that he didn't want to think about it.

Recruitment: He had recently had the church approve two new staff positions with part-time salaries. He was not good at identifying and training lay people to use their secular gifts at church, so he had encouraged the selection of two men in his network.

Eric put down his pen. As he reflected on Ezra 8-10, the odds of success seemed long and the obstacles insurmountable. The same could be said about his own situation. But the story didn't end there. Ezra got to stand shoulder-to-shoulder with Nehemiah at the Water Gate on a day of great celebration. How did Ezra's pastoral leadership survive to see that day? Then he recalled the repetition of the phrase, "The gracious hand of God was on him." That was it. That is going to be how he would make it. Eric smiled and he sensed the Lord's presence, bringing Eric a sense of calm, of purpose, and of reassurance. He would remain faithful.

1. As you look over Eric's shoulder and skim his notes, which points appear to you to be of major concern and require immediate attention? Which ones do you evaluate as being of secondary importance?
2. Would the order and strategic plan for working on these issues change if the church was an established church of 500 members as opposed to a new church plant meeting in the home of one of his church members? Compare and contrast the realities of the different contexts.

RESOURCE LIST

Adams, Jay E. *Handbook of Church Discipline.* Grand Rapids: Zondervan, 1974.

Akin, Daniel L., ed. *A Theology for the Church.* Nashville: B&H Academic, 2007.

Alford, Chip. "Reducing the Risk of Sexual Abuse at Church," *Facts and Trends.* May 1998.

Amen, D. G. *Use Your Brain to Change Your Age.* New York: Harmony Books, 2012.

American Psychiatric Association. *Diagnostic and Statistical Manual of Mental Disorders* (5 ed.). Washington, DC: American Psychiatric Publishers, 2013.

Anthony, Michael J., and James Estep Jr., eds. *Management Essentials for Christian Ministries.* Nashville, TN: Broadman & Holman Publishers, 2005.

Ash, Christopher. *The Priority of Preaching.* Ross-Shire: Christian Focus, 2009.

Bacher, Robert N., and Michael L. Cooper-White. *Church Administration: Programs, Process, Purpose.* Minneapolis, MN: Fortress Press, 2007.

Baker, Joseph S. "Queries Considered, or an Investigation of Various Subjects Involved in the Exercise of Church Discipline," reprinted in *Polity: Biblical Arguments on How to Conduct Church Life*, edited by

Mark Dever (Nashville: Nine Marks Ministries, 2001).

Baptist Faith and Message, 2000 (Nashville: Lifeway, 2000).

Barclay, William. *The Acts of the Apostles*. Rev. ed. The Daily Study Bible Series. Philadelphia, PA: The Westminster Press, 1976.

Barkley, Elizabeth F. *Student Engagement Techniques: A Handbook for College Faculty*. The Jossey-Bass Higher and Adult Education Series. San Francisco, CA.: Jossey-Bass, 2010.

Bennis, Warren and Robert Thomas. *Crucibles of Leadership*. Location 1640

Berkley, James D. *Leadership Handbook of Management and Administration: Practical Insights from a Cross Section of Ministry Leaders*. Grand Rapids, MI: Christianity Today, Inc., and Baker Book House, 1997.

Berg, Jeff, and Jim Burgess. *The Debt-Free Church*. Chicago: Moody Press, 1996.

Best, Harold. *Music through the Eyes of Faith*. New York: HarperOne, 1993.

Black, David Alan. "Exegesis for the Text-Driven Sermon," in *Text-Driven Preaching: God's Word at the Heart of Every Sermon*, edited by Daniel L. Akin, David L. Allen, and Ned L. Mathews (Nashville: Broadman & Holman, 2010).

Black, Lindsay. *Be Thou My Vision: Devotions from the Lyrics of Popular Christian Music*. Cincinnati: Standard Publishing, 2005.

Blanchard, Ken, Patricia Zigarmi, and Drea Zigarmi. "Leadership and the One Minute Manager: Increasing Effectiveness through Situational Leadership." New York, NY: HarperCollins Publishers, 2000. Quoted in Cousins, Don, Leith Anderson, and Arthur H. DeKruyter. *Mastering Church Management*. Portland, OR: Multnomah, 1990. Quoted in Kenneth S. Coley, *Navigating the Storms: Leading Christian Schools with Character and Conviction*. Colorado Springs, CO: Purposeful

Design Publications, 2010.

Blanchard, Ken, Susan Fowler, and Laurence Hawkins. *Self Leadership and the One Minute Manager: Increasing Effectiveness Through Situational Self Leadership*. New York, NY.: HarperCollins Publishers Inc., 2005.

Blue, Ron, and Jeremy White. *The New Master Your Money*. Chicago: Moody, 2004.

Boice, J. M. *Nehemiah: an expositional commentary*.

Braddy, Ken. "Six Marks of a Healthy Group." *Facts and Trends* 61, no. 6 (Fall 2015): 24-26.

Breneman, M. *Ezra, Nehemiah, Esther* (electronic ed., Vol. 10).

Breneman, Mervin. *The New American Commentary*, vol. 10, *Ezra, Nehemiah, Esther*. Edited by E. Ray Clendenen et al. Nashville, TN.: Broadman & Holman Publishers, 1993.

Brown, Gordon B. *Guiding Faculty to Excellence: Instructional Supervision in the Christian School*, 2nd ed. Colorado Springs, CO: Purposeful Design Publications, 2002.

Burkett, Larry. *Using Your Money Wisely*. Chicago: Moody Press, 1990.

Busby, Dan J., Michael Martin, and John Van Drunen. *Ministers Tax and Financial Guide*. Grand Rapids: Zondervan, 2015.

Buzzard, Lynn R. *Church Policy Manual Guidebook*. Cary: BSCNC, 2004.

Buzzard, Lynn R. *With Liberty and Justice*. Wheaton: Victor Books, 1984.

Buzzell, S. S. *Proverbs*. In J. F. Walvoord and R. B. Zuck (Ed.), *The Bible Knowledge Commentary, Old Testament* p. 955. Wheaton: Victor Books, 1985.

Caldwell, William G. "Legal Matters," in *Church Administration Handbook*, edited by Bruce P. Powers, 3rd Edition (Nashville: B & H, 2008).

Carson, D.A. *Exegetical Fallacies*. 2nd ed. Grand Rapids: Baker, 1996.

Carson, D. A. *The Gospel According to John*, Pillar New Testament

Commentary. Grand Rapids: Eerdmans, 1991.

Chaffee, Paul. *Accountable Leadership: A Resource Guide for Sustaining Legal, Financial, and Ethical Integrity in Today's Congregations.* San Francisco, CA: Jossey-Bass Inc., Publishers, 1997.

Chapell, Bryan. *Christ-Centered Preaching: Redeeming the Expository Sermon.* 2nd ed. Grand Rapids, Baker, 2005.

Christensen, D. L. *Word Biblical Commentary, volume* 6A, *Deuteronomy* 1-11. Dallas: Word Books. 1991.

Cobble, James, and Richard Hammer. *Risk Management Handbook for Churches and Schools.* Matthias: Christian Ministry Resources, 2001.

Cole, F. A. *Galatians. Tyndale New Testament Commentaries.* Downers Grove: IVP Academic, 1989.

Coley, Kenneth S. "Excels in Teaching God's Word." In *Sunday School that Really Excels: Real Life Examples of Churches with Healthy Sunday Schools*, edited by Steve R. Parr, 179-188. Grand Rapids, MI: Kregel Ministry Publications, 2013.

Conrad, Rita-Marie, and J. Ana Donaldson. *Engaging the Online Learner: Activities and Resources for Creative Instruction.* Updated ed. Jossey-Bass Guides to Online Teaching and Learning. San Francisco, CA.: Jossey-Bass, 2011.

Croft, Brian, and Phil A. Newton. *Conduct Gospel-Centered Funerals: Applying the Gospel at the Unique Challenges of Death.* Leominster, UK: Day One Publications, 2011.

Culpepper, R. Alan. "Peter as Exemplary Disciple in John 21:15-19," *Perspectives in Religious Studies* 37 (Summer 2010), 165-178.

Dacus, Brad. "Navigating Legal Challenges to Churches" *Ministry in the New Marriage Culture.*

Davey, Stephen. *In Pursuit of Prodigals: A Primer on Church Discipline and*

Reconciliation. The Woodlands, TX: Kress, 2010.

Davidson, Valeria and J. Gregory Lawson, "Children at Church, Protecting" in *Encyclopedia of Christian Education*, v. 1, edited by George Thomas Kurian and Mack A Lamport (Lanham: Rowman & Littlefield, 2015).

Dayton, Howard. *Free and Clear: God's Road Map to Debt-Free Living*. Chicago: Moody, 2006.

Dever, Mark, and Paul Alexander. *The Deliberate Church: Building Your Ministry on the Gospel*. Wheaton: Crossway, 2005.

Dimos, Rollie. *Integrity at Stake*. Grand Rapids: Zondervan, 2016.

Dodson, Mike, and Ed Stetzer. *Comeback Churches: How 300 Churches Turned Around and Yours Can Too*. Nashville: B. and H Publishing Group, 2007.

Drucker, Peter, et al. *The Five Most Important Questions You Will Ever Ask About Your Organization*. 1,

Fortunato, Frank. "Declare God's Glory: A Vision for Global Worship," *Worship Leader*, November/December, 2009.

Gaebelein, F. E., Carson, D. A., Wessel, W. W., & Liefeld, W. L. *The Expositor's Bible Commentary: Matthew, Mark, Luke* (Vol. 8).

Gaebelein, F. E., Harrison, E. F., Mare, W. H., Harris, M. J., & Boice, J. M. *The Expositor's Bible Commentary: Romans through Galatians* (Vol. 10).

Gaebelin, F. E., Patterson, R. D., Austel, H. J., Payne, J. B., Yamauchi, E., Huey, F. B., Jr, & Smick, E. B., Zondervan Publishing House. *The Expositor's Bible Commentary: 1 & 2 Kings, 1 & 2 Chronicles, Ezra, Nehemiah, Esther, Job* (Vol. 4).

Garland, D. E. 2 *Corinthians* (Vol. 29).

Garrison, D. Randy, and Norman D Vaughan. *Blended Learning in Higher Education: Framework, Principles, and Guidelines*. The Jossey-Bass Higher and Adult Education Series. San Francisco, CA.: Jossey-Bass, 2008.

Glover, Voyle A. *Protecting Your Church Against Sexual Predators*. Grand Rapids: Kregel, 2005.

Goetzmann, J. *Care, Anxiety*. In Colin Brown (Ed.), *The New International Dictionary of New Testament Theology, second edition pp.* 276-279. Grand Rapids: Zondervan, 1986.

Golding, Thomas A., "The Imagery of Shepherding in the Bible, part 1" *Bibliotheca Sacra* 163, no. 649 (January 2006):18-28.

Grenz, Arlo. *The Confident Leader: Getting A Good Start As A Christian Minister*. Nashville, TN.: Broadman and Holman Publishers, 1994.

Grudem, Wayne. *Systematic Theology: An Introduction to Biblical Doctrine*. Grand Rapids: Zondervan, 1994.

Guthrie, Donald. *The Pastoral Epistles*. Grand Rapids, MI.: Eerdmans Publishing CO., 1989.

Guthrie, G.H. 2 *Corinthians. Baker Exegetical Commentary On The New Testament*. Grand Rapids: Baker Academic, 2015.

Hammar, Richard R. "2016 Tax Return Preparation & Federal Reporting Guide," Christianity Today International, 2016.

Hammar, Richard. *Legal Issues for Pastors*, v. 1. (Carol Stream: Christianity Today International, 2008).

Hammar, Richard, Steven W. Klipowiez, and James F. Cobble, Jr. *Reducing the Risk of Child Sexual Abuse in Your Church*. Mathews: Christian Ministry Resources, 1993.

Hammet, John S. 40 *Questions About Baptism and the Lord's Supper*. Grand Rapids, MI: Kregel, 2015.

________. *Biblical Foundations for Baptist Churches: A Contemporary Ecclesiology*. Grand Rapids, MI: Kregel, 2005.

Harris, Robin. "We Being Many, Are One: A Fresh Look at a Global Understanding of Worship," *Worship Leader*, November/December, 2009.

Hart, A. D. *Adrenalin and Stress*. Dallas: Word Publishing, 1991.

Harvard Health Publications. Harvard Medical School. Learning while you Sleep: Dream or reality? *Harvard Men's Health Watch. February* 1, 2012. http://www.health.harvard.edu/staying-healthy/learning-while-you-sleep-dream-or-reality, 2012.

Henry, Jack A. *Basic Budgeting for Churches: A Complete Guide*. Nashville: B&H, 1995.

Henry, Jim. *In Remembrance of Me: A Manual on Observing the Lord's Supper*. Nashville, TN: Broadman & Holman, 1998.

Holman Christian Standard Bible.

Hopkins, Bruce R., and David O. Middlebrook. *Nonprofit Law for Religious Organization: Essential Questions and Answers*. Hoboken: John Wiley & Sons, 2008.

Horner, David. A *Practical Guide for Life and Ministry: Overcoming 7 challenges pastors face.*

House, H. Wayne. *Christian Ministries and the Law: What Church and Para-Church Leaders Should Know*. 2nd ed. Grand Rapids: Baker, 1999.

Hughes, R. K. 2 *Corinthians Power in Weakness*. Wheaton: Crossway, 2006.

Hughes, R. Kent. *The Pastor's Book: A Comprehensive and Practical Guide to Pastoral Ministry*. Wheaton, IL: Crossway, 2015.

Hustad, Donald P. *Jubilate II: Church Music in Worship and Renewal*. Carol Stream, IL: Hope Music, 1993.

"Incorporating Your Non-Profit in North Carolina.", www.secstate.state.nc.us.

Iorg, Jeff. *The Painful Side of Leadership: Moving forward when it hurts.*

Jobes, Karen, H. 1 *Peter*, Baker Exegetical Commentary on the New Testament. Grand Rapids: Baker Academic, 2005.

Johnson, Bob I. "Planning and Budgeting," in *Church Administration*

Handbook, edited by Bruce P. Powers, 3rd Edition (Nashville: B&H, 2008).

Johnson, Dennis E. *Him We Proclaim: Preaching Christ from All the Scriptures*. Phillipsburg, NJ: P&R, 2007.

Kahoe, R. D. *Fear*. In D. G. Benner D. G. and P. C. Hill (Ed.), *Baker Encyclopedia of Psychology and Counseling, second edition p.* 451. Grand Rapids: Baker Books, 1999.

Kaiser, Walter. *Toward an Exegetical Theology: Biblical Exegesis for Preaching and Teaching*. Grand Rapids: Baker, 1981.

Keach, Benjamin. "The Glory of a True Church, and its Discipline Display'd," 1697, reprinted in *Polity*.

Keil C. F. *Commentary on the Old Testament* (Vol. 3. Pp. 252-255). Grand Rapids: William B. Eerdmans Publishing Company, 1980.

Kidner, D. *Psalms 1-72 An Introduction and Commentary on Books I and II of The Psalms*. Downers Grove: Inter Varsity Press, 1978.

Kidner, D. *The Proverbs An Introduction and Commentary*. Downers Grove: Inter Varsity Press, 1973.

Kniskern, J. Warren. *Courting Disaster*. Wake Forest: Church Initiative, 2002.

Köstenberger, Andreas J. "Shepherds and Shepherding in the Gospels" in Benjamin L. Merkle and Thomas R. Schreiner, eds. *Shepherding God's Flock: Biblical Leadership in the New Testament and Beyond*. Grand Rapids: Kregel, 2014, pp. 33-58.

Kotter, John. A Sense of Urgency. Chapter 2, chapter 1,

Kotter, John. *Leading Change*. 33-158,

Kotter, John and Dan S. Cohen. *The Heart of Change: Real-life stories of how people change their organizations*.

Kouzes, James M. and Barry Z. Posner. *The Truth About Leadership: The no-fads heart-of-the-matter facts you need to know*. 46, 58, 59, 86,

Kraeuter, Tom. *Guiding Your Church Through a Worship Transition: A Practical Handbook for Worship Renewal*. Lynnwood, WA: Emerald Books, 2003.

Lane, Timothy S., and Paul David Tripp. *How People Change*. Winston-Salem, NC: Punch Press, 2006.

Laniak, Timothy S. *Shepherds after My own Heart: Pastoral Traditions and Leadership in the Bible*, NSBT 20, Downers Grove, Illinois: IVP, 2006.

Lauterbach, Mark. *The Transforming Community: The Practice of the Gospel in Church Discipline*. Carol Stream, IL: Christian Focus, 2003.

Leeman, Jonathan. *Church Discipline: How The Church Protects The Name Of Jesus*. Wheaton: Crossway, 2012.

Leeman, Jonathan. *Church Membership*. Wheaton: Crossway, 2012.

Lea, Thomas D. and Hayne P. Griffin, Jr., 1,2 *Timothy Titus*, New American Commentary. Nashville: Broadman Press, 1992.

Liefeld, Walter. *New Testament Exposition*. Grand Rapids: Zondervan, 1989.

Lloyd, Dan S. *Leading Today's Funerals: A Pastoral Guide for Improving Bereavement Ministry*. Baker Books, 1997.

Lloyd-Jones, D. Martin. *Preaching and Preachers*. Grand Rapids: Zondervan, 1972.

Long, Thomas G. *Preaching and the Literary Forms of the Bible*. Philadelphia: Fortress, 1989.

Lott, David ed. *Conflict Management in Congregations*. 16, 24, 45-53,

MacArthur, John. *Whose Money is it Anyway*? Nashville: Ward, 2000.

Madsen, Suzanne. "Why Is Organizational Change so Hard?" *Liquid Planner*. Available from: http://www.liquidplanner.com/blog/why-is-organizational-change-so-hard, June 10, 2015. Viewed August 12, 2015.

Malphurs, Aubrey. A *Contemporary Handbook for Weddings and Funerals: And Other Occasions*. Kregel Academic & Professional, 2003.

Martin, R. P. *The Epistle of Paul to the Philippians*. Grand Rapids: Eerdmans, 1978.

Maxwell, John C. *Developing the Leaders Around You: How to Help Others Reach Their Full Potential*. Nashville, TN: Thomas Nelson, Inc., 1995.

Mayo Clinic. *Panic Attacks and Panic Disorder* in http://www.mayoclinic.org/diseases-conditions/panic-attacks/basics/symptoms/con-20020825, 2002.

Mazur, Cynthia, and Ronald Bullis. *Legal Guide for Day-to-Day Church Matters*. Cleveland: The Pilgrim Press, 2003.

McConville, J. G. *Ezra, Nehemiah, and Esther*. Edited by John C. L. Gibson. The Daily Study Bible Series. Philadelphia, PA: West Minister Press, 1985.

Merrill, E.H. *Deuteronomy* (Vol. 4) In *The New American Commentary*. Nashville: B&H Publishing Group, 1994.

Meyer, Jason. *Preaching: A Biblical Theology*. Wheaton: Crossway, 2013.

Mohler, R. Albert. *The Conviction to Lead: 25 Principles for Leadership that Matters*. Minneapolis, MN.: Bethany House, 2012.

Moo, D. J. *James. Tyndale New Testament Commentaries*. Downers Grove: IVP Academic, 2015.

Morgan, Robert J. *Then Sings My Soul: 150 of the World's Greatest Hymn Stories*. Nashville: Thomas Nelson Publishers, 2003.

Moseley, Allan. *Thinking Against the Grain*. Grand Rapids: Kregel, 2003.

Morris, Leon, ed. *The Epistles of Paul to the Thessalonians: An Introduction and Commentary* Rev. ed. Tyndale New Testament Commentaries. Grand Rapids, MI: William B. Eerdmans Publishing Company, 1984.

Mounce, William D. *Mounce's Complete Expository Dictionary of Old and*

New Testament Words. Grand Rapids, Zondervan, 2006.

Murray, David. *Jesus on Every Page*. Nashville: Thomas Nelson, 2013.

Newman, Barclay M., ed. A *Concise Greek-English Dictionary of the New Testament*. Stuttgart: German Bible Society, 1993.

Norman, R. Stanton. "The Reestablishment of Proper Church Discipline," in *Restoring Integrity in Baptist Churches* (Grand Rapids: Kregel, 2008).

O'Brien, Peter T. *The Letter to the Ephesians*, The Pillar New Testament Commentary. Grand Rapids: Eerdmans, 1999.

Osbreck, Kenneth W. *Amazing Grace: 366 Inspiring Hymn Stories for Daily Devotions*. Grand Rapids: Kregel Publications, 1990.

Osbreck, Kenneth W. 101 *Hymn Stories: The Inspiring True Stories Behind* 101 *Favorite Hymns*. Grand Rapids: Kregel Publications, 1982.

Osbreck, Kenneth W. 101 *More Hymn Stories: The Inspiring True Stories Behind* 101 *Favorite Hymns*. Grand Rapids: Kregel Publications, 1985.

Owen, Marvin. "Basics of Budgeting," Leaderlife, Fall 2005.

Palloff, Rena M, and Keith Pratt. *Collaborating Online: Learning Together in Community*. Jossey-Bass Guides to Online Teaching and Learning Volume 2. San Francisco, CA.: Jossey-Bass, 2005.

Paproski, Darren. "Common Errors in Analyzing Case Studies." Power Point Slides, Adapted from the University of Technology Sydney Writing Guide, Sydney, Australia. Accessed May 22, 2015. https://web.viu.ca/theuerkof/resources/Steps4AnalyzingCaseStudies.ppt.

Parr, Steve. R. *Sunday School That Really Works: A Strategy for Connecting Congregations and Communities*. Grand Rapids, MI: Kregel Academic and Professional Publications, 2010.

Parr, Steve. R. ed. *Sunday School that Really Excels: Real Life Examples of Churches with Healthy Sunday Schools*. Grand Rapids, MI: Kregel Ministry Publications, 2013.

Pentecost, J. D. *The Words and Works of Jesus Christ*. Grand Rapids: Zondervan, 1981.

Peters, B. A. What are the Consequences of Sleep Deprivation? Scope, Stanford Medicine. 08/26/14. http://scopeblog.stanford.edu/2013/07/11/what-are-the-consequences-of-sleep-deprivation/, 2014.

Peterson, Eugene. *Eat This Book: A Conversation in the Art of Spiritual Reading*. Grand Rapids: Eerdmans, 2009.

Piper, John. *The Supremacy of God in Preaching*. Rev. ed. Grand Rapids: Baker, 2004.

Platt, David, Daniel Akin and Tony Merida. *Christ-Centered Exposition: Exalting Jesus in 1 & 2 Timothy and Titus*.

Poirier, Alfred. *The Peace Making Pastor: A biblical guide to resolving church conflict*. 244

Rainer, Art. *The Minister's Salary and Other Challenges in Ministry Finance*. Rainer Publishing, 2015.

Rainer, Thom. *Effective Evangelistic Churches: Successful Churches Reveal What Works and What Doesn't*. Nashville: B and H Publishers, 1996.

Reynolds, William J., ed. *Baptist Hymnal: 1975 Edition*. Nashville, TN.: Convention Press, 1975.

Roach, David. "Public Apologies Spur Church Discipline Warnings," *Baptist Press*, posted June 1, 2015. Accessed August 1, 2015.

Robinson, Haddon W. In the Foreword to Steven D. Mathewson, *The Art of Preaching Old Testament Narrative*. Grand Rapids: Baker, 2002.

Roebert, Ed. *Mastering Management in the Church*. Kent: Sovereign World, 1996.

Roll A, Colas D, Adamantidis A, Carter M, Lanre-Amos T, Heller HC, de Lecea L. (2011). Optogenetic Disruption of Sleep Continuity Impairs

Memory Consolidation. *Proceedings of the National Academy of Sciences*. 108(32): 13305-10.

Ross, A.P. *Psalms*. In J. F. Walvoord and R. B. Zuck (Ed.), *The Bible Knowledge Commentary, Old Testament p*. 818. Wheaton: Victor Books, 1985.

Ross, A. P. *Psalms*. In J. F. Walvoord and R. B. Zuck (Ed.), *The Bible Knowledge Commentary, Old Testament p*. 838. Wheaton: Victor Books, 1985.

Rouse, M. *Stress Testing Definition* in http://searchsoftwarequality.techtarget.com/definition/stress-testing, 2007.

Rush, Myron. *Management, a Biblical Approach*. Wheaton, IL: Victor Books, 1983.

"Sample: Accountable Reimbursement Plan," www.guidestone.org accessed March 22, 2016.

Sande, Ken. *Managing Conflict in your Church*. Billings: Peacemaker Ministries, 1999.

Sanders, J. Oswald. *Spiritual Leadership: Responding to God's call*. 99-105

SBC Life http://www.sbclife.net/Articles/2012/10/sla7

Schreiner, Thomas R., and Shawn D. Wright, eds. *Believer's Baptism: Sign of the New Covenant in Christ*. NAC Studies in Bible and Theology, ed., E. Ray Clendenen. Nashville, TN: Broadman & Holman, 2006.

Shapiro, Emily. "Planet Fitness Revokes Woman's Membership after She Complained about Transgender Person," March 7, 2015. http://abcnews.go.com/Health/planet-fitness-revokes-womans-membership-transgender-complaint/story?id=29465983, accessed July 27, 2015.

Shelley, M. *Leading your church through conflict and reconciliation: 30 strategies to transform your ministry* (Vol. 1).

Sinek, Simon. *Start with Why: How Great Leaders Inspire Everyone to Take Action*. New York, NY: The Penguin Group, 2009.

Smith, Justin Allen. *Following the Ways of Ezra: An Exploratory Study of the Relationship Between a Senior Pastor's Involvement in Leading Sunday School and Church Health*. Wake Forest, NC: Justin Allen Smith, 2014.

Southern Baptist Convention. "Baptist Faith and Message, 2000." Statement of Faith. http://www.sbc.net/bfm/default.asp (accessed April 3, 2016).

Southwell, P. *Bible Study Commentary: Ezra-Job*. City Road, London: Scripture Union, 1982.

Stavredes, Tina. *Effective Online Teaching: Foundations and Strategies for Student Success*. The Jossey-Bass Higher and Adult Education Series. San Francisco, CA.: Jossey-Bass, 2011.

Stein, Robert. *A Basic Guide to Interpreting the Bible: Playing by the Rules*. 2nd ed. Grand Rapids: Baker, 2011.

Stott, J. R. W. *The Message of the Sermon on the Mount*. Downers Grove: IVP Academic, 1978.

Tautges, Paul. *Comfort the Grieving: Ministering God's Grace in Times of* Loss, Revised and Updated. Grand Rapids: Zondervan, 2014.

Taylor, Allan. *The Six Core Values of Sunday School: A Philosophical, Practical, and Passionate Approach to Sunday School*. Woodstock, GA: Allan Taylor, 2003.

Terry, Lindsay. *I Could Sing of Your Love Forever: The Stories Behind 100 of the World's Most Popular Worship Songs*. Nashville: Thomas Nelson, 2008.

Terry, Lindsay. *Stories Behind Popular Songs and Hymns*. Grand Rapids: Baker Book House, 1990.

Thompson J.A. *Deuteronomy Tyndale Old Testament Commentaries*. Downers Grove: Inter Varsity Press, 1974.

Tidball, Derek, *Ministry by the Book: New Testament Patterns for Pastoral*

Leadership. Downers Grove: IVP Academic, 2008.

Tiemann, William Harold, and John C. Bush. *The Right to Silence*. Nashville: Abington, 1983.

Tokuhama-Espinosa, Tracey. *Making Classrooms Better: 50 Practical Applications of Mind, Brain, and Education Science*. Norton Books in Education. New York, NY.: W.W. Norton & Company, Inc., 2014.

Tripp, Paul David. *Instruments in the Redeemer's Hands: People in Need of Change Helping People in Need of Change*. Phillipsburg, NJ: P & R Publishing, 2002.

VanGemerman Willem A. *Psalms*, The Expositor's Bible Commentary, revised edition. Grand Rapids: Zondervan, 2008.

Van Yperen, Jim. *Making Peace: A guide to overcoming church conflict*. 246-249

Watson, G. B., and S. E. Gro. *Faculty Mentoring Faculty*. Quoted in Barbara J Duch, Susan E. Groh, and Deborah E. Allen, eds., *The Power of Problem-Based Learning: A Practical "How to" for Teaching Undergraduate Courses in Any Discipline*. Sterling, VA.: Stylus, 2001. Quoted in Rita-Marie Conrad and J. Ana Donaldson, *Engaging the Online Learner: Activities and Resources for Creative Instruction*. Jossey-Bass Guides to Online Teaching and Learning. San Francisco, CA.: Jossey-Bass, 2004.

Watson, Richard. *Why Good Ideas Go Bad: Why Do Some Smart People Make Stupid Mistakes?* Fast Company Leaders; available from http://www.fastcompany.com/1718105/why-good-ideas-go-bad, January 18, 2011. Accessed August 12, 2015.

Wegner, Paul. "Ministry Foundations in the Old Testament" in *Ministry in the New Marriage Culture* edited by Jeff Iorg (Nashville: B&H Publishing, 2015).

Welch, Robert H. *Church Administration.* 2nd ed. Nashville: B&H Publishing, 2001.

Welch, Robert H. *Church Administration.* 2nd ed. Nashville: B&H Publishing, 2011.

Wiarda, Timothy "John 21:1-23: Narrative Unity and its Implications," *Journal for The Study Of The New Testament* 46 (June 1992): 53-71.

Williams, Michael. *How to Read the Bible through the Jesus Lens.* Grand Rapids: Zondervan, 2012.

Williamson, H.G.M. *Biblical World Commentary: Ezra, Nehemiah.* Edited by David A. Hubbard et al. Waco, TX.: Word Books, 1985.

Wills, Gregory A. "Southern Baptists and Church Discipline," in *Restoring Integrity in Baptist Churches* (Grand Rapids: Kregel, 2008).

Worth, B. J. *Worth's Income Tax Guide for Ministers.* Nappanee: Evangel Publishing House, 2009.

Young D.J. *The Book of Isaiah, vol.* 3. Grand Rapids: Eerdmans, 1997.

Yount, William. R. ed. *The Teaching Ministry of the Church.* 2nd ed. Nashville, TN: B&H Academic Publishing Group, 2008.

Zigarelli, Michael A. *Management by Proverbs: Applying Timeless Wisdom in the Workplace.* Chicago, IL: Moody Press, 1999.

ENDNOTES

1 R. Albert Mohler, *The Conviction to Lead: 25 Principles for Leadership that Matters* (Minneapolis, MN.: Bethany House, 2012), 83.

2 Ibid., 84.

3 Donald Guthrie, *The Pastoral Epistles* (Grand Rapids, MI.: Eerdmans Publishing CO., 1989), 138.

4 Elizabeth F. Barkley, *Student Engagement Techniques: A Handbook for College Faculty*, The Jossey-Bass Higher and Adult Education Series (San Francisco, CA.: Jossey-Bass, 2010), 17.

5 Tina Stavredes, *Effective Online Teaching: Foundations and Strategies for Student Success*, The Jossey-Bass Higher and Adult Education Series (San Francisco, CA.: Jossey-Bass, 2011), 13-14.

6 D. Randy Garrison and Norman D. Vaughan, *Blended Learning in Higher Education: Framework, Principles, and Guidelines*, The Jossey-Bass Higher and Adult Education Series (San Francisco, CA.: Jossey-Bass, 2008), 35).

7 Rita-Marie Conrad and J. Ana Donaldson, *Engaging the Online Learner: Activities and Resources for Creative Instruction*. Updated ed. Jossey-Bass Guides to Online Teaching and Learning (San Francisco, CA.: Jossey-Bass, 2011), 5.

8 Tracey Tokuhama-Espinsosa, *Making Classrooms Better: 50 Practical Applications of Mind, Brain, and Education Science*, Norton Books in

Education (New York, NY.: W.W. Norton & Company, Inc., 2014), 173.

9 Ibid., 203.

10 G. B. Watson, and Groh, S. (2001). Faculty mentoring faculty. In Duch, B., Groh, S., & Allen, D. (Eds.), *The power of problem-based learning.* Sterling, VA.: Stylus. Cited in Conrad and Donaldson, *Engaging the Online Learner*, 3.

11 Rena M. Palloff and Keith Pratt, *Collaborating Online: Learning Together in Community*, Jossey-Bass Guides to Online Teaching and Learning Volume 2 (San Francisco, CA.: Jossey-Bass, 2005), 8.

12 Ibid., 63.

13 Ibid., 63-4.

14 Darren Paproski, "Common Errors in Analyzing Case Studies." Power Point Slides, Adapted from the University of Technology Sydney Writing Guide, Sydney, Australia. Accessed May 22, 2015. https://web.viu.ca/theuerkof/resources/Steps4AnalyzingCaseStudies.ppt.

15 Andreas J. Köstenberger, "Shepherds and Shepherding in the Gospels" in Benjamin L. Merkle and Thomas R. Schreiner, eds. *Shepherding God's Flock: Biblical Leadership in the New Testament and Beyond* (Grand Rapids: Kregel, 2014), 53.

16 Timothy S. Laniak, *Shepherds after My Own Heart: Pastoral Traditions and Leadership in the Bible*, NSBT 20 (Downers Grove, Illinois: IVP, 2006), 21.

17 Willem A. VanGemeren, *Psalms*, The Expositor's Bible Commentary, Revised Edition (Grand Rapids: Zondervan, 2008), 251–3.

18 i.e., Paul's prayers for the Ephesian believers in Ephesians 1:17–19 and 3:16–19.

19 The form of the demonstrative pronoun in the Greek text, *toutōn*, could be either masculine or neuter, hence the interpretive options.

See D. A. Carson, *The Gospel According to John*, Pillar New Testament Commentary (Grand Rapids: Eerdmans, 1991), 675–676.

20 Timothy Wiarda, "John 21:1–23: Narrative Unity and Its Implications," *Journal for the Study of the New Testament* 46 (June 1992), 64.

21 R. Alan Culpepper, "Peter as Exemplary Disciple in John 21:15–19," *Perspectives in Religious Studies* 37 (Summer 2010), 166–171.

22 Karen H. Jobes, *1 Peter*, Baker Exegetical Commentary on the New Testament (Grand Rapids: Baker Academic, 2005), 303–306.

23 i.e., Galatians 6:6; 1 Corinthians 9:9–14; 1 Timothy 5:17–18.

24 Clinton E. Arnold, *Ephesians*, Zondervan Exegetical Commentary on the New Testament (Grand Rapids: Zondervan, 2010), 260.

25 Thomas D. Lea and Hayne P. Griffin, Jr., *1,2 Timothy Titus*, New American Commentary (Nashville: Broadman Press, 1992), 243.

26 Thomas A. Golding, "The Imagery of Shepherding in the Bible, part 1" *Bibliotheca Sacra* 163, no. 649 (January 2006), 22.

27 Ibid.

28 Derek Tidball, *Ministry by the Book: New Testament Patterns for Pastoral Leadership* (Downers Grove: IVP Academic, 2008), 81.

29 D. Martin Lloyd-Jones, *Preaching and Preachers* (Grand Rapids: Zondervan, 1972), 9.

30 For a recent and more comprehensive review of the biblical record of preaching, see Jason Meyer, *Preaching: A Biblical Theology* (Wheaton: Crossway, 2013).

31 For a fuller presentation of the importance of preaching, see Christopher Ash, *The Priority of Preaching* (Ross-Shire: Christian Focus, 2009).

32 David Alan Black, "Exegesis for the Text-Driven Sermon," *Text-Driven Preaching: God's Word at the Heart of Every Sermon*, ed. Daniel L. Akin,

David L. Allen, and Ned L. Mathews (Nashville: B&H, 2010), 159.

33 For an extended discussion of the "one meaning but many applications" idea, see Walter Kaiser, *Toward an Exegetical Theology: Biblical Exegesis for Preaching and Teaching* (Grand Rapids: Baker, 1981), 24–47.

34 John Piper, *The Supremacy of God in Preaching*, rev. ed. (Grand Rapids: Baker, 2004), 23.

35 Eugene Peterson, *Eat This Book: A Conversation in the Art of Spiritual Reading* (Grand Rapids: Eerdmans, 2009), 50–53.

36 For help in doing this, see Bryan Chapell, *Christ-Centered Preaching: Redeeming the Expository Sermon*, 2nd ed. (Grand Rapids, Baker, 2005); Dennis E. Johnson, *Him We Proclaim: Preaching Christ from All the Scriptures* (Phillipsburg, NJ: P&R, 2007); David Murray, *Jesus on Every Page* (Nashville: Thomas Nelson, 2013); and Michael Williams, *How to Read the Bible through the Jesus Lens* (Grand Rapids: Zondervan, 2012).

37 Walter Liefeld, *New Testament Exposition* (Grand Rapids: Zondervan, 1989), 45.

38 For help with this, see the *Christ-Centered Exposition* series of commentaries on biblical books. For example, this author's *Leviticus* volume is an effort to teach the meaning of that Old Testament book and to show its relevance and importance for followers of Jesus.

39 Haddon W. Robinson, in the Foreword to Steven D. Mathewson, *The Art of Preaching Old Testament Narrative* (Grand Rapids: Baker, 2002), 12.

40 Mastering two sources could help in this task: D.A. Carson, *Exegetical Fallacies*, 2nd ed. (Grand Rapids: Baker, 1996) and William D. Mounce, *Mounce's Complete Expository Dictionary of Old and New Testament Words* (Grand Rapids, Zondervan, 2006), xiii–xxvi.

41 For help with interpreting and applying the various genres of

Scripture, see Thomas G. Long, *Preaching and the Literary Forms of the Bible* (Philadelphia: Fortress, 1989) and Robert Stein, *A Basic Guide to Interpreting the Bible: Playing by the Rules*, 2nd edition (Grand Rapids: Baker, 2011).

42 Emily Shapiro, "Planet Fitness Revokes Woman's Membership after She Complained about Transgender Person," *ABC News*, March 7, 2015, http://abcnews.go.com/Health/planet-fitness-revokes-womans-membership-transgender-complaint/story?id=29465983.

43 For an extended discussion of Western culture's worldviews and their effects on moral thinking and acting, see Allan Moseley, *Thinking Against the Grain* (Grand Rapids: Kregel, 2003).

44 Gregory A. Wills, "Southern Baptists and Church Discipline," *Restoring Integrity in Baptist Churches* (Grand Rapids: Kregel, 2008), 182.

45 Some standard that defines primary doctrines is necessary and has always been used by the confessing church. One such standard is the *Baptist Faith and Message*, 2000 (Nashville: Lifeway, 2000).

46 Joseph S. Baker, "Queries Considered, or an Investigation of Various Subjects Involved in the Exercise of Church Discipline," reprinted in *Polity: Biblical Arguments on How to Conduct Church Life*, ed. Mark Dever (Nashville: Nine Marks Ministries, 2001), 256.

47 Mark Lauterbach, *The Transforming Community: The Practice of the Gospel in Church Discipline* (Carol Stream, IL: Christian Focus, 2003), 158.

48 Barclay M. Newman, ed., *A Concise Greek-English Dictionary of the New Testament* (Stuttgart: German Bible Society, 1993), 57.

49 Stephen Davey, *In Pursuit of Prodigals: A Primer on Church Discipline and Reconciliation* (The Woodlands, TX: Kress, 2010), 42.

50 Other works that provide discussions of the process of church discipline are Jay E. Adams, *Handbook of Church Discipline* (Grand Rapids: Zondervan, 1974); Mark Dever and Paul Alexander, *The Deliberate Church: Building Your Ministry on the Gospel* (Wheaton: Crossway, 2005), 67–73; John S. Hammett, *Biblical Foundations for Baptist Churches: A Contemporary Ecclesiology* (Grand Rapids: Kregel, 2005), 124–129; Jonathan Leeman, *Church Discipline: How the Church Protects the Name of Jesus* (Wheaton: Crossway, 2012); and R. Stanton Norman, "The Reestablishment of Proper Church Discipline," *Restoring Integrity in Baptist Churches* (Grand Rapids: Kregel, 2008), 214–219.

51 Benjamin Keach, "The Glory of a True Church, and Its Discipline Display'd," 1697, reprinted in *Polity* (year of reprint), 70.

52 See, for example, the documents on church order from the Charleston and Philadelphia Baptist associations, written in 1774 and 1805, respectively, in *Polity*, pp. 115–158.

53 For examples of the negative consequences of a lack of care and compassion in the church discipline process, see David Roach, "Public Apologies Spur Church Discipline Warnings," *Baptist Press*, June 1, 2015, http://www.bpnews.net/44855/public-apologies-spur-church-discipline-warnings.

54 John S. Hammett, *40 Questions About Baptism and the Lord's Supper* (Grand Rapids: Kregel, 2015), 22.

55 Ibid, 23–24.

56 See Augustine of Hippo, "On the Catechising of the Uninstructed," *St. Augustine: On the Holy Trinity, Doctrinal Treatises, Moral Treatises*, vol. 3., ed. Philip Schaff, trans. S. D. F. Salmond. A Select Library of the Nicene and Post-Nicene Fathers of the Christian Church, First Series (Buffalo, NY: Christian Literature Company, 1887), 312.

57 In the chapter on baptism in a recent book by Kent Hughes and Douglas O'Donnell, the issue of the subjects of baptism is addressed. Hughes is a Baptist while O'Donnell is a paedobaptist. This makes for an interesting chapter in which these authors who are "nearly identical in the classical theological categories and share similar approaches to ministry" firmly, yet humbly disagree over key issues related to baptism. See Kent Hughes, *The Pastor's Book: A Comprehensive and Practical Guide to Pastoral Ministry* (Wheaton, IL: Crossway, 2015), 373.

58 John S. Hammett, *Biblical Foundations for Baptist Churches: A Contemporary Ecclesiology* (Grand Rapids: Kregel, 2005), 267.

59 Gerhard Kittel, Geoffrey W. Bromiley, and Gerhard Friedrich, eds. *Theological Dictionary of the New Testament*, vol. 1 (Grand Rapids: Eerdmans, 1964), 529.

60 Hughes, *The Pastor's Book*, 426–427.

61 Ibid., 425–426.

62 Mark Dever, "The Church" *The Doctrine of the Church*, ed. Daniel L. Akin (Nashville: B&H Academic, 2007), 790.

63 For a discussion on the presence of Christ in the elements, see Wayne Grudem, *Systematic Theology: An Introduction to Biblical Doctrine* (Grand Rapids: Zondervan, 1994), 991–996.

64 Grudem, *Systematic Theology*, 990.

65 1 Corinthians 11:26.

66 Southern Baptist Convention, "The Baptist Faith & Message, 2000" http://www.sbc.net/bfm2000/bfm2000.asp (accessed April 3, 2016).

67 Hammett, 40 *Questions*, 259–265.

68 For a good discussion on this issue, see Hammett, 40 *Questions*, 267–272.

69 See Hughes, *The Pastor's Book*, 458–459; Hammett, 40 *Questions*,

291–292.

70 Hammett, *40 Questions*, 292–293.

71 Hammett, *40 Questions*, 294.

72 Paul Tautges, *Comfort the Grieving: Ministering God's Grace in Times of Loss*, Revised and Updated (Grand Rapids: Zondervan, 2014), 14.

73 Brian Croft and Phil A. Newton, *Conduct Gospel-Centered Funerals: Applying the Gospel at the Unique Challenges of Death* (Leominster, UK: Day One Publications, 2011), 22–23.

74 Tautges, *Comfort the Grieving*, 47.

75 Ibid., 15.

76 Timothy S. Lane and Paul David Tripp, *How People Change* (Winston-Salem, NC: Punch Press, 2006).

77 Paul David Tripp, *Instruments in the Redeemer's Hands: People in Need of Change Helping People in Need of Change* (Phillipsburg, NJ: P & R Publishing, 2002). Tripp explains the methodology briefly in chapter 6 and then expounds each aspect in chapters 7–14.

78 Tautges, *Comfort the Grieving*, 58–59.

79 C. F. Keil, *Commentary on the Old Testament*, vol. 3. (Grand Rapids: William B. Eerdmans Publishing Company, 1980), 252–255.

80 Harvard Men's Health Watch, "Learning while you sleep: Dream or reality?" *Harvard Health Publications*, February 1, 2012, http://www.health.harvard.edu/staying-healthy/learning-while-you-sleep-dream-or-reality.

81 Daniel G. Amen, *Use Your Brain to Change Your Age* (New York: Harmony Books, 2012).

82 R. Kent Hughes, *2 Corinthians: Power in Weakness* (Wheaton: Crossway, 2006), 23–24.

83 George H. Guthrie, *2 Corinthians: Baker Exegetical Commentary on the*

New Testament. (Grand Rapids: Baker Academic, 2015).

84 Derek Kidner, *Psalms 1–72: An Introduction and Commentary on Books I and II of The Psalms* (Downers Grove: Inter Varsity Press, 1978), 165.

85 Adapted from the American Psychiatric Association, *Diagnostic and Statistical Manual of Mental Disorders* (DSM-5), 2013.

86 Sid S. Buzzell, "Proverbs," *The Bible Knowledge Commentary, Old Testament*, ed. John F. Walvoord and Roy B. Zuck, (Wheaton: Victor Books, 1985), 955.

87 Allen P. Ross, "Psalms," *The Bible Knowledge Commentary, Old Testament*, ed. John F. Walvoord and Roy B. Zuck (Wheaton: Victor Books, 1985), 818.

88 Duane L. Christensen, *Word Biblical Commentary, volume* 6A, *Deuteronomy* 1–11 (Dallas: Word Books, 1991), 143.

89 Eugene H. Merrill, The *New American Commentary: Deuteronomy*, Vol. 4 (Nashville: B&H Publishing Group, 1994), 167.

90 J. A. Thompson, *Deuteronomy: Tyndale Old Testament Commentaries* (Downers Grove: Inter-Varsity Press, 1974), 121.

91 Richard D. Kahoe, "Fear," *Baker Encyclopedia of Psychology and Counseling, Second Edition*, ed. David G. Benner and Peter C. Hill (Grand Rapids: Baker Books, 1999), 451.

92 Derek Kidner, *The Proverbs: An Introduction and Commentary* (Downers Grove: InterVarsity Press, 1973), 59.

93 J. Goetzmann, "Care, Anxiety," *The New International Dictionary of New Testament Theology, Second Edition*, ed. Colin Brown (Grand Rapids: Zondervan, 1986), 276–279.

94 John R. W. Stott, *The Message of the Sermon on the Mount* (Downers Grove: IVP Academic, 1978), 168–169.

95 J. Dwight Pentecost, *The Words and Works of Jesus Christ* (Grand

Rapids: Zondervan, 1981), 185.

96 John R. W. Stott, *The Message of the Sermon on the Mount* (Downers Grove: IVP Academic, 1978), 222.

97 "Panic Attacks and Panic Disorder," Mayo Clinic, 2002, http://www.mayoclinic.org/diseases-conditions/panic-attacks/basics/symptoms/con-20020825.

98 Archibald D. Hart, *Adrenalin and Stress* (Dallas: Word Publishing, 1991), 6.

99 Edward J. Young, *The Book of Isaiah*, Vol. 3, (Grand Rapids: Eerdmans, 1997), 84.

100 Brandon Peters, MD, "What are the Consequences of Sleep Deprivation?" *Scope, Stanford Medicine*, August 26, 2014, http://scopeblog.stanford.edu/2013/07/11/what-are-the-consequences-of-sleep-deprivation/.

101 Ralph P. Martin, *The Epistle of Paul to the Philippians* (Grand Rapids: Eerdmans, 1978), 168–169.

102 Margaret Rouse, "Stress Testing Definition," *Tech Target*, June 2007, http://searchsoftwarequality.techtarget.com/definition/stress-testing.

103 Douglas J. Moo, *James (Tyndale New Testament Commentaries)* (Downers Grove: IVP Academic, 2015), 198.

104 Allen P. Ross, "Psalms," *The Bible Knowledge Commentary, Old Testament*, ed. John F. Walvoord and Roy B. Zuck (Wheaton: Victor Books, 1985), 838.

105 R. Alan Cole, *Galatians (Tyndale New Testament Commentaries)* (Downers Grove: IVP Academic, 2015), 126.

106 James M. Kouzes and Barry Z. Posner, *The Truth about Leadership: The No-fads Heart-of-the-Matter Facts You Need to Know* (San Francisco:

Jossey-Bass, 2010), 46.

107 Ibid., 58–59

108 John Kotter, A *Sense of Urgency* (Boston: Harvard Business Review Press, 2008).

109 Ibid., Chapter One

110 John Kotter, *Leading Change* (Boston: Harvard Business Review Press, 1996), 33–158.

111 All Scriptural references are found in: *Holman Christian Standard Bible*. 2003. Holman Bible Publishers.

112 Peter Drucker, et al. *The Five Most Important Questions You Will Ever Ask About Your Organization* (San Francisco: Jossey-Bass, 2008), 1.

113 Kouzes and Posner, *The Truth About Leadership*, 86.

114 Warren Bennis and Robert Thomas, "Crucibles of Leadership," *HBR's 10 Must Reads on Leadership* (Boston: Harvard Business Review Press, 2011), Kindle location 1,640.

115 All Scriptural references are from: *Holman Christian Standard Bible*. 2003. Holman Bible Publishers.

116 Roy Pneuman, "Nine Common Sources of Conflict in Congregations," *Conflict Management in Congregations*, ed. David Lott (Virginia: The Alban Institute, 2001), 45–53.

117 Ibid., 45–53

118 Ibid., 50

119 Speed Leas, "The Basics of Conflict Management in Congregations," *Conflict Management in Congregations*, ed. David Lott (Virginia: The Alban Institute, 2001), 24.

120 Ibid., 16

121 Chris Turner, "Control Issues Head List for Pastoral Terminations," SBC LIFE, October 2012, http://www.sbclife.net/Articles/2012/10/

sla7.

[122] Alfred Poirier, *The Peace Making Pastor: A Biblical Guide to Resolving Church Conflict* (Grand Rapids: Baker Books, 2006), 244.

[123] Jim Van Yperen, *Making Peace: A Guide to Overcoming Church Conflict* (Chicago: Moody Publishers, 2002), 246–249

[124] Ibid., 246–249

[125] Oswald J. Sanders, *Spiritual Leadership: Responding to God's Call.* (Nashville: LifeWay Christian Resources, 1999), 99–105.

[126] Simon Sinek, *Start With Why: How Great Leaders Inspire Everyone to Take Action* (New York: The Penguin Group, 2009), 39.

[127] William Barclay, *The Acts of the Apostles*, Revised edition (Philadelphia, PA: The Westminster Press, 1976), 30–31.

[128] Allan Taylor, *The Six Core Values of Sunday School: A Philosophical, Practical, and Passionate Approach to Sunday School* (Woodstock, GA: Allan Taylor, 2003), 8–9.

[129] Ibid., 33.

[130] Steve R. Parr, ed., *Sunday School That Really Excels: Real Life Examples of Churches with Healthy Sunday Schools* (Grand Rapids: Kregel Ministry, 2013), 23–24.

[131] Leon Morris, ed., *The Epistles of Paul to the Thessalonians: An Introduction and Commentary* (Grand Rapids: William B. Eerdmans Publishing Company, 1984), 18.

[132] Ibid., 19.

[133] Ibid., 58.

[134] Ibid., 60.

[135] Ibid.

[136] Ibid., 63.

[137] Taylor, *The Six Core Values*, 59.

138 Arlo Grenz, *The Confident Leader: Getting a Good Start as a Christian Minister*. (Nashville: Broadman and Holman Publishers, 1994), 113-116.

139 Taylor, *The Six Core Principles*, 62–69.

140 Ibid., 147.

141 Ken Braddy, "Six Marks of a Healthy Group," *Facts and Trends*, Fall 2015, 24–26.

142 William R. Yount, ed., *The Teaching Ministry of the Church*, 2nd ed. (Nashville: B&H Academic, 2008), 62.

143 Kenneth S. Coley, "Excels in Teaching God's Word," *Sunday School that Really Excels*, ed. Steve R. Parr (Grand Rapids: Kregel Publications, 2013), 185–87.

144 Steve R. Parr, *Sunday School that Really Works: A Strategy for Connecting Congregations and Communities* (Grand Rapids: Kregel Academic & Professional Publications, 2010), 23–24.

145 James D. Berkley, ed. *Leadership Handbook of Management and Administration: Practical Insights from a Cross Section of Ministry Leaders* (Grand Rapids: Baker Books, 1994), 203.

146 Michael J. Anthony and James Estep Jr., eds., *Management Essentials for Christian Ministries* (Nashville: B&H Publishers, 2005), 391.

147 Anthony, *Management Essentials*, 393.

148 Robert N. Bacher and Michael L. Cooper-White, *Church Administration: Programs, Process, Purpose* (Minneapolis: Fortress Press, 2007), 156.

149 Ibid.

150 Myron Rush, *Management: A Biblical Approach* (Wheaton: Victor Books, 1983), 195.

151 Gordon B. Brown, *Guiding Faculty to Excellence: Instructional Supervision in the Christian School*, 2nd ed. (Colorado Springs: Purposeful Design Publications, 2002), 180.

152 Ken Blanchard, *Self-Leadership and The One Minute Manager* (New York: HarperCollins, 2005), 77.

153 Bacher, *Church Administration*, 154.

154 John C. Maxwell, *Developing the Leaders Around You: How to Help Others Reach Their Full Potential* (Nashville: Thomas Nelson, Inc., 1995), 99–101.

155 Bacher, *Church Administration*, 158.

156 Michael A. Zigarelli, *Management by Proverbs: Applying Timeless Wisdom in the Workplace* (Chicago: Moody Press, 1999), 267.

157 Berkley, *Leadership Handbook*, 250.

158 Paul Chaffee, *Accountable Leadership: A Resource Guide for Sustaining Legal, Financial, and Ethical Integrity in Today's Congregations* (San Francisco: Jossey-Bass, 1997), 127.

159 Paul Wegner, "Ministry Foundations in the Old Testament," *Ministry in the New Marriage Culture*, ed. Jeff Iorg (Nashville: B&H Publishing, 2015), 13.

160 Ken Sande, *Managing Conflict in Your Church* (Billings: Peacemaker Ministries, 1999), 57–58.

161 James Cobble and Richard Hammer, *Risk Management Handbook for Churches and Schools.* (Matthias: Christian Ministry Resources, 2001), 7.

162 Robert H. Welch, *Church Administration*, 2nd ed. (Nashville: B&H Publishing, 2011), 272.

163 Lynn R. Buzzard, *With Liberty and Justice* (Wheaton: Victor Books, 1984), 122

164 William G. Caldwell, "Legal Matters," *Church Administration Handbook*, 3rd ed., ed. Bruce P. Powers (Nashville: B & H, 2008), 219

165 Ibid., 219–220.

166 J. Warren Kniskern, *Courting Disaster* (Wake Forest: Church Initiative, 2002), 184.

167 Jonathan Leeman, *Church Membership* (Wheaton: Crossway, 2012), 24.

168 Brad Dacus, "Navigating Legal Challenges to Churches," *Ministry in the New Marriage Culture*, ed. Jeff Iorg (Nashville: B&H Publishing, 2015), 211–12.

169 Ibid., 212.

170 Ibid., 213.

171 Cobble and Hammar, *Risk Management Handbook for Churches and Schools* (Matthias: Christian Ministry Resources, 2001), 296.

172 Jonathan Leeman, *Church Discipline: How the Church Protects the Name of Jesus* (Wheaton: Crossway, 2012), 28.

173 H. Wayne House, *Christian Ministries and the Law* (Grand Rapids: Kregel, 1999), 70–71.

174 Cobble and Hammar, *Risk Management Handbook for Churches and Schools*, 272.

175 Ibid.

176 Ibid.

177 Bruce R. Hopkins and David O. Middlebrook, *Nonprofit Law For Religious Organization: Essential Questions and Answers* (Hoboken: John Wiley & Sons, 2008), 7.

178 North Carolina Department of the Secretary of State, "Incorporating Your Non-Profit in North Carolina," www.secstate.state.nc.us.

179 Ibid.

180 Cynthia Mazur and Ronald Bullis, *Legal Guide for Day-to-Day Church Matters* (Cleveland: The Pilgrim Press, 2003), 101–102.

181 James F. Cobble and Richard Hammar, *Risk Management Handbook for Churches and Schools*, 278.

182 Ibid.

183 Ibid.

184 William Harold Tiemann and John C. Bush, *The Right to Silence* (Nashville: Abington, 1983), 33

185 Richard Hammar, *Legal Issues For Pastors*, vol. 1. (Carol Stream: Christianity Today International, 2008), 153.

186 Hammar, 57.

187 Voyle A. Glover, *Protecting Your Church Against Sexual Predators* (Grand Rapids: Kregel, 2005), 13.

188 Chip Alford, "Reducing the Risk of Sexual Abuse at Church," *Facts and Trends*, May 1998, 7.

189 Ibid.

190 Richard R. Hammar, Steven W. Klipowiez, and James F. Cobble, Jr., *Reducing the Risk of Child Sexual Abuse in Your Church* (Mathews: Christian Ministry Resources, 1993), 15.

191 Ibid, 15, 17.

192 Ibid, 17.

193 Lynn R. Buzzard, *Church Policy Manual Guidebook* (Cary: BSCNC, 2004), 152.

194 Ibid., 105.

195 Hammar, Klipowiez, and Cobble, *Reducing the Risk of Child Sexual Abuse in Your Church*, 45

196 Ibid, 46–49.

197 Ken Sande, *Managing Conflict In Your Church* (Billings: Peacemaker Ministries, 1999), 90.

198 Valeria Davidson and J. Gregory Lawson, "Children at Church, Protecting," *Encyclopedia of Christian Education*, vol. 1, ed. George Thomas Kurian and Mack A Lamport (Lanham: Rowman & Littlefield,

2015), 224–26.

199 Ibid.

200 Howard Dayton, *Free and Clear: God's Road Map to Debt-Free Living* (Chicago: Moody, 2006), 26.

201 John MacArthur, *Whose Money Is It Anyway?* (Nashville: Ward, 2000), 3.

202 Ron Blue with Jeremy White, *The New Master Your Money* (Chicago: Moody, 2004), 27.

203 Ibid.

204 Ed Roebert, *Mastering Management in the Church* (Kent: Sovereign World, 1996), 21.

205 Rollie Dimos, *Integrity at Stake* (Grand Rapids: Zondervan, 2016), 19–21.

206 Jack A. Henry, *Basic Budgeting for Churches: A Complete Guide* (Nashville: B&H, 1995), 14.

207 Ibid., 16.

208 Bob I. Johnson, "Planning and Budgeting," *Church Administration Handbook*, 3rd ed., ed. Bruce P. Powers (Nashville: B&H, 2008), 156.

209 Robert H. Welch, *Church Administration*, 2nd ed. (Nashville: B&H, 2001), 169.

210 Johnson, "Planning and Budgeting," 156–58.

211 Marvin Owen, "Basics of Budgeting," *LeaderLife*, Fall 2005, 14–15, http://www.lifeway.com/lwc/files/lwcF_PDF_Budget_Basics_LeaderLife.pdf .

212 Ibid.

213 Larry Burkett, *Using Your Money Wisely* (Chicago: Moody Press, 1990), 82.

214 Jeff Berg and Jim Burgess, *The Debt-Free Church* (Chicago: Moody Press, 1996), 13.

215 Art Rainer, *The Minister's Salary and Other Challenges in Ministry*

Finance (Nashville: Rainer Publishing, 2015), 46.

216 Richard R. Hammar, "2016 Tax Return Preparation & Federal Reporting Guide," *Christianity Today International*, 2016, 11.

217 Ibid., 12.

218 Ibid.

219 B. J. Worth, *Worth's Income Tax Guide for Ministers* (Nappanee: Evangel Publishing House, 2009), 73.

220 Ibid., 37–38.

221 Dan Busby, J. Michael Martin and John Van Drunen, *Ministers Tax and Financial Guide* (Grand Rapids: Zondervan, 2015), 76.

222 Ibid., 44.

223 Ibid.

224 "Sample: Accountable Reimbursement Plan," www.guidestone.org, accessed March 22, 2016, http://www.guidestoneretirement.org/~/media/Retirement/Flash/2156x_AcctReimbPlan%20pdf.pdf?_ga=1.87818715.2143054132.1465337351.

225 Suzanne Madsen, "Why Is Organizational Change So Hard?" *The Liquid Planner* (blog), June 10, 2015, http://www.liquidplanner.com/blog/why-is-organizational-change-so-hard.

226 Mike Dodson and Ed Stetzer, *Comeback Churches: How 300 Churches Turned Around and Yours Can Too* (Nashville: B&H Publishing Group, 2007), 197.

227 Richard Watson, "Why Good Ideas Go Bad: Why Do Some Smart People Make Stupid Mistakes?" *Fast Company Leaders*, January 18, 2011, http://www.fastcompany.com/1718105/why-good-ideas-go-bad.

228 Ibid.

229 Thom Rainer, *Effective Evangelistic Churches: Successful Churches Reveal What Works and What Doesn't* (Nashville: B&H Publishers,

1996), 22.

230 Psalms 135:3, 147:1; Genesis 13:6, 36:7, 49:15; and Job 36:11.

231 Donald P. Hustad, *Jubilate II: Church Music in Worship and Renewal* (Carol Stream, IL: Hope Music, 1993), 64.

232 Hustad, 157.

233 Madsen.

234 Harold Best, *Music through the Eyes of Faith*, (New York: HarperOne, 1993), 175.

235 Urbana is a major Christian student missions conference sponsored by InterVarsity Christian Fellowship for college students interested in missions. For more information, access their website at https://urbana.org.

236 Frank Fortunato, "Declare God's Glory: A Vision for Global Worship," *Worship Leader*, November/December, 2009, 28–29.

237 Ibid.

238 Robin Harris, "We Being Many, Are One: A Fresh Look at a Global Understanding of Worship," *Worship Leader*, November/December, 2009, 27.

239 There are many books on this subject, including:

Terry Lindsay, *I Could Sing of Your Love Forever: The Stories Behind 100 of the World's Most Popular Worship Songs* (Nashville: Thomas Nelson, 2008).

Kenneth Osbeck, 101 *Hymn Stories: The Inspiring True Stories Behind 101 Favorite Hymns* (Grand Rapids: Kregel Publications, 2012).

Lindsay Black, *Be Thou My Vision: Devotions From the Lyrics of Popular Christian Music* (Cincinnati: Standard Publishing, 2005).

Charles E. Fromm, ed., *Song Stories: The Stories Behind Worship's Best Loved Songs*, Vol. 1, 2 (Amazon digital services, 2012).

240 Madsen.

241 Hustad, 68–69.

242 Tom Kraeuter, *Guiding Your Church Through a Worship Transition: A Practical Handbook for Worship Renewal* (Lynnwood, WA: Emerald Books, 2003), 84.

243 Reynolds, William J., editor. *Baptist Hymnal: 1975 Edition.* Nashville: Convention Press, 1975.

244 Justin Allen Smith, *Following the Ways of Ezra: An Exploratory Study of the Relationship between a Senior Pastor's Involvement in Leading Sunday School and Church Health* (Wake Forest, NC: Justin Allen Smith, 2014), 102.

245 J. G. McConville, *Ezra, Nehemiah, and Esther*, ed. John C. L. Gibson, The Daily Study Bible Series (Philadelphia, PA: West Minister Press, 1985), 45.

246 Ibid., 56-57.

247 Ibid., 46.

248 Ibid., 47.

249 H.G.M. Williamson, *Biblical World Commentary: Ezra, Nehemiah*, eds. David A. Hubbard et al. (Waco, TX.: Word Books, 1985), 111.

250 P. Southwell, *Bible Study Commentary: Ezra-Job* (City Road, London: Scripture Union, 1982), 13.

251 Williamson, *Biblical World* Commentary, 123-124.

252 Mervin Breneman, *The New American Commentary*, vol. 10, *Ezra, Nehemiah, Esther*, ed. E. Ray Clendenen et al. (Nashville, TN.: Broadman & Holman Publishers, 1993), 143.

253 McConville, *Ezra, Nehemiah, and Esther*, 59.

254 Williamson, *Biblical World Commentary*, 129.

255 Breneman, *The New American Commentary*, 158.

256 Ibid., 159.

257 Ibid., 160.

258 McConville, *Esther, Nehemiah, and Esther*, 68-69.

259 Breneman, *The New American Commentary*, 224.

260 Ibid., 226.

261 Williamson, *Biblical World Commentary*, 298.

Made in the USA
Columbia, SC
19 August 2021